Tales of an Unsociable Traveller:

The Road from Wigan Pier to Tsukiji Fish Market

David R.Y.W. Chapman

To Mum, Dad and Carol. Thank you for showing me unconditional love and support throughout the months that I have spent writing this book. I shall always cherish these precious memories.

My appreciation must also be extended to Bert, Michelle, John, Ellie and the rest of my wonderful family who have provided invaluable inspiration and encouragement.

CONTENTS

CHAPTER 1: A WHOLE NEW WORLD
AN INTRODUCTION FROM THE UNITED KINGDOM
MARCH 2012

Carol and I were walking down a street in Wigan, hand in hand, when we encountered a man who was heading in the opposite direction. I could see that if we carried on travelling along our current course, we would be less than one metre apart from him when our paths crossed. Recognising the danger ahead, I took decisive action by guiding us away from this stranger. Given that this episode occurred in 2012, I am unable to attribute my behaviour to the social distancing guidelines that were introduced following a global pandemic. I was just continuing the habit of a lifetime by avoiding unnecessary social interaction with other human beings.

"Why did you lead us away from that guy? Do you think that he looked dodgy?" Carol asked.

"Not particularly. I just prefer to keep my distance from people."

"Do you always do that?"

"Not always. If I feel that there is a good chance that a stranger will, heaven forbid, attempt to strike up a conversation about the weather or some other form of small talk, then I will usually try to avoid them," I explained.

Carol seemed curious: "Do you not like people?"

"I do like people. I even have an interest in humanitarian work. I just find that making small talk with strangers is really awkward."

This rather peculiar incident occurred during the first few weeks of our relationship. Thankfully, it was not enough to put Carol off. She even went on to marry me! I had been tempted to avoid revealing any spoilers and instead build up the identity of my wife for a dramatic reveal like in the television show *How I Met Your Mother,* but I doubt that anyone is remotely interested in my love life.

"You seem to know a lot of people," I said to Carol after she had

1

exchanged greetings with several passers-by.

"I don't know any of the people that have said hello."

"So why did you return the greeting?"

"That's just what us Wiganers do. We're friendly folk, you know."

"Let me get this straight: you quite happily say hello to strangers?"

"Yes. That is what it is like here. It's a friendly town."

"I have never heard of such an absurd concept!"

Although I had been raised in North-West England, which is known for being a friendly region, this seemed rather extreme to me. Perhaps this was because I am an introvert. My instincts have always been to escape each scenario that I find myself in without suffering any embarrassment or physical harm.

During my school days, I would literally keep my head down and try to keep social interaction to an absolute minimum. One could say that I have been practicing a form of social distancing my whole life. I would be wary if a stranger said hello to me: are they going to attempt to murder me, commit a violent robbery, or just lure me into a financial scam?

A simple walk to the shops would become a mission which consisted of avoiding anything unpleasant transpiring during those five minutes spent outside of the safety of my family home. The strange thing is that nothing of this nature has ever happened to me. I have been fortunate enough to have had a life free from humiliation, pain or anguish.

* * *

I soon discovered that Wigan is indeed a friendly town in which strangers will often exchange a kind word or two. This became even more apparent after I moved here in 2017. Despite the welcoming locals, it almost felt like I was relocating to another country. It often seems that Wiganers are speaking a totally different language from the rest of England.

Consequently, there have been many occasions where I have had to ask Carol to translate for me! Given that she is fluent in Spanish, I had always assumed that if she were ever required to help me understand the locals it would be because we had moved to Spain rather than a town that is only twenty-five miles from where I spent my formative years in Altrincham.

I have been able to decipher some phrases such as, 'Put wood in th'ole,' which means, 'Shut the door.' However, there have been many comments that have left me dumbfounded. It is common for a Wiganer to say something along the lines of, 'Am feelin' reet klempt, I need jackbit.' The first time that I heard someone say this I thought that they were adopting something similar to Cockney rhyme, and that they were declaring their need to use the toilet. It actually translates as, 'I am really hungry. I need to get something to eat.'

I was unsure if I was being subjected to homophobic abuse when I heard someone say 'powfagged,' but this apparently means 'extremely tired.'

'Tha's gerrin' on mi wazz!' caused me similar exasperation. Outside of Wigan, people are more likely to say: 'You are getting on my nerves!'

There are also occasions where the Wiganese vocabulary seems somewhat limited. Any positive situation is invariably described as 'beltin!' If something has exceeded expectation this may be upgraded to 'bloody beltin!'

The food in Wigan can add to the feeling that you are in an entirely separate country from the rest of England. One of the town's signature dishes is the Wigan kebab, which consists of a pie served in a barm. You may call this a bap, a bun or a roll depending on what part of the nation you are from. There are even some insane people who refer to this form of bread as a cob, a muffin or, believe it or not, a bin lid. In upmarket food establishments, the Wigan kebab is often topped with tomato ketchup. Despite my initial reservations, I must admit that I have grown rather fond of this delicacy! Perhaps this is because I live within a few hundred yards of The Trawlerman, which is not only the finest chip shop in the universe but also the spiritual home of the Wigan kebab.

Staying on the subject of food, I was astonished to discover the sheer amount of pie shops in the town. I had always assumed that people had exaggerated the extent of Wiganers' love for pies, but since moving here there are times when I have pondered whether there is a local regulation in place stating that there must be at least two pie shops in every row of retail units. Given that Wigan is home to the annual World Pie Eating Championship, perhaps this is to help the town's competitors prepare for this prestigious event.

A Wiganer will often devour a baby's head, or a 'babby's yed' as it is known in these parts. Alternatively, people may opt for 'pey wet' and a 'smack.' Although this sounds like a menu that was designed by a masochistic cannibal, babby's yed is how Wigan folk describe a steak and kidney pudding. It is a sentence that I never imagined composing, but pey wet is the discharge from mushy peas. A smack is a potato fritter, which is often served in a barm and covered in pey wet. Of course. A Wiganer would probably receive a bemused look, or a punch to the face, if they tried to order a Wigan kebab or a 'smack barm, pey wet' in another part of the country!

Perhaps Wiganers' love of food is reflected by the fact that the Heinz factory in Kitt Green is the largest food processing plant in Europe. It produces more than a billion cans of food each year. Forget London, Paris or Berlin; the tins of baked beans and soup in your kitchen cupboards were probably made in Kitt Green!

I sincerely hope that my father-in-law's eating habits are not the norm for people in Wigan. If so, they are missing out on the joys of sampling food from around the world. Remarkably, Bert has never tried rice, pasta, Indian cuisine or Chinese food! He has not even had a cup of coffee during his seventy-plus years on this planet! His diet consists of the traditional British fare of meat and vegetables. And pies, of course. I have seen many surprising things during my travels around the globe, but Bert's reluctance to taste unfamiliar food has been one of my most shocking discoveries.

Wigan's quirky culinary preferences should not come as too much of a surprise; after all, this is the town that is famous for having a pier that is not a pier. This was originally a coal-loading staithe, estimated to be around twenty metres long, where wagons from a nearby colliery were unloaded onto waiting barges on the Leeds and Liverpool Canal.

It was jokingly referred to as a pier by locals, with George Formby Sr. popularising this term. His son, also called George Formby, would go on to become one of the town's most celebrated residents due to his humorous songs which often incorporated the use of a ukulele. One of his biggest hits was "When I'm Cleaning Windows."

Another George immortalised the 'pier' in *The Road to Wigan Pier*. Orwell painted a rather bleak picture of Wigan in his 1937 book, and he once mischievously stated: "I liked Wigan very much - the people, not the scenery."

Despite the less than flattering description, the town embraced the notoriety that the book brought. This is probably because Wiganers have a reputation for having a sense of humour and for not taking themselves too seriously.

Before moving to the area, I was unaware that the artistic heritage of Wigan included notable names such as The Verve and Sir Ian McKellen. Nor did I know that Wigan Casino was regarded as the spiritual home of the Northern Soul music movement. The sight of one local institution has been unavoidable though, as I pass the Uncle Joe's Mint Balls factory every working day after I return to Wallgate Station in the evening. The sweet manufacturer has been producing the popular mints since 1898, with the factory existing in its current location since 1919. It was certainly strange to see Prince Charles visit this aging building as part of the site's centenary celebrations. Perhaps Uncle Joe's Mint Balls keep the Duke of Edinburgh all aglow.

I have enjoyed seeing the town celebrate its sporting success in recent years. Wigan Warriors have won three Super League titles, a Challenge Cup and a World Club Challenge since I first stepped foot in the town.

4

Meanwhile, the local football team, Wigan Athletic, stunned big-spending Manchester City in the 2013 FA Cup final. Not that I am suggesting that my arrival had anything to do with an upturn in the town's fortunes.

*   *   *

If someone had told a younger version of me that I would spend months stuck in my home in Wigan, I would have wondered what sins I had committed to warrant such punishment. As it turns out, I am lucky to have moved to such a friendly town. I would also have scoffed at the notion that I would travel through six continents; however, my love of exploring the planet has become one of the defining aspects of my life.

Thinking back to that afternoon walking through Wigan with Carol, and the subsequent years spent in the town, makes me realise how much more I could have experienced during my early years of travelling if I had been willing to engage in conversation with other human beings. After all, one of the best ways of discovering a regional culture is through interaction with the local people. One can learn about history and tradition whilst meeting fascinating individuals who provide a different perspective on the world around us. As well as discovering unexpected gems such as the Wigan kebab!

The trips detailed in this book were not my first overseas excursions. My initial jaunts to foreign lands involved less planning; thus, I went along with the flow, experienced unforeseen events and relied on the kindness of other human beings. Unfortunately, after these more off-the-cuff adventures, I became almost too efficient and prepared for such journeys. I no longer needed to depend on the help of others when navigating foreign cities, which unbeknown to me at the time, deprived me of the opportunity to learn more about the places that I visited.

I have been fortunate enough to meet many interesting people during my travels, but it has become apparent that keeping social interaction to a minimum was a key feature of these early trips. I poke fun at my father-in-law for sticking to the food that he is familiar with, but I was often guilty of doing the same. Sampling local food is one of the joys of visiting new countries. Sadly, I was too risk-averse to enjoy more than a sporadic venture into the culinary scene of my host nation.

Another realisation is that I often declined the opportunity to enter historic buildings. Whether this was because of my dislike of large crowds or my habit of adding too much to my itinerary, and consequently depriving myself of the time required to explore all of them in depth, I missed out on some potentially invaluable experiences. Strangely, my inept social skills and the occasional blunder unwittingly led to the creation of memories that will last a lifetime. Regardless, it was impossible not to appreciate the beauty of the places I visited.

I am sure that I am not the only one who has at some stage succumbed to this form of travelling which only scratches the surface. It can be argued that we live in a new 'Golden Age of Travel' due to the low costs involved and the ease of access to different countries, at least for those of us lucky enough to hold a passport issued by a country from the so-called developed world.

The flip side to this is that because travelling has become so easy, one can arrange flights and accommodation without having to interact with another human being. All for a similar price to a train ticket between British cities, and a local hotel. Itineraries can be pieced together using internet research or pocket guidebooks; however, sometimes the best adventures occur when you do not know exactly what to expect and you allow yourself to be swept up in the moment, often forging a bond with other human beings in the process.

This somewhat unsociable form of travel does not lend itself to a more personal and deeper experience; however, the journeys that I describe in this book still evoke vivid and thrilling memories each time that I think of them. In the end, travelling can take whatever form you like, as you are the author of your own story.

Hopefully, my inability to truly immerse myself in the various cultures featured in this book inspire you to take a different path to the one that I chose. I may have spent time in beautiful cities and expanded my knowledge along the way, but I undoubtedly could have delved deeper into the places that I visited. It is much more rewarding when you take the time to talk to the locals, learn some of the language and introduce new flavours to your palate.

Travelling has given me a broader understanding of different cultures and it has caused me to consider global issues in a way that I would not have been able to comprehend without seeing such contrasting places and meeting such inspiring people. It has also aided my development as a human being. I will always be shy and feel slightly awkward in social situations, but I no longer hide away from the world. In fact, I take every opportunity to roam the planet. Even if I still struggle to make small talk with strangers.

CHAPTER 2: LOCKED IN A CAGE AFTER AN ENCOUNTER WITH A FAT POLICEMAN
BUDAPEST, HUNGARY
APRIL 2012

My first overseas trip of 2012 was the second successive city break that did not involve a sporting event. Progress was being made, both in terms of the nature of my travelling and in my personal life. I had received a promotion at work before embarking on this Easter weekend trip, I had set the wheels in motion to finally move out of the family home, and I was now dating the lady that would one day become my wife.

Although Carol and I had only been romantically involved for around three weeks, I was already jetting off to Central Europe with another woman. Carol was kind enough to forgive me, which was probably because the other woman in question was my mother. In hindsight, perhaps I was lucky that she was not put off by the thought of dating a grown man who was still going on holidays with his mum.

Once our flight had arrived at Budapest Ferenc Liszt International Airport, which was named after Hungary's most famous composer, I was faced with the task of guiding us to our accommodation in the city centre. I had assigned myself this responsibility and I was determined to use public transport rather than relying on a taxi to deliver us to the front entrance of our hotel. It was about time that I proved myself, both as a capable traveller and more generally as an adult. The skill of navigating my way around foreign cities via public transport would surely be essential for future trips, so this was a good test for myself.

Fortunately, the airport and the city centre are well connected by a regular rail service. Our old-fashioned train had a functional rather than stylish appearance, which is perhaps fitting for a country that had once been in the grasp of the Soviet Union for four decades. Our thirty-minute journey was straightforward, with the only moment of confusion coming when an elderly woman began to speak to us in broken English.

"You Japanese?" she asked.

We shook our heads before Mum responded, "No, we are Chinese."

Our fellow passenger seemed surprisingly jovial as she enthusiastically nodded and said, "Yes. Korean."

I was unsure whether to consider this woman to be a positive indicator of a friendly nation or a worrying sign of a troubled people. In the end, my aversion to making small talk meant that I did not engage in enough conversation to form a conclusion. For all I know, she could have turned out to have had an inspirational life story or been someone capable of providing us with information that could have enriched our trip.

Nyugati Pályaudvar, which roughly translates as Western Railway Station, is a large rail terminal with seventeen platforms that mostly service routes within Hungary. As we stepped out of our carriage, it felt like we could have been in any generic transport hub in Europe. Upon entering the main body of the station, however, it became clear that this was a grand building that served as a reminder of the more luxurious age of train travel.

The station, which opened in 1877, has a rich history. It was designed by the Eiffel Company. I believe that you may have heard of some of the other projects associated with the company, such as the Eiffel Tower and the Statue of Liberty.

Dragging our hand luggage behind us, we embarked on a straightforward ten-minute walk to our accommodation. The weather was agreeable enough to feel comfortable whilst wearing a T-shirt and jeans, as it would be for the majority of our trip. Upon arrival, Hotel President seemed to be a decent establishment. Located next to the Hungarian National Bank and the Chamber of Commerce, the building did not look out of place amongst such esteemed company.

Despite the various flags that were proudly on display above the main entrance, I had a pretty good idea that the name of the hotel was not an indication of a meaningful link with any national president. It was more than adequate to serve as our temporary home for the next three nights though.

We were pleased with the hotel we had chosen, or to be more accurate, the hotel booking that we had decided to keep. I say this because I had initially booked two different hotels, with each having the option to cancel the reservation free of charge. This bought me some time and allowed me to weigh up the pros and cons of each whilst avoiding the risk of being left with neither. The other property looked just as nice but was located on the other side of the Danube. I was pleased with my final decision, although I realise that this behaviour was less than exemplary and was unfair on the hotel that I eventually snubbed.

This reminded me of how I handled the dilemma of Games lessons during my school days. If the condition of the sports fields were decent, we would play football. If bad weather had caused the pitches to become frozen or waterlogged, we would go for a cross-country run instead. The final decision was often made just before the lesson was due to commence.

Faced with the uncertainty of whether we would be playing an enjoyable football match or enduring a gruelling one-hour run, I devised a plan that provided me with a favourable outcome from either scenario. I would ask Dad to write a note which requested that I be excused from physical activity due to my asthma; however, I would also bring my football kit. If it were decided that we would play football, I would throw the note away. But if we were told that we were required to go on a cross-country run, I would hide my kit and hand in the note instead!

Others were not so fortunate. Some of my classmates who were in poor physical condition would often take so long completing the cross-country route that the rest of us would be home by the time that they finished. I remember that one boy used to take an eternity to finish. Urban legend states that if you travel past my old school grounds on a clear day, and if you look hard enough, you can still see him struggling to complete the cross-country session that he began almost twenty years ago.

After entering our hotel room, Mum and I unpacked our small cases before heading out for an evening meal. We soon found a small restaurant that appeared to serve traditional Hungarian food and seemed reasonably priced enough to leave us with plenty of Forint for the rest of the trip. Goulash was the obvious choice for tourists like us, so we opted for a portion each. I imagine that it was so predictable that we were going to choose this dish that the waiter had started to write down our order before we had even placed it.

As religion had not been part of my upbringing, I was oblivious to the Catholic requirement of avoiding eating the meat of warm-blooded animals on Good Friday. Fish is the popular choice of many on this day, with even non-religious people adopting this tradition. Here we were, ordering beef dishes in a predominantly Roman Catholic country. Oh, the shame! It was probably for the best that I had not realised this at the time, for my over-active mind may have started to worry that I would somehow fall foul of the law due to my meal selection. Or that an angry mob of people would turn up at the restaurant baying for blood. At least they would not try to eat me!

With a consistency sitting somewhere between a soup and a stew, goulash can be traced back to the ninth century when shepherds used to consume something similar. For this reason, the Hungarian name for the dish, Gulyás, loosely translates as 'herdsmen.' There is a plethora of different variations to this hearty dish, but our meal definitely contained paprika, beef, peppers, carrots and potatoes. Another certainty is that we both thoroughly enjoyed our food.

During our walk back to the hotel, we passed St. Stephen's Basilica, which was being illuminated by artificial lighting against the pitch-black sky. We decided to return in the morning and have a better look in daylight. It was the first historic site that we had encountered, and it would also serve as a good marker between our hotel and one of the main bridges that connected the two halves of the city.

Day one had been a success. I had managed to guide us through part of the Hungarian public transport system, we had tried some Gulyás, and I had led us back to the hotel without incident. I almost felt like an adult. Apart from the lack of interaction with the locals, of course. I began to think about the woman on the train. Travel documentaries are littered with such chance encounters in which the likes of Michael Palin or Simon Reeve are able to entice someone into recounting their life story in a manner that provides a better understanding of the country in question. Had I missed out on an opportunity to gain insight into the Hungarian population or had I dodged a prolonged conversation with a deranged woman? Either way, it was clear that I was not confident enough to speak to a stranger.

* * *

After a satisfying continental breakfast, we returned to St. Stephen's Basilica. We could now appreciate the beauty of the neoclassical building which stood before us. The central dome of the basilica is flanked by two bell towers, with the southern one, for what it is worth, containing Hungary's largest bell.

We did not enter the building but if we had, we would have been presented with the opportunity to be in the presence of what is regarded as one of the country's most sacred relics. The item in question is the "incorruptible" right hand of Saint Stephen I of Hungary, who was the nation's first King. This piqued Mum's interest, although she did not exactly seem ecstatic at the prospect of coming into contact with a thousand-year-old hand.

"Why is there a hand from the Middle Ages in the church?" she asked.

Given that I did not really know how to answer Mum's question, I tried my best to sound as confident and assured as I could when providing my response: "He was the first King of Hungary. And they made him into a saint. So, he must hold a special place in their hearts."

Mum was not satisfied with this answer though: "But why preserve his hand? It's a bit weird."

She was only echoing my thoughts, but I carried on regardless: "When they exhumed his body, his right hand was apparently the only part that had not decayed, leading many to believe it was holy."

I think my rather rushed telling of the legend was enough to appease Mum's curiosity, but her position remained the same: "I would not want to be near the hand!"

It is a good job that we were not there in August, as there is an annual procession in which the hand is proudly displayed and carried through the city.

I had a quick read of my guidebook and I saw that there was another quirky fact about the basilica. With a height of ninety-six metres, it shares the honour of being the city's tallest building with the Hungarian Parliament. This was a deliberate design feature, as the number ninety-six represents the founding year of the Hungarian nation in 896, and the equal height of the buildings is supposed to symbolise how the religious and government institutions were the most important bodies in shaping the identity of Hungary.

This sentiment remains in place today, with regulations dictating that no building in Budapest can exceed this height. It seems inevitable that this will one day be scrapped and that high-rise buildings will eventually dominate the skyline, but I was pleased not to see a mass of skyscrapers during our visit. I found this traditional regulation to be intriguing, although I did not dare mention this to Mum as it would almost certainly lead to a series of difficult questions that I would be unable to answer.

If the basilica is considered to be elegant and important in equal measure, the same could not be said for the next tourist attraction that we encountered. The curious looking *Fat Policeman Statue* is located in the area between the basilica and the Széchenyi Chain Bridge. He is thought to have been a local officer who had two passions in his life: protecting his community and indulging in Hungarian cuisine. The statue's popularity with tourists was clear to see, as his bronze belly was shiny from all the times that it had been rubbed for good luck.

"David, do you want your photograph taken with the statue?" Mum asked.

I gladly accepted her invitation, but I soon felt awkward posing next to the rotund officer whilst a crowd of tourists waited for their turn to do the same. My paranoia kicked in as I began to imagine a scenario in which I was getting heckled by the crowd. 'Which one of them is the Fat Policeman?' and, 'They make a nice couple,' were the type of comments that crossed my mind, even if it was extremely unlikely that they would enter the thoughts of anyone from the crowd of onlookers.

This is not the only bizarre statue in Budapest. A couple of years after our visit, a bronze figure depicting Peter Falk's character from the long-running television show *Columbo* was unveiled. Although the statue is located on Falk street and the actor is thought to have Hungarian ancestry, it is not entirely clear why the local authorities decided to create this peculiar statue. The street is named in honour of the nineteenth-century Hungarian politician Miksa Falk, but there are no confirmed links between the two.

The part of me which enjoys quirky attractions like this would probably relish a return to Budapest in order to explore its other unusual statues. There are also works of art that represent former U.S. President Ronald Reagan, iconic footballer Ferenc Puskás and the artist Attila József. Perhaps in an attempt to escape the city's communist past, contemporary statues that appeal to everyday Hungarians have been erected instead of the usual fare of historical and political figures. Lázló Marton's *Little Princess* was created for his daughter who used to dress up as royalty by using a makeshift outfit consisting of newspaper and a bathrobe. Another installation portrays a hooded and faceless individual who represents the anonymous author of the *Deeds of the Hungarians,* which details the early history of the nation.

We moved on from the local 'bobby on the beat' and began to cross the Széchenyi Chain Bridge that connects Pest to Buda on the other side of the Danube River. I am not trying to be cute; the two sides of the city are indeed called Buda and Pest. The bridge that we were now walking across was completed shortly after the Hungarian Revolution of 1848, but it was not until 1873 that the separate cities of Buda and Pest were merged.

Hotel President and St. Stephen's Basilica are located in Pest, which is the flatter and more vibrant side of the combined city. What awaited us in Buda appeared to be a place that once housed the important and rich people on its hilly terrain. The castle overlooking the Danube provided the biggest clue.

"So, we are leaving Pest behind and going to Buda? David, does that mean we are travelling to another city?" Mum asked.

"No, they used to be separate but now they are part of one city," I explained.

Mum paused before posing her next question: "So, could Manchester be a merged city? Did there used to be separate places called Man and Chester?"

I shook my head. "No, Chester is near Wales and... well, there is the Isle of Man, but neither has anything to do with Manchester. I believe that Manchester was known as Mamucium during Roman times. Most merged cities that I can think of have rather clumsy names like Dallas/Fort Worth, but Budapest has a nice ring to it."

Mum nodded in agreement before concurring that, "Budapest does sound good."

I could not resist passing further comment on the city's name: "It certainly sounds better than Pestbuda anyway!"

Mum looked puzzled as she asked: "What do you mean? Is there a place called Pestbuda?"

I knew that I should have stayed quiet.

The stone pillars that hold the iron chains reminded me of Brooklyn Bridge, which Mum and I had visited the previous year. Like its famous equivalent in New York, Széchenyi Chain Bridge is one of the most recognisable sights within the city and it has become a tourist attraction in its own right.

There were a couple of stone statues of lions at each end of the bridge that had a similar look to those found in Trafalgar Square. Any feeling of being back in London was strengthened by the knowledge that the bridge was designed by an Englishman. Along with the Marlow Bridge over the River Thames, it is one of only two remaining bridges that were designed by William Tierney Clark. There was certainly a strong British influence, as construction of the suspension bridge was overseen by a Scotsman by the name of Adam Clark.

A plaque that we had walked past on the Pest side confirmed the English engineer's role in the bridge's design and more importantly meant that I did not have to explain this to Mum. There were also inscriptions to commemorate the Scottish Clark and a Greek merchant named Georgios Sinas, who helped finance the project.

Unfortunately, we did not see these inscriptions, so it was up to me to explain their roles to Mum: "A Scottish engineer called Adam Clark built the bridge."

Mum asked the obvious question: "Clark again. Does that mean that they are related?"

"No. One was from England and the other from Scotland. Also, a Greek merchant helped to fund the bridge's construction."

"Why did a Greek person fund it?"

My guidebook provided me with the information to answer this: "He had financial interests in the area, so a link between Buda and Pest was beneficial to his business. As well as many other citizens."

This led to Mum posing the following question: "So if an Englishman designed the bridge, a Scotsman built it and a Greek businessman funded it, why does it have a Hungarian name?"

It sounded like the opening line of a joke; albeit one for which I did not know the punchline. At least I was able to make up a response that was not too far from the truth: "You know how it works: a ruler of the country, usually a King or a politician, takes credit for the construction of an important project."

In fact, Count Ivan Széchenyi is considered by many to be one of the most important Hungarians in history. He donated large sums of money towards the modernisation of Hungary and through his political writing, he encouraged other wealthy members of society to give up some of their economic privileges for the sake of the advancement of the country. Due to his belief that transport infrastructure was key to the economic future of the nation, he supported projects like the construction of the bridge that now bears his name.

The first tourist attraction that I wished to visit in Buda was called Fisherman's Bastion. As I had seen lots of beautiful pictures of the bastion whilst searching online for places of interest within Budapest, I was full of excitement. We soon reached our desired location after crossing the Széchenyi Chain Bridge.

"Fisherman's Bastion. That's an interesting name. What do fisherman have to do with it?" Mum asked.

I tried my best to explain the origin of the name without sounding like I had just read about it in my guidebook: "The bastion was built on the walls of Buda Castle at the turn of the twentieth century. The name comes from various historical accounts which state that the castle was defended by fishermen who lived under the castle walls. I am not sure how accurate that is though."

It was clear by the look on Mum's face that she was going to ask a follow-up question, and she duly obliged.

"What is a bastion?"

This was the question that I feared she would ask. It was not exactly my area of expertise, but I made an attempt to give an acceptable answer: "A bastion is part of a defensive fortification of a tower."

Thankfully, this seemed to temporarily satisfy Mum's curiosity. We climbed the stairs and began to walk along the bastion. It was as impressive in the physical form as it had appeared in the images that I had seen online. Fisherman's Bastion, like the Széchenyi Chain Bridge, was extensively damaged during the sieges of Budapest during the Second World War.

The subsequent restoration work has resulted in an area that seems well suited as a tourist attraction but is a little too polished for an historic fortification. In any case, this may have always been the intention, as many people suspect that Fisherman's Bastion was built to celebrate the history of the castle and the city rather than to defend it.

Nevertheless, a sense of history is provided by some of the architectural elements, such as the seven towers which represent each of the ninth-century Magyar tribes who settled in the area that would one day become Budapest. If the sense of authenticity was diminished somewhat by the tourist-friendly, smooth and accessible walkways, the view overlooking the Danube and across to Pest on the other side remained as spectacular as they surely were at the time of construction.

Although this view would have been strategically advantageous if the castle needed to be defended from invading forces, Mum and I were content to simply stand in awe and enjoy this visual treat.

"Mum, this is why I was so eager to visit here" I remarked.

She smiled and confirmed her approval by simply stating that, "It is beautiful."

We could see the imposing and majestic Hungarian Parliament Building by the bank of the Danube, which was glistening in the sun, as well as the familiar sights of Széchenyi Chain Bridge and St. Stephen's Basilica. It all looked so much prettier from this vantage point. Even the bastion itself enhanced the view, with the stone towers and walls providing a charming frame for the image in front of us.

We headed over to Matthias Church, which is located in the Holy Trinity Square in front of the bastion. Before reaching the church, we bumped into our old friend St. Stephen I. This time he appeared in the form of a bronze equestrian statue. It had an elevated position thanks to the stone pedestal that it rested upon. I resisted the urge to knock him off his pedestal, instead opting to take a photograph of the statue against the backdrop of the church.

Originally built in the eleventh century, it has undergone many transformations during its lifetime, including being converted into a Mosque following the Ottoman invasion in the sixteenth century. The building has suffered significant damage over the course of its history, most notably after the Mongol invasion in the thirteenth century and during the Second World War. The subsequent restorations added a different dimension each time, incorporating a range of architectural styles such as Gothic and Baroque.

The appearance of the church matched that of Fisherman's Bastion: it was pretty, but it almost seemed a little too polished to reflect its storied past. After all, this was the site of several royal weddings and coronations, including the crowning of Franz Joseph and Elizabeth, which effectively marked the establishment of the Austro-Hungarian Empire.

Mum and I did not have such grand ambitions; locating our next tourist attraction was all that was on our agenda. The imposing Buda Castle was the obvious choice, but we decided to give it a miss. We had been afforded a clear view of it during our walk across Széchenyi Chain Bridge, and its position at the top of Castle Hill made it, like most castles, visible from many parts of the city.

Instead, we went in search of something that was designed to be more discreet. The 'Hospital in the Rock' was built in the caverns of Castle Hill as the Second World War was about to break out across Europe in 1939. The existing tunnels of the castle complex were extended so that the makeshift hospital could be accessed in this way. A collection of dedicated workers, including around forty doctors and the head nurse of the Hungarian Red Cross, were on hand to tend to wounded soldiers and civilians.

This was used most notably during the fifty-day siege of Budapest which began in December 1944. The hospital was equipped to treat around seventy patients, but they were swamped by around six hundred people at the height of the suffering. Approximately 38,000 civilians died as a result of the siege by the Allied Forces. The number of deaths doubles when you factor in those who perished in the labour and prisoner of war camps. The unusual history of the 'Hospital in the Rock' continued, as it was transformed into a nuclear bunker during the Cold War era.

We initially struggled to locate it, which I guess is to be expected when trying to find a secret hospital hidden in the caverns of a hill in a foreign country. Eventually, we found the modest entrance and had a read of the information that was alongside it. A description of life inside the hospital was accompanied by photographs that provided a glimpse of the conditions that the doctors, nurses and patients were faced with.

There was a sign which informed us that there was an entrance fee and that a guided tour was required. Some of the photos showed what the hospital museum now looks like, with waxwork figures filling the rooms in order to recreate scenes that one would expect to find inside. We took a moment to try to picture what it would have been like to work in such a location whilst terrible things were happening within the city on a daily basis.

"Mum, you were a nurse for many years in Manchester. Imagine treating patients in there. Do you think that you could do it?" I asked.

"I could not. It was difficult at times in Manchester, where we had top-class equipment and were in a fairly wealthy, peaceful city. I could not imagine being faced with so many injured people whilst trapped inside a cave."

We decided not to enter, as we did not particularly fancy looking at a collection of waxworks. Instead, we headed to a different entrance point to the network of underground tunnels known as 'The Labyrinth.' We paid the modest entrance fee and descended the steps into near darkness.

Thankfully, there was just enough lighting to prevent either of us falling down the stairs and requiring medical treatment. It would have been most unfortunate to have been injured whilst navigating the tunnels that lead to a disused hospital. It was at this point that I decided to tell Mum that Vlad the Impaler had been held captive here in the fifteenth century.

"So, he could be waiting for us in these dark tunnels? Why have you taken me here? Are you trying to get rid of your poor old mum?" she asked.

I chuckled and reassured her that this was not my plan. My laughter was short lived though, as the darkness soon put us on edge. Every little sound made us twitchy. We eventually stumbled upon a metal structure that looked like a giant birdcage, which prompted me to ask Mum to take a photograph whilst I stood inside of it.

"Is it not a bit dark for photos?" she asked.

"The flash is on. If this were a horror movie, a semi-decomposed woman would appear next to me as the camera flash lights up the cavern!"

Mum looked a bit worried. "I hope that does not happen," she remarked.

I locked myself in the cage and clung on to the metal frame with both hands, mimicking a prisoner who was unfortunate enough to have found themselves held captive here. The flash went off but there was no sign of anyone that resembled a member of the undead. Apart from the dopey Englishman who was posing for photographs inside a cage.

"You look scary...like Dracula!" Mum cheekily suggested.

In fairness, she was probably right. A close-up picture of me locked up in a cage with the flash on was not likely to be a pretty sight. The Labyrinth is around six miles long, but we did not explore much of it. We barely covered one per cent of the network of tunnels before we decided to return to daylight and civilisation. We were satisfied with sampling a small section and taking a cringe-worthy tourist photograph. Or perhaps we were just terrified at the prospect of bumping into Vlad the Impaler.

The cover of my guidebook featured a photo of a statue of Saint Gerard overlooking another of the Danube's great bridges, known locally as Erzsébet Híd. I informed Mum of my desire to recreate this image and she was happy to go along with this plan. It seemed that she had put her complete faith in my leadership. Hopefully, she would not regret that decision.

We made our way back to the Danube before following the riverbank until we reached Gellért Hill. It was bigger than I had expected.

"How high is that?" Mum asked.

Unsure of the answer, I glumly stated: "It looks like it will be a long walk to the top."

In fact, the height of the hill is 235 metres. We had travelled this far, so we may as well go the extra mile. Or the extra 235 metres in this case. We climbed the steps, passing people who were making their way back down to street level. As they did not appear to be tired, I told myself that this must mean that the walk to the top is not so taxing. Unless they had given up and aborted their journey before exhaustion had taken hold of them.

The statue of Saint Gerard was the first point of interest that we encountered. Gerard was part of the nobility in Venice, but he had ended up in Hungary after embarking on a pilgrimage in the eleventh century. King Stephen I, whose legacy was becoming evident to us, appointed Gerard as a bishop and convinced him to help with the conversion of the Hungarian population to Catholicism. Gerard, or Gellért as he is known in Hungarian, lived on the hill until he met a rather unpleasant death there following a Pagan uprising.

One legend states that he was stoned and lanced before being thrown from the hilltop into the Danube. Another account declares that he was placed in a cart and pushed down the hill, before being beaten to death at the bottom. Alternatively, it is claimed that he was rolled down the hill in a spiked barrel. Either way, it seems that he was thrown down the hill in some form or another and that his death was horrific. At least he had a hill named after him. And a statue.

It was fairly challenging to recreate the photograph that I had in mind. It was taken from behind the statue, as if to position the Saint, who is holding a cross in his hand, so that he is overlooking the city and the Danube.

"You have got to give it to him. He is a stubborn and determined fellow. Long after he was thrown from the top of the hill, here he is, still spreading his religious message," I joked.

This left Mum with a blank expression on her face.

"I have no idea what you are talking about, David."

"That makes two of us."

I managed to capture the image that I wanted, even if it was vastly inferior to the one from the guidebook. We then continued our uphill journey until we reached another statue. This time it depicted a woman stood on a pedestal whilst holding a palm leaf. The combined height of *The Liberty Statue* and pedestal is forty metres, making it visible from much of the surrounding area. It was erected in 1947 after what was at the time regarded as the Soviet liberation from Nazi rule.

Within a decade, resentment towards the communist Soviet regime resulted in the Hungarian Revolution of 1956. The fact that the Soviets bombarded the city and its dissenting population from the hill where a statue honoured the Soviet liberation was most ironic. And incredibly sad, of course. Following the fall of communism, the wording of the statue's inscriptions was changed to honour those who had sacrificed their lives for the freedom and liberty of Hungarians rather than paying homage to the Soviets.

The statue stood in front of the Citadel, which we had walked around in order to avoid paying the entrance fee. The fortress was built by the Habsburgs after the uprising of 1848 to 1849, who had chosen this location as it was ideal for launching strikes into Buda or Pest in the event of any more trouble from the local population. The Soviets certainly approved of this strategic decision.

Not for the first time that day, we took in a spectacular view of the Danube and the city that straddles both sides of it. This was enough to justify the arduous trek up the hill and left us satisfied with what we had seen, to the extent that we did not feel the need to explore what was behind the walls of the Citadel.

In fact, we did not even check out the interesting sounding Cave Church. As the name suggests, this is a church that was built within the caves of the hill. Inspired by a visit to Lourdes, returning Hungarian pilgrims chose the St. Ivan Cave due to the belief that its thermal water had healing powers. The Soviets, delightful as always, executed the monks and sealed the entrance to the cave. It was eventually reopened after the fall of the Soviet Union. The prospect of making my mum walk further along the hill and possibly having to pay an entrance fee was enough to dissuade me from visiting. Besides, we were unsure whether it would even be open over Easter weekend.

With our sightseeing for the day complete, we made our way back down the hill and retraced our steps along the riverbank until we reached the Széchenyi Chain Bridge. We could have crossed Erzsébet Híd, otherwise known as Elisabeth Bridge, but my overly cautious brain was telling me not to risk the possibility of losing my bearings and getting us lost in a foreign country. Mum and I left Buda behind after a thoroughly good day exploring its major landmarks.

One quirky tourist attraction on this side of the city that I was not aware of at the time was the Children's Railway. Gyermekvasút is a seven-mile narrow-gauge rail line that is operated by children aged between ten and fourteen. Adults drive the train and supervise the children though, so you are not putting your life in too much danger by using this form of transport. This originated from a project that was introduced during communist rule. Like other initiatives introduced across the Soviet Union, it was intended to instil discipline and a variety of other desired attributes amongst the younger members of society who would spend time in youth camps.

I doubt that I would have been able to resist the urge to have a ride along this unusual rail service If I had known about it at the time of our visit. Apparently, the children of today, who work there one day out of every fifteen, dress up in smart uniforms and greet passengers in a professional manner at each station. They are even known to burst into song on occasion. The railway provides some of the older members of the city's population with a sense of nostalgia, whilst it has proven to be a popular tourist gimmick.

In some way, I feel disappointed to have missed out on travelling along a railway operated by children. But then again, I use Northern Rail trains during my daily commute, so there is probably not much difference. That is rather unfair, and I should apologise. I am sure that the Children's Railway is far more efficient and pleasant.

We found a reasonable looking restaurant on the way back to the hotel, where we enjoyed another tasty evening meal. This time we plumped for a different traditional Hungarian dish called Csirke Paprikás, or Chicken Paprikash. Unsurprisingly, our meal had a strong flavour of paprika, along with peppers, onions, tomatoes and a serving of egg dumplings. It had been a pleasant but tiring day in which we had enjoyed taking in the many sights of the city. Aside from St. Stephen's Basilica, we had only really explored Buda. Pest was still to come!

*　　*　　*

Margaret Island was the first port of call for the following day's sightseeing. This is not located in either Buda or Pest. Instead, it is a sliver of land, 500 metres in width, which sits in the Danube between the two sides of the city. Fortunately, the weather was suitably pleasant for exploring the 2.5-kilometre length of the island.

As well as the scenic parkland, there was also a fair amount of history to explore. The Knights of St. John settled on the island in the twelfth century and the ruins of numerous religious buildings can be found here. The first interesting thing that we encountered was the Centenary Monument, which marked one hundred years since Buda merged with Pest. It is a rather unusual sculpture, with what are supposed to be two bronze leaves that start off as separate entities but intertwine at the top. The symbolism was clear to see but they looked more like rusty pieces of scrap metal rather than leaves.

"What is that?" Mum asked.

"It is supposed to be two leaves that are intertwined, representing the merger between..."

"Buda and Pest! See, I have been listening and I have learned something this weekend. Thank you for teaching me."

I was being given far too much credit, since it was our guidebook that had provided most of the information over the course of the weekend, but her response demonstrated how travelling can be an effective form of education. And that at least someone had benefitted from me waffling on about tourist attractions and churning out regurgitated historical facts all weekend.

The tiny island was an amiable place to travel around on foot. It was essentially a park in the middle of the Danube that provided an escape from the surrounding city. Feeling relaxed and carefree, we strolled through the central pathway and rose garden, passing the swimming pools and a prominent fountain. The ruins of some religious buildings caught our eye, so we approached them for a closer inspection.

Although the few remaining crumbling walls were not much to look at, the Dominican Convent had an interesting backstory. King Béla IV is said to have vowed to dedicate his daughter's life to religion if the Hungarians were able to repel the Mongol invasion. True to his word, he founded the convent and sent his young daughter Margit, known in English as Margaret, there in 1251.

Years later, he would request for her to leave behind her religious life and marry King Ottokar II of Bohemia. Margit, however, disobeyed her father's wishes and chose to serve God for the entirety of her life. She apparently opted to perform the most menial and physically draining duties, often neglecting her health in the process. She died before she had even turned thirty, but her memory lives on forever through her Sainthood. The island, known as Margit-sziget in Hungarian, was also named after her. As I mentioned earlier, there was not much to look at, but it is always interesting to stand before the ruins of a structure that was built hundreds of years ago, especially if there is an intriguing story behind it.

I posed a question for Mum: "How would you have felt if I had dedicated myself to God at the expense of my health and personal happiness?"

Mum paused before answering: "Well, I cannot imagine that you would do that. You are not religious, you go to the gym every day, and you like travelling."

I put the question to her again: "But what if I did? How would you feel about it?"

"I would not be happy. That girl died when she was just a couple of years older than you are now."

Her answer was certainly understandable, as I cannot imagine that many parents would be happy to see their child die at such a young age.

The nearby Premonstratensian Church was more substantial than the ruins that we had just visited. The remains of this thirteenth-century building, which was once used as a monastery, were rediscovered in 1914 when a storm knocked over a walnut tree and uncovered a church bell.

Excavation work then revealed the ruins of the building, which was eventually reconstructed.

It looked like an old church that one would expect to find in a small village in the English countryside. It was bigger than the one that is featured in *Emmerdale*, for example, but it would not seem out of place in that particular television show. We were now in proximity to the fifty-seven-metre-high water tower that had been visible from afar. Built in 1911, the octagonal tower had the dual purpose of supplying water for the inhabitants of the island whilst serving as a lookout station. It was reopened to the public a month after our visit, with exhibitions regularly being held there.

We were unconcerned about not being able to enter the pale-yellow tower, as we were more than happy to just admire it from ground level before strolling back through the gardens that belong to the island. Mum and I also neglected to visit the Japanese garden or musical well. Given that the island is regarded by many Catholics as a place to reaffirm their devotion to God, it seemed a suitable place for Mum and I to reflect on the virtues of life and the complexity of the world that we live in. I began by asking Mum about her thoughts on communism.

She responded by saying: "Communism is a difficult thing to endure. I was lucky that I grew up in Hong Kong, but life would have been much tougher in mainland China."

I delved further into the subject: "There are lots of examples of communist regimes that have caused suffering, but do you think that is due to the system itself or because of the corrupt leaders involved?"

Mum shrugged her shoulders and said: "I don't know. Does it matter?"

I thought about this before replying: "I think it does. At least the principle of Communism has some good aspects. If there was ever a well-intentioned and efficient regime in place, then it could work. I am not keen on the materialistic aspect of capitalism."

"David, you may not think that you are materialistic, but your obsession with travelling works in a similar way."

Mum's response caused me to engage in a moment of introspection. She was right. My desire to travel was becoming insatiable, and this had resulted in a self-centred way of thinking that was aligned with the world of capitalism.

Furthermore, I had been convincing myself that travelling was some form of noble quest, but the truth was that my trips abroad had allowed me to temporarily lead a hedonistic lifestyle. When travelling, I would eat whatever I wanted, I would do as I pleased, and I would not be overly concerned about the time or money being spent. Only my inner cheapskate kept me in check.

Feeling somewhat disappointed with my selfish ways, I suggested that we should visit Heroes' Square. After a long walk towards the central districts of Pest, passing the station where we had arrived by train on our first day, we stumbled upon the House of Terror. This large building stood out from its surroundings, as it had what appeared to be a black entablature with a stencil design featuring some cut-out letters.

Mum and I looked up towards the top of the building to try to make out what word the letters formed. We initially thought that it may be something from the Russian language, but we eventually realised that it was 'Terror' written upside down from our perspective. This would appear as normal from above, but nobody apart from the caped hero of the *Superman* films would benefit from this. It took longer than it should have to notice that the stencil produces the word, this time reading the correct way from our perspective, in the form of sunlight on the side of the building; hence, why the letters were positioned this way on the stencil design.

It looked an impressive building, but it was one that contained an extensive collection of artefacts that highlight some of the darkest periods in Hungarian and European history. In 1944, during the final months of the Second World War, the far-right Arrow Cross Party came to power. This fascist regime, which was the de-facto Nazi party of Hungary, inflicted large-scale suffering on its own population, particularly in relation to the Jewish community and ethnic minorities.

It is estimated that up to 15,000 people were murdered during this brief period, with another 80,000 sent to concentration camps. The building in front of us served as the party's headquarters, with the cellar being used to torture and kill people.

The building's dark history is not confined to the short-lived era of the Arrow Cross Party rule. The State Security Authority, known as the ÁVH, also set up camp here during the Communist era. Hungary was a satellite state of the Soviet Union, so the ÁVH was effectively the local version of the KGB. Anyone who dissented against the regime was likely to be held here and tortured. It is thought that many thousands endured this fate. The Soviets ruled with an iron fist, with the ÁVH instilling a sense of fear across the Hungarian population. It certainly makes me appreciate the freedom that I have been blessed with.

I asked Mum if she wanted to go inside but she said that she did not fancy looking at the many exhibits which detail the atrocities that were committed. I would probably have found it interesting, but it was understandable that Mum did not wish to explore the horrific world of torture and murder. Instead, we continued our journey towards Heroes' Square.

This entailed a pleasant fifteen-minute walk along Andrássy út, which is a 2.5-kilometre boulevard named after former Hungarian Prime Minister Gyula Andrássy. If we had visited during the communist era, we would have been walking down Sztálin út, as it was, unsurprisingly, renamed after Joseph Stalin. There were a couple of further changes before the original street name was restored following the fall of the Soviet Union.

"It is a nice road. It reminds me of the Champs-Élysees."

Mum had made an apt comparison. The wide boulevard that we were walking along was lined with trees, grand buildings, restaurants and fashionable shops. I had vague memories of the famous avenue in Paris from a school trip that I went on when I was thirteen. My French teacher, Mr Green, had told us all about how the Champs-Élysees had become a sea of triumphant football fans celebrating their national team's victory at the World Cup that had been held in France a few weeks before our visit in 1998. The mood of celebration had dampened somewhat by the time of our trip, but I remember trying to picture the scene from our coach. Whilst the Champs-Élysées leads to the Arc de Triomphe, Heroes Square is the crowning glory at the end of Andrássy út.

It was not too long before we were making our way through the open space of the square, dodging a plethora of skateboarders and fellow tourists in the process. The Millennium Monument is the dominant feature of the square, with a thirty-six-metre column occupying its centre. A statue of the Archangel Gabriel rests on top, and the Memorial Stone of Heroes sits at its base. This serves as a tribute to those who have died defending the country since the tenth century. The monument was adorned with statues depicting the leaders of the seven tribes who claimed the land that one day would become Hungary. Semi-circular arcades framed the square and provided a spectacular backdrop for the column and memorial stone.

Mum provided her assessment: "The memorial looks nice, but it is similar to many others that you find across Europe. It is probably better looking than most though. The open square and the arcades give it a nice look."

I concurred, before providing some additional information: "The communist politician Imre Nagy was reburied here in 1989."

"If he was a Communist, wouldn't he be unpopular though?"

"It is fairly complicated, but it appears that he was seen as being someone who tried to scale back the harsher aspects of the Soviet regime."

Nagy was a figurehead for the 1956 revolution, but he was executed a couple of years later. The Soviets did not permit him a burial place accessible to the public. In a highly symbolic and defining moment in the final days of Soviet-led communist rule, a crowd of over 100,000 people gathered to witness the body of Nagy being reburied along with those of other prominent individuals who had been executed following the revolution.

Viktor Orbán, who was a young politician at the time, gave a rousing speech calling for the end of Soviet control over Hungary. He is currently serving his fourth term as Prime Minister. His political views have shifted considerably since that day in 1989, with his government pursuing an increasingly far-right agenda and clamping down on civil liberties.

Before making the return journey along Andrássy út, we refuelled with some cake and a cup of tea in one of the nearby cafes. Mum and I shared a slice of a layered chocolate buttercream sponge cake, called Dobos Torte, and a portion of a walnut-based cake, known as Esterházy Torte. Both are popular and traditional dishes within Hungary. They were certainly tasty, and they provided us with enough energy for our walk back to the area near our hotel.

We were soon eating again, this time within the WestEnd City Shopping Mall located next door to Nyugati Train Station. If we would have chosen to find a restaurant in the latter, we may have ended up in what is regarded as one of the grandest McDonald's in the world. I would have found it strange to devour a Big Mac whilst sat in an historic station hall which has such immense architectural value. The décor is apparently more in line with a restaurant boasting a Michelin Star or two rather than a fast-food outlet.

As it turned out, we ended up eating in a less glamorous and unusual setting, although the quality of food was probably better. Mum had chosen a Chinese vendor within the food court of the shopping mall. She had a long conversation with the owner in Mandarin, which mostly entailed him telling her about how he had travelled from China to start a new life within Hungary. Prime Minister Orbán's anti-immigrant rhetoric and right-wing policies have been stepped up in recent years, so perhaps our vendor would not have enjoyed such a pleasant transition into Hungarian society if he had begun his new life in Europe more recently.

I had again failed to engage with a resident of Budapest, leaving it to Mum to talk to him about his interesting personal story. I could have discovered more about life for immigrants in Hungary and perhaps heard something unexpected that changed my understanding of the city, but I had once more shied away from this possibility.

Instead, I happily consumed my noodles with the knowledge that Manchester United had just extended their lead over Manchester City at the top of the Premier League to eight points with just six games remaining of the season. Being a pessimist, I was one of the few fans who had doubts that the team would go on to win the trophy. For once, it turned out that my negativity was well placed on this occasion. I would like to say that pessimism prepares you for disappointment, but unfortunately this is not the case. All it does is provide you with an appetiser of apprehension to compliment your main course of agony.

We stopped by the Hungarian State Opera House on our way back to the hotel. The facade of the Neo-Renaissance building was impressive, but its real beauty was concealed from us. If we had booked tickets for a show that was being held there, we would have been able to admire its opulent interior. The auditorium may not be the biggest, but it is claimed that the acoustics are only bettered by the respective opera houses in Paris and Milan. In any case, it was time to get some sleep on our last night in Budapest.

*   *   *

I woke up on our final morning in the Hungarian capital with the realisation that we had not visited the most iconic sight of the city. Although we had admired the Hungarian Parliament Building from afar, we had not yet stopped by for a closer look. Fortunately, as we were flying back to Manchester later in the afternoon, the morning was free for a final sightseeing session.

With our woollen hats on due to there being a slight chill in the air, we headed towards the huge building that was situated by the bank of the Danube. We had admired the white facade and burgundy dome from Buda on our first day, but the sheer size of it was more apparent now that we were in its shadow.

It may only be the third biggest parliamentary building in the world, but it can certainly stake a claim for being the most beautiful. Inspired by the Palace of Westminster's proximity to the River Thames, the location by the Danube adds to the splendour of the architectural design. The main facade faces the river, but the main entrance is on the other side by Kossuth Lajos Square. It was from one of the balconies here that, following the fall of the Communist regime, the Hungarian Republic was declared on the Twenty-Third of October in 1989.

"It is a beautiful building," Mum remarked.

I agreed with her assessment and perhaps due to recency bias, went a step further: "It is one of the most beautiful buildings that I have seen, and I prefer it to Westminster."

This was a little unfair to the historic equivalent in London, which is even more iconic and has a history that goes back a further nine hundred years. In any case, both are wonderful buildings and I felt blessed to be stood in front of such grandeur. I tried my best to use the extensive arrangement of colourful flowers in front of the entrance to enhance my photograph, but this was unnecessary; the building was majestic enough that it did not need additional features to improve its splendour.

Whilst its aesthetic quality cannot be questioned, the lavish design and cost involved in the construction merits a certain amount of scrutiny. The interior is adorned by around half a million precious stones, in addition to over forty kilograms of gold, and there is a turret for every day of the year incorporated into the design. I am not sure how this works during a leap year though.

The Hungarian Parliament Building may be the most revered tourist attraction in the city, but we soon unwittingly discovered what we would come to regard as its most memorable feature. Our decision to take one last walk along the Danube resulted in a chance encounter with sixty pairs of iron shoes by the riverbank. We were most intrigued by this and wondered why they had been placed there. A nearby plaque revealed the harrowing reason behind their installation: "To the memory of the victims shot into the Danube by Arrow Cross militiamen in 1944-45."

A quick scan through my guidebook provided further information. The pro-Nazi Arrow Cross fascist regime executed many people by the bank of the Danube by making them take off their shoes before shooting them. Their bodies would fall into the river and be washed away whilst their shoes were left behind on the riverbank.

It has been suggested that around 3,500 people were killed in this manner during this short reign of terror, with the Jewish population comprising the highest percentage of victims. Less conservative estimates indicate that around 20,000 Jews were executed along the Danube and that over 80,000 were led on death marches to the Austrian border. We will never know the exact figure, only that there was a tragically high number of people who suffered this horrific fate.

The *Shoes on the Danube Bank* memorial, which was created by film director Can Togay and sculptor Gyula Pauer in 2005, is such a powerful and moving way to commemorate the victims of the atrocities that occurred here. The level of detail further enhances the human connection that one can make with the memorial. The iron shoes offer an insight into the vast array of victims; there are shoes that resemble the appearance of those worn by men, women and children from both rich and poor backgrounds, and from a variety of professions.

After reading about the dark history that inspired this creation, the sight of a pair of child's shoes by the riverbank is about as sad and sombre as it can get. Of all the memorials that I have seen around the world, this was certainly one of the most effective in evoking emotion and illustrating the depressing reality of past events. It further underlined the importance of learning about human stories whilst travelling, whether this is in the form of history or from people currently living in the place one is visiting.

It turns out that the last thing that we saw in Budapest left the biggest impression, and I do not think that recency bias can be attributed on this occasion. Despite the sobering experience, this enhanced what had already been an outstanding trip. The only thing that was missing was a trip to the famed thermal baths located within the city. As that would have involved seeing my mother in a swimming costume, perhaps it was for the best that we did not visit any of them.

CHAPTER 3: THE BIRTH OF THE FLAG COLLECTION!
STOCKHOLM, SWEDEN
APRIL 2012

Three days after returning from Budapest with my mother, I was heading to Sweden with my father. As I had only transferred to a new department at work the previous week, my new colleagues were immediately alerted to the fact that I was a frequent traveller. If I was not at my desk by the start of my shift, there was a good chance that I was roaming around a city in some foreign land. This is a bit of an exaggeration, but my first few weeks in the job saw me venture overseas on numerous occasions.

Our journey involved SAS involvement. Unfortunately, my anecdote is not interesting enough to be referring to the special forces unit of the British Army. Instead, my rather tepid tale involves a flight with Scandinavian Airlines System rather than a hostage rescue or a highly classified counter-terrorism mission. Mind you, it would be rather terrifying to experience a holiday that involved an armed siege. This would have been more likely in the 1960s, when hijacking was frighteningly common. At one point, a plane was held up on average once every six days in the United States alone.

Dad and I were sat next to a fellow British tourist during our flight to Stockholm. He seemed a friendly guy, but this did not stop me from choosing to have a nap rather than make small talk with him for three hours. Before falling asleep, I heard him tell Dad about how he was going to watch the same two sporting events as we were. The Swedish capital was hosting a football match between two of the country's most successful teams that evening and *UFC on Fuel TV: Gustafsson vs. Silva* a couple of days later. My interest in mixed martial arts had already begun to diminish by 2012, but I still held sufficient interest to travel to another country in order to watch a live show.

31

Our fellow passenger's revelation was not enough to entice me to speak to him though. I would sooner rest my head against the side of the plane and have it jolted every few seconds than engage in the dreaded activity of chatting to a stranger. In order to indicate that I was not open to the prospect of joining the conversation, I kept my eyes firmly closed, despite not being able to nod off for more than a few seconds at a time.

At one point, I heard him inform Dad that he was hoping to add to his collection of football shirts: "I buy the local team's jersey whenever I travel abroad."

I found this quite interesting and wondered whether I should start building a similar collection. After all, I did not possess any physical items to represent the different places that I had previously travelled to. I was tempted to ask him about the average cost of the football shirts, but I had firmly committed myself to avoiding small talk at any cost. We had not even arrived in Sweden, yet I was already choosing to limit my contact with others.

After a smooth landing at Stockholm Arlanda Airport, we politely said our goodbyes to the man that I had been ignoring for the past three hours. Following my trip to Budapest, I was feeling confident enough to use public transport to reach our hotel. I had read that the Arlanda Express was a direct train service that connected the airport to central Stockholm. It seemed idiot-proof. I guess we were the perfect candidates to put this to the test! If this was not quite simple enough for a couple of hapless chaps like us, I had decided to book a hotel that was next door to the train station. We arrived safely at our hotel around twenty minutes after boarding the train, which hopefully demonstrated that we were not complete idiots.

I gave myself a pat on the back for my wise choice of accommodation. Hotel C had been easy to locate, it had a McDonald's directly opposite it, and it even had its own ice bar.

"Just imagine how good Hotel A must be?!" I told myself.

Thankfully, I did not embarrass myself by announcing my joke to anyone in the lobby. After dropping off our luggage in our rather nice-looking hotel room, we made our way to the ice bar that was situated close to the lobby of the hotel. It was being marketed as the world's first permanent ice bar, which was enough to entice us into visiting it. In any case, the entry fee only permits visitors to stay for forty-five minutes in the bar area, which is kept at a constant temperature of -5°C.

We were given gloves and an 'ice cape' that resembled the shiny, padded and hooded coats that East 17 wore in the video for the 1994 Christmas number one single, "Stay Another Day." They may have fallen on hard times recently, but I doubt that they require a father and son combination to be added to their line-up.

In keeping with the bar's theme, the glasses that contained our fruit juice were made from ice. It seems bizarre that people pay to spend three quarters of an hour in sub-freezing temperatures whilst clutching a block of ice to drink from, but I certainly appreciated the novelty factor. We took the obligatory photographs in our borrowed clothing whilst stood next to several ice sculptures that were dotted around the room.

We probably only used up half of our allotted time, but it was, nevertheless, an enjoyable experience. The people who designed the ice bar were also responsible for creating the world's first hotel made entirely from ice. The Ice Hotel in Jukkasjärvi has been rebuilt every year since it opened in 1990. Although I can understand why this unique building captures the imagination of tourists, the prospect of sleeping on a bed made from ice is a ghastly thought. I imagine that the novelty soon runs out and that guests are left cursing how everything that they touch is made from ice. Even Elsa got sick of that in the Disney film *Frozen*. Or so I have been told.

Upon our exit, we spoke to one of the members of staff in reception about our visit to the ice bar and our upcoming plans in Stockholm. The friendly worker offered his thoughts on the ice bar: "It is pretty cool, right? I mean, it's actually very cold not cool!"

"It is nice. That is nice, not ice!" Dad replied.

I sincerely hoped that someone would just say something that did not involve a joke or a pun about ice. The hotel worker obliged by asking us what we planned to do with our time in Stockholm. We duly informed him that we were going to watch the UFC show on Saturday night and that we were attending the big football match that evening.

This seemed to pique his interest: "Nice. I think Gustafsson is really good and he will become champion one day. It is quite a big deal here. The show sold out quicker than any other European UFC event. Also, AIK vs Göteborg is one of Sweden's biggest football matches, so you have chosen well."

"What is the standard of football like here?" I tentatively enquired.

"It is pretty good, I think. Not at the same level as the Premier League but we have some good players. You are from Manchester. Do you support United or City?"

He seemed pleased that I had indicated that I supported the former.

"Am I right to say that the stadium has lots of history?" I asked.

"For sure. The Råsunda Stadium hosted the World Cup final between Sweden and Brazil in 1958. Sadly, we lost 5-2 but we are proud to have played such an important match against a great team. We did well but Pele scored twice, and they were just too good. Unfortunately, the stadium is going to be torn down later this year, so you are lucky that you will get to see it."

I had not been aware of its impending demolition; thus, I felt even more pleased with our decision to visit this historic football ground. We thanked him for the information before leaving the hotel. It was time to watch some football.

We were not going to the match alone though. I had arranged to meet up with a fellow UFC Fight Club member called Christoph. We had briefly met following a UFC show in his home country of Germany a couple of years earlier and we had just about kept in touch through Facebook. This scenario gave me conflicting emotions. On the one hand, it provided a layer of comfort, as I could rely on someone else to guide us to the stadium. However, it also meant that I would have to engage in conversation with an individual who I was only vaguely familiar with.

"Hi David."

"Hi Christoph. This is my dad, Barry."

"Hi Barry."

"Hi Christoph."

This was going as badly as expected. Now that we had exchanged pleasantries, it was time to turn to the task at hand.

"I hope you know your way to the stadium!" I joked.

"Yeah, I made a note of which train we need to take," Christoph replied.

"Good, because that is the only reason why I agreed to meet up!"

My comment may have been laced with humour but there was certainly an element of truth behind it. I could put up with the small talk if Christoph made my life easier by safely leading us to the stadium. We followed our German friend through the station, purchasing tickets along the way. The metro stations within Stockholm are surprisingly pleasant on the eye. In most cities around the world, metro or underground stations are drab places that seem to suck the life out of the commuters that pass through. However, the stations in Stockholm have been transformed into art exhibitions. Over ninety of the one hundred metro stations are adorned with sculptures and colourful mosaics.

As we made our way down the escalators and through T-Centralen station, we were surrounded by the type of blue and white patterns that one has become accustomed to seeing on crockery. It certainly made a charming first impression and it eased my anxiety about the upcoming journey.

"This train will take us there directly," Christoph confidently proclaimed.

We followed him onto a train carriage and exchanged a few brief sentences about the upcoming football match. I looked around and noted how there did not seem to be any football fans onboard. We examined the map of the rail network and looked at each other nervously.

"I think we are on the wrong train," Christoph declared.

34

"Great. You had the one job of leading us to the football ground, but you have failed miserably. I was willing to put up with the awkward conversation and extended periods of silence in exchange for this service, but now I have nothing to show for this painful experience."

Of course, I did not vocalise these thoughts. Instead, we all shared a polite chuckle before heading towards another platform. Finally, we were on the right train. The negative aspect of this was that we were now in a more crowded carriage. Still, I think the benefits of switching to a train that was actually travelling to where we needed to go far outweighed the negative aspect of feeling less comfortable!

Upon arrival at our destination of Solna Centrum, it was clear that the artwork within the different metro stations varied significantly. In contrast with the blue and white colour scheme that we had left behind at T-Centralen, we were greeted with striking red and green patterns. The green depicted a forest scene, whilst the red represented an evening sun behind the treetops. Any feeling of unpleasantness caused by a crowded journey on the metro was quickly forgotten after seeing our colourful surroundings.

I think that other cities around the world should take inspiration from the metro stations in Stockholm. If this helps ease the misery of the daily commute, then why not install similar artwork in London or New York? The designs also highlight how metro stations provide a large canvas for artistic expression that have not been taken advantage of in most cities throughout the world.

As the Råsunda Stadium was located within walking distance of Solna Centrum, it was straightforward to locate. This also meant that we did not have to endure an extended period of small talk before reaching the stadium. We were sat in a different section to Christoph, so we said goodbye for now and arranged to meet outside the ground following the conclusion of the match. Although it may have been due to the fact that we had just visited an ice bar, the weather seemed milder than what I had anticipated.

The stadium had the appearance of an old-fashioned English football ground, with four distinctively separate stands, and pillars obscuring some supporters' view of the pitch. Dad and I noticed that there were rolls of blue and yellow paper underneath our seats, which we assumed were there so that fans could display the colours of the AIK Fotboll team. I certainly hoped that it was not complimentary toilet paper, as this would hardly be a positive endorsement of the quality of the hotdogs that we had just purchased.

As kick-off approached and the stands began to fill, the atmosphere was starting to become more intense. Several flares were set off, filling the air with smoke, and the supporters in our section had started throwing their rolls of coloured paper towards the pitch. Dad and I did the same with the paper that had been placed under our seats. What rebels we were! In truth, this orchestrated activity was probably the closest that either of us would ever get to experiencing the life of a football hooligan.

If the pre-match activities were this exciting, then surely the action on the pitch would be even more thrilling? Sadly, this was most certainly not the case. What followed was one of the worst games of football that I have ever witnessed. There were not any players close to the calibre of Zlatan Ibrahimović or Henrik Larsson strutting their stuff on the pitch. If this match was a fair representation of Swedish football, then our friend at the hotel must have worryingly low standards if he thinks that the quality of the league is good. Perhaps the rules are different in Sweden: maybe each team is only permitted to complete one successful pass to a teammate before they must relinquish possession?

As a Manchester United supporter, it has often been painfully boring and frustrating in equal measure to watch the team play so poorly since Sir Alex Ferguson retired in 2013. Whenever United are enduring a particularly bad spell, I just remind myself of the match that we watched in Stockholm. However bad it gets, the memory of that turgid encounter makes me count my blessings that I do not have to watch Swedish football on a weekly basis.

Following an abysmal ninety minutes, AIK were on the verge of securing a 1-0 victory against their bitter rivals.

"At least the home fans will be happy and there will be a good atmosphere amongst the supporters who join us on the metro journey back to our hotel," I reasoned.

Almost immediately after I uttered those words, the AIK goalkeeper decided to drop the football at the feet of an IFK Göteborg player, gifting him an easy goal. The mood inside the stadium was now in keeping with the action on the pitch. I just hoped that there was not enough time for the visitors to pinch another goal and send the home supporters into a collective violent rage. Thankfully, the referee must have been thinking the same thing, as he almost immediately blew his whistle to signal the end of the match.

We trudged out of the stadium with the AIK supporters, who seemed more despondent than angry. Judging by the quality of the football on display, they were probably used to such disappointment. In case any of you are dying to know the outcome of the 2012 Swedish football season, which I am sure that many of you are, AIK Fotboll had to settle for fourth place in the league whilst IFK Göteborg finished seventh. Remarkably, there were nine teams that finished below Göteborg.

"Did you enjoy the game?" Christoph asked upon our reunion.

"It wasn't the best, but I enjoyed the experience. How about you?" I replied.

"It was not great. I am used to watching good football. My team, Borussia Dortmund, are playing really well at the moment."

"Shall we head back?" Dad suggested.

This was music to my ears. It was cold and dark, and I had more or less exhausted my repertoire of small talk. We made our way back to the metro station and boarded the first train that arrived, which was not as crowded as I had feared. We said our goodbyes to Christoph at T-Centralen before returning to our hotel. I could now relax with the knowledge that I would not be required to engage in such prolonged periods of awkward conversation for the rest of the trip. Overall, our first day in Sweden had been a success. We had conquered public transport, visited an ice bar and attended a football match.

Once again, my most significant failings were based on my reluctance to speak to other human beings. The guy on the plane. The hotel worker. Christoph. They had all been helpful, yet I had spurned their friendliness to varying degrees. Perhaps our experience of Stockholm could have been more rewarding if I had shown a higher level of engagement. The football match highlighted the importance of human interaction. Whilst the game had been excruciatingly boring, the atmosphere generated by the supporters, including the collective pre-match throwing of coloured tissue paper, was rather thrilling. I did not dwell on this for too long though.

"I had a good day. Did you?" I asked Dad.

"Yeah, it was nice. It was a shame that the home team did not hold on for the win. The ice bar was interesting too. What's on tomorrow's agenda?"

"We have the UFC weigh-ins in the afternoon, of course. I think that we will visit an outdoor museum in the morning. Goodnight Dad."

"Goodnight son."

*   *   *

Although I was intrigued by the breakfast options on offer the following morning, I was not brave enough to deviate from my standard choice of cereal and a croissant. I declined to take the opportunity to sample a traditional Swedish breakfast by choosing some items from the Smörgåsbord. I liked the look of the cheese, the cold cuts and the open-faced sandwiches but it felt slightly alien to consider eating them so early in the morning. I suppose that this was a natural consequence of growing up in Britain, where such items are usually eaten later in the day. I have become more accustomed to this practice over the years, so I am more likely to consume these breakfast options nowadays.

Our plan was to visit the open-air museum of Skansen after breakfast. This is located on the island of Djurgården, which meant that we would have to make our way there from central Stockholm. We decided to take the ferry from the old town, known as Gamla stan. A straightforward ten-minute walk took us from our hotel to the old town, which is located on an island. This is not particularly surprising, given that the city of Stockholm sits upon fourteen islands that are connected by over fifty bridges. We did not spend much time in Gamla stan, as we did not want to deviate from our plan. The morning was all about visiting Skansen.

We soon located the departure point for the ferry to Djurgården and boarded the first available vessel. The journey was a rather cold one, which had been exacerbated by our foolish decision to stand outside and take photographs of the surrounding area. The boat trip took less than ten minutes, but this was still long enough for us to almost make a costly error by disembarking at the first of the two scheduled stops.

Before reaching Djurgården, the ferry stops at Skeppsholmen. If we had left the boat there, we would have found ourselves on a small island that contained nothing of interest to us. I do not imagine that Dad would have enjoyed a morning exploring the Museum of Modern Art or the East-Asian Museum. The most interesting sounding attraction was an old sailing ship named *af Chapman*. Even if we had decided to explore the ship that shared our family name, we would have been left disappointed, given that it now serves as a youth hostel.

The entrance to Skansen was visible upon disembarkation. We paid the entrance fee, which I believe was around 150 Swedish Krona. This equates to about £12. Considering that we were in Scandinavia, which is renowned for its extremely high prices, I guess that this was not too bad. As we made our way through this hilly area, we had a look at the wooden houses and old-fashioned farming equipment that formed this replica nineteenth-century Swedish town. It had been opened by Artur Hazelius, who wanted to demonstrate what life was like in pre-industrial times. It has often been labelled as the oldest open-air museum in the world, but I am not sure of the accuracy of this claim.

It was interested in examining the level of detail that had gone into creating this replica town, including having the workers dress in period costume, all playing their part in attempting to provide visitors with an interactive way of learning about the past. There were even various animal enclosures containing brown bears, European bison, moose, reindeer and other Nordic species. This recreation of pre-industrial Scandinavian life was rather charming. I just hoped that there was nothing disturbing behind it all, like in the M. Night Shyamalan film *The Village*.

As we started walking back towards the ferry embarkation point, Dad asked whether there was anything else to see in Djurgården. I had not heard of the area aside from the world of football. Djurgårdens IF Fotboll had enjoyed a successful spell during the early 2000s that saw them win three national league titles and three Swedish cups. I remember watching highlights of their famous 2-2 draw away to Italian giants Juventus in 2004. More importantly, I had engaged in numerous battles with them in the *Football Manager* video game series.

In truth, I had not bothered to research things to do on the island as I had only anticipated a brief visit. I was unaware that there is a royal park, or a nineteenth-century amusement park called Gröna Lund. The ABBA Museum opened a year after our visit, depriving us of the opportunity to sing and dance with holograms of the band. What a shame!

Following another straightforward ferry journey, we were soon back in Gamla stan, where we took another metro journey to the Ericsson Globe arena. Unfortunately, Globen Station was rather bland, which was in keeping with what I was used to back in Britain. I had hoped for something similar to the visually impressive stations that we had seen the previous day. It does feel unusual to be critiquing the artistic value of subway stations, but that is what happens to you after being spoilt by the beauty of the Stockholm metro network.

The appearance of the Ericsson Globe looked exactly like one would expect from a sporting arena whose name consisted of a Swedish telecommunications company and the word 'globe.' A modern but simple white globe-shaped building. For what it is worth, its diameter of 110 metres makes it the largest hemispherical building on earth. Judging by the lucrative sponsorship deal that was struck between the arena and Ericsson, you could say that it is worth quite a lot. Whilst the external features of the arena were relatively interesting, the interior had a fairly generic appearance. I guess that this is to be expected, as most international arena events require a similar configuration.

The weigh-ins involved the usual routine of twenty-four male competitors taking to the stage one by one and proceeding to strip down to their underwear whilst the mostly male crowd cheered on vociferously. As usual, most of the fighters looked drawn-out after depleting their bodies in order to make the required weight. They would down a bottle of water as soon as they were notified that they had cleared the scales. I can only imagine how dismayed they would be if an official then informed them that there had been an error, meaning that they would have to burn off the water weight that they had just consumed.

The weigh-ins also involved 'stare-downs' between the competitors of each bout. Some of them looked slightly uncomfortable whilst they looked into the eyes of their opponent. It would be my worst nightmare to be forced to make prolonged and intense eye contact with a guy who was going to be paid thousands of dollars to rearrange my face. Whilst we both stood in our shorts. With a couple of thousand people cheering us on. And the television cameras focused on our every move.

Following the conclusion of the weigh-ins, we made our way back to the area near our hotel. There was a meet and greet with legendary mixed martial artist Tito Ortiz and heavyweight contender Stefan Struve scheduled to take place in the electronics store Webhallen. The shop was located on Sveavägen, which is the street where former Swedish Prime Minister Olof Palme was assassinated in 1986.

Palme had been an outspoken critic of the aggressive foreign policies of the competing world superpowers, such as the Soviet Union and the United States. He was a consistent critic of dictatorships such as the Franco regime in Spain. Palme was also notable for protesting against the United States' role in the Vietnam War and he was the first Western leader to visit post-revolutionary Cuba.

The prospect of assassination was not my most pressing concern though. Sveavägen is regarded as Sweden's busiest road, which meant that it was likely to be heaving with a mixture of shoppers and mixed martial arts enthusiasts. I felt relieved that we had managed to reach the store before there were many people waiting. Crucially, the queue was small enough for us to be able to stand inside the store rather than out in the cold.

It took around thirty minutes for us to negotiate the queue and meet the fighters, which is not too bad going for this type of event. I noticed that every single fan was taking the opportunity to talk to Tito Ortiz, so I decided that I would pay Stefan Struve some attention. He had probably become so accustomed to being ignored that he did not respond to my opening remark. Mind you, this may have been because he was unable to hear the softly spoken voice of a man who is a foot and a half shorter than him.

Standing at a fraction under seven feet tall, he was the largest competitor on the UFC roster. Once he had realised that the mumbling that he could hear was coming from my mouth rather than a dog scurrying around his feet, he engaged in a brief but polite conversation with me. This consisted of me making the clichéd quips regarding his height and asking predictable questions about his future opponents. Dad and I looked ridiculous in the photograph that was taken of us. We are both around five feet, five inches tall, which made us look like small children when stood next to Stefan and Tito.

We went for a quick walk before attempting to find somewhere to eat. I say this but it was obvious that we were always going to eat at the McDonald's that was located opposite our accommodation. Dad has always enjoyed this fast-food franchise, and I was a lazy swine who could not be bothered to search for alternatives.

Surprisingly, Sweden has one of the highest numbers of McDonald's restaurants per capita in Europe. I had read that it occupied the top spot in all of Europe, but I cannot be sure of the accuracy of this claim due to a lack of available data. This was an unexpected fact about Sweden that did not seem to fit the image of a healthy, nature-loving country. However, one must remember that the population is relatively small compared to the size of the land mass. Most Swedes live in cities, so perhaps this 'nugget' of information should not come as too much of a surprise.

Other facts that I have read about Sweden are more in keeping with the liberal image of the country. In 1979, it became the first nation in the world to introduce legislation that prohibited parents from smacking their children. Sweden was also amongst the first countries to declassify homosexuality as an illness and to allow transgender people to legally change their gender. It is also one of the most generous donors of foreign aid in the world. For example, it was the first country to meet the United Nations' target of donating 0.7% of its Gross National Income. It has since surpassed the one per cent mark.

None of this information was in our thoughts as we devoured our burgers though. Instead, we reflected upon our second day in Stockholm.

"The trip is going rather well," I declared.

"Yes. We have seen lots of interesting things. We made it to the football match. Let's hope that we make the UFC show," Dad replied.

"We will explore the old town before the show tomorrow night. Does that sound ok?"

"I leave it in your capable hands. What is in the old town?"

"Well, I really want to see the narrowest street in Stockholm."

"OK, whatever floats your boat," Dad chuckled.

*   *   *

The UFC show was not scheduled to commence until around five or six in the evening; therefore, we had most of the day to explore the city. There was only one place to start: it was time to visit Stockholm's narrowest street! Dad did his best to hide his excitement, but I imagine that he was as thrilled as I was.

Located in the old town, Mårten Trotzigs Gränd was named after a German merchant who moved to Sweden in the sixteenth century. I held

41

little interest in this information; all that I cared about was the width of the street. At its narrowest point, it has a width of just thirty-five inches. In reality, the street is little more than an alleyway with some stairs. I did not let this dampen my spirits as I proudly posed between the two walls of the alley. Dad somehow contained his enthusiasm and declined the opportunity to have his photograph taken on this narrow street. What a missed opportunity!

The Stockholm Cathedral was never going to be able to live up to the splendour of Mårten Trotzigs Gränd but we paid it a visit in any case. This thirteenth-century building was originally designed in the Gothic style before it was given a Baroque makeover around five hundred years later.

I took photographs of all the notable landmarks, but I found that the charm of the old town lay in its cobbled streets and some of its less significant pastel-coloured buildings. Like many other successful old towns throughout the world, it has succeeded in retaining a vintage appeal for tourists whilst existing within a modern city.

Snow gradually began to fall as the day progressed, giving a pleasant look to the many photographs that I took. As we crossed the bridge that lead us out of the old town, the red brick building of the City Hall looked even more impressive with a sprinkling of snow on its roof. It was not enough to entice us into visiting the site of the annual Nobel Prize banquet, as it was located on yet another island. I suggested that we should check it out on our way back, but we failed to do so.

Whilst the smattering of snow looked pretty in my photographs, it was rather less agreeable under foot. We were now walking through sludge. This had managed to retain enough of its original white colour that it did not ruin the images that I had captured, but my feet were starting to feel cold and wet.

I am not a fan of snow. It may be pretty to look at, but it brings such misery. Aside from the inevitably low temperatures that accompany it, snow eventually melts and turns into ice or sludge. Public transport grinds to a halt and everyday life becomes impossible. At least that is what happens when we get the slightest bit of snow in Britain.

'Nice to look at but horrible to experience' has always been my opinion of snow. Perhaps my perspective would be different if I had grown up in a country that could handle extreme weather. Even after a night of heavy snowfall, Swedish roads are often cleared by the morning, which means that cars can travel as normal just hours after a blizzard.

Then again, at least we get the benefit of having a bonus day off work or school when the weather is bad in Britain. The Swedish population must make their way through the snow, or sludge, and do a full day's work as usual. The excuse of 'I could not make it into the office due to the snow' is less likely to cut it in Scandinavia.

I wonder how the people of Sweden would have coped with the British winters in the 1960s though. After all, my father's generation often regale stories about how it heavily snowed every winter during their childhood, and that you were guaranteed a 'White Christmas.' Conversely, every summer was apparently filled with constant sunshine and scorching temperatures. This rather dubious account of days gone by is not a new phenomenon; it seems that it is an unwritten rule that each generation must tell a similar tale. No doubt that I will say the same when I am older. If you encounter me waffling on about freezing winters and unbearably hot summers during my latter years, please do not hesitate to present these pages as evidence that the seasons were rather mild and ordinary when I was a young man.

We returned to the McDonald's restaurant opposite our hotel for a late lunch. I regret not trying Swedish food during our time in Stockholm, but our wallets probably appreciated our decision to frequent this cheap establishment. Mind you, even fast food in Sweden can cost the equivalent of £10. If there is one thing that I have learned from my travels around the globe, it is that Scandinavia is expensive. No wonder why gap-year students go backpacking around South-East Asia rather than this part of the world. You could probably spend the same amount of money in one week in Sweden as you would in two months in Vietnam.

I checked the football results back in England and discovered that Manchester City had won their match against Norwich by a score of 6-1. Whilst most people were still confident that Manchester United would maintain their lead at the top of the league and remain champions, my negativity was telling me that it was inevitable that this would be squandered.

The metro journey to the venue was straightforward, although a little crowded. After all, we had been advised by one of the hotel workers that the event had sold out in record time. Over 15,000 people were packed inside the Ericsson Globe for *UFC on Fuel TV: Gustafsson vs. Silva.*

As usual, I did not drink anything for the duration of the show, as I did not want to have to use one of the public toilets that were being frequented by the thousands of people in attendance. What a horrific thought! Instead, I sat there dehydrated for seven hours whilst we were surrounded by noisy drunkards. It was more obvious than ever that the live shows were not my scene; therefore, this would turn out to be one of the final mixed martial arts shows that I attended.

Following Alexander Gustafsson's victory over Thiago Silva, the crowd left the arena in much higher spirits than the AIK supporters had done following the football match on Thursday evening. The return metro journey was uneventful, which is exactly what one wishes for when travelling on crowded public transport. I had substantial experience of the methods that are required to survive such journeys: keep your head down, avoid eye contact, and try not to touch too many germ-infested handrails.

We were glad to be back in the warmth of our hotel room before long. Dad and I felt pleased that we had achieved everything that we had wanted to on this trip. We had attended a football match and a mixed martial arts show, visited the island of Djurgården, and we had explored the historic old town. We had even walked along Stockholm's narrowest street!

* * *

As our flight home was scheduled for the early evening, we had a few hours to explore Stockholm on Sunday. I decided that the best option would be to head back to the old town to meander through the charming cobbled streets. Whilst aimlessly walking through Gamla stan, we decided to enter a souvenir store. After browsing the mass-manufactured goods for a few minutes, I decided to buy a teddy bear for Carol. This would prove to be the start of a tradition that would continue for a couple of years; one which saw me bring back a cuddly toy every time that I ventured overseas. They all eventually ended up in a bin bag in the spare room, of course, but it seemed quite a cute thing to do at the time. For the record, I believe that the teddy that I brought back from Stockholm was a moose. I am unable to recall his name though.

The other souvenir that I bought resulted in me starting a collection that would become an obsession. I purchased a small Swedish flag and instantly realised that I would now have to obtain the equivalent item for all the countries that I had previously visited. Once I had returned home, it became clear that I would also have to buy another Swedish flag. If I was going to start collecting flags, I needed them all to be of uniform size and style; therefore, I found an online supplier who could meet all of my nerdy needs.

It would drive me crazy if I had to look at a collection of different sized flags with dissimilar shaped stands. It also became clear that there would have to be clearly defined and strictly enforced rules. I had always had an obsessive personality, at least in terms of building collections. The flag collection would be no different. Only countries or sovereign states that were recognised by the United Nations were allowed, which meant that early additions such as England and Wales were soon discarded.

As it turns out, the changing of the guard occurs at the Royal Palace on Sundays, so we were treated to the unexpected sight of the formal handover of duties outside of the official residence of King Carl XVI Gustaf and

Queen Silvia. The brick and sandstone palace, which was inaugurated in the eighteenth century, is one of the largest in Europe. I assume that the interior is more extravagant. Mind you, the King and Queen reside at Drottningholm Palace, which appears to have a more lavish setting.

In contrast to the previous day, the sun was shining brightly, and the temperature was most agreeable. We joined the substantial crowd that had gathered to witness this event, which was carried out with the discipline and precision that one would expect from such an occasion. I do have to say that it was not quite as regimented as the flag collection that I would go on to build, but few things in life are.

I thought that the event seemed to last a fair amount of time, but this was just the scaled-down winter version. Apparently, summer ceremonies can go on for around forty minutes, with a military band also marching through central Stockholm during the day. I watched the guards perform their duties without showing a flicker of emotion, which resembled the collective expression belonging a group of people who had just listened to one of my hopeless attempts at telling a joke.

Our time in the Swedish capital had been splendid, but all good things must come to an end. We returned to the hotel to collect our things before taking the Arlanda Express to the airport. Whilst preparing to board the plane, we bumped into the guy who had been sat next to us during the outbound journey. He informed us that he had purchased a Swedish football shirt for the equivalent of £50. At least my collection would prove to be a much cheaper way of marking my adventures around the world. Spending a couple of quid each time that I visit a new country seems a better choice than purchasing a ridiculously expensive football shirt on each occasion. My bank balance and wardrobe certainly approve of my choice.

The flag collection would also prove to be a driving force behind my newfound desire to visit as many countries as possible. Previously, I had travelled to visit new cities; now the focus was on ticking off new countries. The flags provided a tangible reward for each trip, and a feeling of euphoria that I would become addicted to. I would only have to wait another two weeks to feed my addiction…

CHAPTER 4: FALSE TEETH AND MISSING HANDS
ROME, ITALY
APRIL 2012

I had only been dating Carol for three weeks when I asked her the big question. She duly said yes and informed me that she was so happy and excited that she had been brought to tears. The question, of course, was: "Would you like to go to Italy with me?"

"Rome or Venice?" was the next question that I asked her. I did not have a preference. Both appeared to be wonderful cities and I would be guaranteed to visit a new country either way.

"Hmmm…they both sound amazing…let's go to Rome!" was Carol's enthusiastic response.

Given the speed and fervor of her response, it was clear that Carol was the one for me! She was thrilled to travel abroad together at such an early stage in our relationship and she seemed to share my passion for exploring different cultures. I was impressed that she was able to communicate in English, Spanish and, most impressively, Wiganese. Her love of Spanish and Latin American culture was something that had grabbed my attention from the moment that we first met.

Three weeks later, we were touching down at Leonardo da Vinci - Fiumicino Airport. The express train was easy to locate and it only took around half an hour to reach the main station in the city centre. The weather was more intense than I had anticipated. It was only mid-morning, but the temperature was already sweltering. Whilst we were happy about the warm weather that greeted us, it meant that our train journey was slightly uncomfortable. A crowded train and high temperatures do not necessarily make the best combination.

We were relieved to alight the vehicle once we had reached the city centre. Having highlighted our nearby accommodation on our map, we found it with ease. Given that everything was going to plan, I braced myself for disappointment upon arrival at Deseo Home. I had chosen to stay at the guesthouse because it was one of the few establishments in Rome that one could temporarily reside at without needing to ask the bank for a sizeable loan.

Unlike with a hotel chain, I had no idea what to expect from the guesthouse. I felt a certain amount of pressure as this was the first trip that I had taken with Carol and I did not want her to be disappointed. We were warmly greeted by a young man who was stationed behind the reception desk. He informed us of the breakfast times and the all-important Wi-Fi code before handing me our key.

We dropped off our luggage in our room, which was surprisingly pleasant and colourful, before heading back out to explore the Italian capital. The friendly member of staff who had welcomed us a few minutes earlier stopped us on our way through reception and dispensed some helpful information. He gave us another map and highlighted several points of interest, suggesting that we should start by visiting the nearby Vittorio Emanuele II monument.

"We call it the 'false teeth' because of its shape and white colour. Some people think it is ugly, but I like it. It is a ten-minute walk from here," he advised.

Ten minutes later, we were approaching the huge monument. Before we could get closer, we would have to cross one of the many chaotic roads in Rome. There seemed to be Vespas whizzing around in every direction and there were hundreds of them parked by the pavement. We also witnessed some of the worst parking that either of us had ever seen. Some cars seemed to have been abandoned, such was the owners' lack of consideration for others. Other vehicles had encroached onto the pavement, often parked at ridiculous angles that achieved little other than making life difficult for all those around them. The chaos of Rome!

After dithering for a few minutes, we finally took our chance to cross the road in order to get a closer look at the immaculate marble building. The giant national flags left us in no doubt as to where we were. The monument is named after the first king of the unified Italy who ruled during the second half of the nineteenth century.

Following the fall of the Roman Empire, the land that now belongs to Italy consisted of numerous city-states and powerful republics. The unification of Italy is often regarded as being completed after the Austro-Hungarian Empire, which had claimed much of what is now Italian land, was defeated during the First World War.

We decided to pay the required number of Euros to take the lift to the panoramic terrace. The early afternoon sun was fierce, so I regretted my decision to not to bring any shorts or sunglasses. There was nothing that I could do to stop me from melting in the sun, but Carol suggested that we should take it in turns to wear her sunglasses so that I was not squinting in all of our photographs. I was reluctant to do this as they were clearly designed for a woman, but I eventually conceded that this was the best option. It may have made me look slightly feminine but at least my eyes would not be half-shut in all of the photos.

"My sunglasses suit you!" Carol mischievously remarked.

I felt exhilarated to be in such a wonderful city with a girlfriend that not only shared my passion for travel, but also put me at ease enough to be able to laugh at each other without fearing that the other person may take offence.

The view of the city from our elevated position seventy metres above street level was certainly worth the admission fee. I had seen countless images of the Colosseum and the Roman Forum during my lifetime; now here they were in clear sight. The equestrian statue of Vittorio Emanuele II and the chariots that were positioned along the edge of the roof provided a further reminder that we were in one of Europe's most historic cities, which was once the centre of the Roman Empire that ruled much of the world from 27 BC until the fall of Constantinople in 1453 AD. It is remarkable, although somewhat tragic, to consider that this empire dominated other civilisations for nearly 1,500 years.

"Shall we go to the Colosseum next?" I asked Carol.

"Yeah, I can't wait to see it."

"You have already seen it. In fact, you are looking at it right now!"

"Don't be silly! You are a cheeky one!" Carol said with a chuckle.

This was another good sign. My woeful attempts at humour were being well received by Carol, which was a new experience for me. The lack of an awkward silence following one of my jokes threw me, so I did not know what to do with myself.

"Are you leading the way then?" Carol suggested.

"Of course. I will get us there, no problem," I confidently proclaimed.

It soon became clear that this would not be quite as simple as I had envisioned. Although the Colosseum was located about a kilometre ahead of us, our path was blocked by the Roman Forum. I kept my cool and reassured Carol that I knew what I was doing and that we just had to walk around the enclosed ruins. Thankfully, we soon arrived at the most recognisable landmark in Rome with my reputation as a competent tour guide intact.

We joined the queue for the ticket office and slowly shuffled along in the searing heat. We were in the Eternal City, and I was starting to think that it had been given this name due to the length of time that it took to gain entrance to tourist sites. By the time that we reached the front of the queue, we were informed that it would close in forty-five minutes. I calculated that this would be just about enough time for us to explore this historic site. Carol agreed, which was a relief considering that I was determined that our time spent in the queue would be rewarded.

The Colosseum is a wonder to behold. The sense of history and importance that it evokes is impossible to ignore. It is an overwhelming feeling to walk through the world's most infamous amphitheatre with the knowledge that it was built nearly two thousand years ago. It is difficult to comprehend how such a large amount of the travertine limestone, volcanic rock and brick-faced concrete has remained standing for so long, even withstanding multiple earthquakes in the process.

It is thought that the Colosseum could once have accommodated between 50,000 and 80,000 spectators, who would watch a variety of events such as gladiatorial contests, animal hunts and executions. Not all of the spectacles were so barbaric; dramas based on classical mythology were also presented to the public.

The bloody history of the Colosseum has made it a focal point for those who have campaigned against capital punishment. Indeed, the local authorities adjust the night-time illumination from white to gold when a death sentence is commuted or overturned, or when a country or region bans capital punishment.

The site holds even greater significance within Christianity, with many believing that the Colosseum was the site of the martyrdom of Christians whose faith contradicted the teachings of the Roman Empire. Failure to acknowledge the Roman Gods often resulted in a gruesome execution, although it is unclear if they were performed in the Colosseum or within another venue in Rome. The term 'fed to the lions' has been attributed to accounts of Christians being sent into the amphitheatre without any clothing or weapons, where they would be torn apart by wild animals such as lions.

The animals also suffered a horrific fate here. Lions, giraffes, elephants, dogs and goats were amongst the animals imported from the far reaches of the Roman Empire for the purpose of being hunted and killed in front of large audiences. The more exotic the animals were, the more impressed the audience would be. Roman leaders would attempt to demonstrate their wealth and power by involving animals that most citizens had never seen before.

The Spanish tradition of bullfighting may seem barbaric, but it rather pales in comparison to the animal hunts of Roman times. Scores of animals are reported to have been killed within the inauguration of the Colosseum, with estimates of the total number of animal deaths here ranging from hundreds of thousands to a million. Hundreds of thousands of humans were also thought to have been killed here for the sake of entertainment and a rudimentary form of 'justice.'

The image of gladiators has been glorified over time, but it must have been horrific to have been enslaved by the Roman authorities before being led to an inevitable and terrifying death.

"Can you imagine what it was like, walking into the amphitheatre to face a gruesome death in front of 50,000 people?" I asked Carol.

"They would be cheering for your death too!"

"My death?! Would you cheer for my death or spare my life?"

We may have only been dating for around six weeks, but I felt that her answer would be a rather important indicator of how our budding relationship was going.

"Of course, I would spare you!" Carol said with laughter.

"Phew! That's reassuring to know. Maybe your answer would have been different if I had failed to lead us to the Colosseum from the false teeth!"

The parts that were still standing demonstrated how there were three floors with colonnades surrounding the arena, and a further level without arches. As we walked through the various sections, I considered how it must have been an awe-inspiring place for the citizens of ancient Rome. The shadow of the imposing walls was now covering the majority of the amphitheatre, which provided a visual clue that it was time to conclude our visit.

As we were leaving, I reflected on how impressive it had been to walk around such a historic place. I wonder if this is still the case after recent restoration work. There was strong criticism after the local authorities announced that the Colosseum would be given a facelift. This involved an extensive cleaning project and rebuilding sections that had previously been destroyed or significantly damaged. I found that part of the charm of our visit was seeing an incomplete structure that had retained an authentic feel to it. Too much restoration risked distorting this. I fear that the newly cleaned Colosseum may look too polished, and that plans to build a new floor that would provide a stage for entertainment performances will further detract from the sense of authenticity.

We were feeling jovial as we walked back, hand in hand, to our accommodation. Carol started swinging our arms up and down in sync with our stride pattern. I laughed and asked her what she was doing.

"My Dad used to do this with us when we were kids," she gleefully informed me.

It was a nice moment. We had already visited a couple of the city's most important and historic monuments and we had grown closer as a couple.

"There is still so much more to see in Rome..." I began.

"And I can't wait to see it all with you," a beaming Carol interjected.

"Me too. We have not had any Italian food yet either."
"Now we're talking!"

After returning to Deseo Home, we indulged in one of the essential activities of an overseas trip: we had a pre-dinner nap. Whether we are on a city break that involves a full day of sightseeing or we have been relaxing on the beach on holiday, we always end up having a little nod before our evening meal. After a few days of this routine, one begins to wonder how it will be possible to cope without this.

Feeling refreshed following our power nap, we headed back towards the historic centre in order to find a restaurant to dine in. We soon encountered another holiday tradition: we had to walk along a street that was full of competing restaurants. Every establishment had a member of staff stood outside the entrance hunting for potential customers, making it impossible to inspect a menu without being accosted.

We were looking for a decent restaurant, but it was difficult to make a considered decision due to the constant harassment. On this street alone, there were a dozen restaurants claiming to offer the best food in Rome at the cheapest price. It can sometimes feel like you are taking part in a game in which the contestants have to time their approach to a restaurant just at the moment when the member of staff working the door is already in the middle of a sales pitch to other tourists. This would only give you a brief window to glance over the menu before making an initial assessment and leaving the scene.

Eventually, it is inevitable that you will be collared by an individual representing one of the restaurants. They must possess superhuman powers, as they seem to be able to put tourists into a trance from which they are able to convince people to dine in their establishment, regardless of whether they like the look of the menu. On this occasion, a slick young man named Giuseppe caught us in his trap. We had not even had a proper look at the menu, but his charm offensive compelled us to enter the restaurant he was pitching. This continued even after we had been led to our outside table.

"The lady looks absolutely beautiful. A beautiful lady in the most beautiful city. You are a lucky man, Sir."

It was still early days in our relationship, so the prospect of Carol running off with a charming Italian waiter was not out of the question. In my mind, Giuseppe had ensured that I would have to raise my game in order to fend off a challenger for Carol's affection.

"Yes. I feel like the luckiest man on earth. Not just a beautiful lady but *the* most beautiful."

Take that, Giuseppe! Just when I thought that I had seen off my rival, he returned for another round of competing compliments.

"She shines brighter than the stars in the sky. Rome is illuminated by her presence."

This was becoming more difficult than I had anticipated. Stumped for a response, I resorted to the tactic of reminding him of his role in this play.

"We'll have a bottle of red wine, please."

Giuseppe returned to our table a defeated man. He poured our drinks before taking our food order.

Carol smiled and stated that, "He seems nice."

Maybe there was still hope for Giuseppe after all. We thoroughly enjoyed our bruschetta and pasta, whilst dining *al fresco*. Incidentally, this phrase refers to something different in Italian. Whilst non-Italians use the term to describe outdoor dining, al fresco, which translates as 'in the fresh (air),' is used by Italians to either describe keeping an item in the correct place or to refer to being in prison due to the cold nature of such places. Italians will say *fuori* or *all'aperto* when talking about eating outside. We were most certainly a pair of clueless tourists, so al fresco was probably the most appropriate term for us to use.

"I must confess that I am not particularly keen on red wine," I cautiously informed Carol.

"Me neither."

"Perhaps I should not have ordered red wine then! At least it is romantic. Dining outside in Rome whilst drinking red wine."

We thoroughly enjoyed our dinner and mildly enjoyed our choice of beverage. It was time to settle our tab and say goodbye to Giuseppe. The bill was more reasonable than I had anticipated. Perhaps our Italian friend had reduced it in order to impress Carol. Or make me look worse by giving the impression that I had taken her to a cheap restaurant.

"Goodbye my friends. Look after her. You are a lucky man, Sir."

Unless Carol turned back and ran towards Giuseppe before declaring her undying love for him, it appeared that I had seen off my love rival. We ambled along the historic streets before stumbling across one of Rome's most iconic attractions. The Trevi Fountain, with the aid of subtle lighting, looked splendid against the backdrop of the night sky.

"Wow! It is beautiful," Carol remarked.

"It appears that one encounters beauty and history around every corner in Rome."

We took some pictures of the fountain, but it was difficult to get the perfect shot due to the throngs of tourists who were attempting to capture the same image. We decided to conclude our sightseeing for the day and return in daylight.

"What a first day. It was wonderful, don't you think?" I asked Carol upon our return to our room.

"I loved every minute of it. And we still have two more days left to explore Rome."

*   *   *

We woke up the following day feeling refreshed and excited. Breakfast arrangements were a little unusual but hugely enjoyable. There was a trolley of food and drink in the reception area for us to select items from and take back to our room. This allowed me to present Carol with breakfast in bed. We may have eaten croissants and cereal, but Deseo Home had given me brownie points with Carol. It was a relaxing way to start our day and it also meant that we did not have to have any awkward social interaction with our fellow guests, such as making sure I did not look impatient whilst waiting for the person in front of me to figure out how to use the coffee machine.

We were soon walking towards the historic centre again. We began our sightseeing by returning to the Trevi Fountain, with the hope that it would be less crowded than it was the previous night. Unfortunately, there were now twice as many people there.

"It looks even more beautiful in daylight. It's just a shame that there are so many tourists," I mused.

"Can you get rid of them for me, please?" Carol cheekily enquired.

"I'm afraid not. Bloody tourists!"

Our conversation highlighted a common problem with popular tourist sites. The more famous and revered an attraction is, the more tourists there are likely to be. It is understandable to be frustrated by the crowds but by visiting the site, one is only adding to the problem that they are complaining about.

After patiently waiting for our opportunity to find somewhere to perch by the fountain, we managed to get a fellow tourist to take the obligatory photograph of us sat in front of the famous landmark. What I really mean to say is that Carol asked someone to take our picture. We would have been there all day if I had been the one tasked with making this request to a stranger.

Men dressed in gladiator costumes asked us several times if we would like to have our picture taken with them. After the umpteenth attempt to entice us into this tourist trap, Carol snapped.

"No!" she sternly informed one of the men.

He sheepishly waddled off with his tail between his legs. I made a mental note not to get on the wrong side of Carol. She is gentle and kind in nature, but she had demonstrated that if you push her far enough, she is capable of defeating a Roman gladiator with just one word.

We then took part in another activity that one almost feels compelled to join. Carol and I each threw a coin from our right hand over our left shoulder into the fountain. This is one of the few locations where it is not frowned upon to commit an act of littering. It is also a rare example of a place where people are happy to literally throw their money away.

The reason for this is that people are embracing the legend which states that performing this action guarantees a return to Rome at some point in the future. This seemed a thoroughly agreeable prospect, so I was happy for us to take part in this tradition. I would have been concerned if Carol had thrown a second coin over her shoulder, as this is supposed to ensure that a new romance comes your way. Perhaps inspired by the 1950s film *Three Coins in the Fountain,* it is said that repeating this ritual three times leads to marriage. As we are now happily married, perhaps Carol chucked in a couple of extra coins without me noticing. We are yet to return to Rome though.

Interestingly, it is estimated that around 3,000 Euros are thrown into the fountain each day, which equates to an annual figure of over one million. This staggering amount of money has customarily been donated to Caritas, which is a charity associated with the Catholic church who have used the money to help the poor and the homeless. The Mayor of Rome sparked a row in 2019 by announcing that the coins would be used to fund the maintenance of cultural sites and social welfare projects instead of being donated to Caritas.

Unfortunately, the Trevi Fountain has attracted opportunistic thieves who fish out as many coins as they can before being caught. There has been a recent crackdown on this criminal practice, with authorities increasing the fines handed out to perpetrators. Fines are also given out when people wade into the fountain. There have been numerous occasions when this has happened, presumably in an attempt to recreate the iconic scene from the 1960s film *La Dolce Vita,* in which Anita Ekberg enters the fountain whilst wearing her evening dress and beckons Marcello Mastroianni to join her. I felt thoroughly relieved that Carol did not leap into the fountain and call for me to accompany her. Or steal any coins.

After leaving the Trevi Fountain, it did not take long before we were stood before another famous landmark. Carol was excited about visiting the Spanish Steps, which are located a short distance away from the fountain. Seeing numerous images of the steps over the years had resulted in her developing a romanticised perception of them, and she also held an interest with anything remotely connected to Spanish culture.

In this case, the link to Spain was a tenuous one. The steps were funded by a French diplomat and designed by Italian architects. The name is attributed to the fact that the Spanish embassy was located at the foot of the stairway at the time of its construction in the eighteenth century.

Nevertheless, our first glimpse of the famous staircase confirmed that they were a beautiful creation that lived up to our lofty expectations. As we stood next to Fontana della Barcaccia in Piazza di Spagna, the most striking feature of the stairs was the arrangement of Azaleas. Displaying the flowers, which my unknowledgeable eyes deemed to be purple in colour, is a long-held tradition that occurs every spring. It certainly enhanced the beauty of the cherished landmark.

As we ascended the steps, a fellow tourist offered to capture an image of the two of us. We were grateful for this act of kindness, although we laughed after noticing that a man was sat down within camera shot, oblivious to the fact that he was now part of a photograph that we will treasure for the rest of our lives.

I noticed that I was squinting in the photograph, which reminded me that I had to buy a pair of sunglasses. A chance to make this purchase presented itself at the top of the 135 stairs. A man with a stall in front of the Trinità dei Monti church was selling an array of sunglasses at an agreeable price. The problem was that the figures were almost too agreeable.

Whilst I was happy to pay ten Euros for a pair of sunglasses that seemed to block out the sunlight, I was dubious as to whether the sticker which indicated that the glasses offered UV protection was legitimate. Given that I did not have many options available to me, I settled for sunglasses that stopped me squinting, even if they offered little to no protection for my eyes. I just crossed my fingers and hoped that I would not do irreparable damage during the next couple of days.

The Italian Renaissance church and the accompanying obelisk that stand proudly at the top of the Spanish Steps were a visual delight. Incidentally, the church and the surrounding area are property of the French state. Mass is most commonly conducted in French. This was all a surprise to me, as I had assumed that it would have links to Spain rather than France.

We attempted to escape the crowds by having a walk through a park. Villa Borghese is the most famous park within the city, so this would have been the logical choice. However, we set off in the opposite direction and after meandering through the city streets, we ended up by a patch of grass that was looking rather bare.

For some unknown reason, I decided to purchase a can of Duff Beer from one of the tourist stalls. Like the well-known saying goes: 'When in Rome, do as Homer Simpson does.' Carol and I sat on the grass whilst we shared a tube of Pringles and a sandwich, as well as the can of novelty beer. This may not have been a feast fit for a Roman Emperor, but we still enjoyed our makeshift lunch. It was just nice to have a break from the hustle and bustle of the Italian capital.

The afternoon was spent wandering around the streets of the historic centre, pointing out beautiful buildings and fountains on every street. Most of them were probably insignificant but they were all attractive in their own right.

At some point, we ended up at the Pantheon, where we took a series of pictures of the church which was once a Roman temple. Its construction was completed in the second century AD for Hadrian. The Roman emperor would surely be pleased that this incredible building is still standing proudly in the centre of Rome nearly two thousand years later.

He would probably be surprised to learn that there are sections of the wall that bears his name still in place in Britain. Then again, he was a Roman emperor, so there is a good chance that he had a bit of an ego. For that reason, I will not mention the structures that were built in his name in places he visited such as Turkey and the Middle East. It seems as though he travelled across the world as much as I have. I would hazard a guess, however, that his voyages resulted in more deaths and misery than mine have.

The Pantheon is a magnificent building. The different architectural elements that were incorporated have resulted in a variety of shapes that complement each other. The cylindrical main section is connected to a rectangular vestibule, which in turn is connected to an impressive portico. This features a series of columns and a pediment, which provides a triangular shape above the entrance.

Whilst I am grateful that I had the privilege of admiring the exterior of the building, I regret not having the patience to join the long queue to enter it in order to explore the beauty that lies within. The opulent decorative features do not particularly interest me, but I do wish we had taken the opportunity to have a look at the most revered aspects of the Pantheon. The world's largest unreinforced dome features an oculus, which provides the building's only source of light.

Pantheon roughly translates as, 'Honour all Gods,' and the oculus was seemingly intended to provide a connection to the Gods above. If any rain falls through the oculus, which has a diameter of nine metres, the gentle slope of the floor ensures that it is drained away. I am sure that I would have been in awe at the sight of daylight entering the Pantheon via the oculus. Hopefully, I will get to see it on my next visit to Rome. It is a good job that I threw that coin in the fountain.

Whilst passing a series of souvenir shops, we decided to purchase some cheap tat to take back to Britain. We picked up the obligatory fridge magnets before continuing the tradition that I had started in Stockholm. I bought an elephant soft toy dressed in an 'I love Rome' T-shirt. Perhaps we mistook his trunk for genitalia, as we decided that our newfound cuddly friend was a male. We also gave him the imaginative name of Roman.

With our new buddy safely stowed in our bag, we treated ourselves to an ice cream from a gelateria on Piazza Navona. I had read about how unusual flavours of gelato, such as olive oil, are popular in parts of Italy, but I resisted the temptation to look for weird and wonderful options. Instead, I followed Carol's lead by plumping for pistachio and coconut flavours.

We enjoyed our ice cream whilst people-watching in the square. The area seemed to be full of tourists, but it is apparently a popular meeting point for locals. It is easy to see why the square is frequented by residents and tourists alike, as it is situated on an historic site that is visually pleasing.

The former location of the Roman Stadium of Domitian now contains numerous landmarks, such as Sant'Agnese in Agone. This seventeenth-century Baroque church dominates the Western side of the piazza. Fontana dei Quattro Fiumi, or the Fountain of the Four Rivers, and its Egyptian obelisk are situated in the centre of the square. Together, these landmarks provided the perfect backdrop for the surprisingly stressful activity of eating an ice cream before it melts in the early evening sun.

The church and the fountain have faced a certain degree of criticism over the years though. A common jibe relates to one of the statues belonging to the fountain. Four great rivers are depicted, highlighting the four major continents of the world as understood by the Romans. The Nile, the Danube, the Ganges and the Plata are each represented by their own God. The figure representing the latter has his hand raised as if he is shielding his eyes. People who disapprove of the appearance or the architectural merits of Sant'Agnese in Agone have been known to suggest that he is covering his eyes due to the ugliness of the church building.

"Shall we take Roman back to our room? I think he needs a nap," I suggested.

"Roman needs a nap?! More like David needs a nap!"

"Guilty as charged!"

We walked back to Deseo Home, each using one hand to swing Roman up and down. We were soon fast asleep in bed, but I felt that we had earned our nap. After all, we had experienced a full day of sightseeing in one of the most beautiful cities on Earth.

A few hours later, we dined in a restaurant that was close by to our accommodation, this time eating indoors.

"What would you like to drink? Perhaps something from the wine list?" the waitress asked.

Neither of us knew much about wine, so we hoped for the best after Carol had ordered a bottle of Frizzante. I was slightly nervous as we both took our first sip.

"It's really nice!" was my expert conclusion.

"I like it too," Carol replied.

"It is a good job that we like it, seeing as we ordered a whole bottle!"

It turns out that Frizzante is a type of semi-sparkling red wine, made from the Lambrusco grape. It was the perfect drink for us, as it was easy to drink and seemed to have a respectable reputation. It was certainly more highly regarded than Lambrini anyway.

I am unable to recall what dishes we selected for our evening meal, which I am assuming has more to do with the length of time that has elapsed rather than the strength of the wine. I remember enjoying the meal though.

* * *

Bocca della Verità was the first port of call the following morning. Carol was excited about visiting this landmark, but I had been oblivious to its existence. It turns out that it is a giant marble mask that is located within the portico of the Santa Maria in Cosmedin minor basilica. The circular carving is thought to depict the face of the Titan God Oceanus.

'The Mouth of Truth,' as it is known in English, was immortalised by the 1953 film *Roman Holiday*. Just as with the landmark itself, I had never heard of the film. The most famous scene sees Gregory Peck play a practical joke with Audrey Hepburn by placing his hand in the mouth of the carving and pretending that it has been bitten off by placing it up his sleeve. A commonly told tale is that Hepburn's shriek was a genuine reaction as she had been unaware of Peck's trick.

This scene was inspired by the centuries-old myth which stated that a liar would lose his or her hand if they placed it in the mouth of the monument; therefore, it was viewed as a rudimentary version of a lie detector. It is thought that during the Middle Ages, trials would involve someone standing behind the carving and using a sword or an axe to chop off the hand of those deemed to have been untruthful.

Judging by the length of the queue, it seemed as if I was the only person in Rome who had been unaware of its existence. To compound matters, we were stood behind a group of young Americans who were travelling around Europe during their gap year. By the time that we had reached the Mouth of Truth, we were familiar with every detail of their itinerary. Due to the volume and frequency of their chatter, we had little choice but to listen to their anecdotes from their travels to the likes of Prague, Budapest and

Krakow. Whilst their incessant yapping was irritating enough, my frustration was amplified by a sense of jealousy.

I could not help but feel envious of their dilemma of whether to make Venice, Florence or Milan their next destination. I had not been interested in travelling when I was their age, so the idea of going on an adventure such as theirs had not crossed my mind. By the time that I had developed a passion for exploring the planet, I was at an age when I was required to earn a living. I could hardly grumble though. I was fortunate to have the money and resources to be able to travel frequently. After all, this was my third overseas trip of the month.

Finally, we were at the front of the queue. The monument was roped off and we were informed that we were only allowed one photograph. This meant that the stakes were high, as we would only get one chance to get this right. Not only was my camera in the hands of a stranger, so was our fate.

I felt nervous as we stood behind the rope and placed our hands within the Mouth of Truth. This was not because I was worried about losing my hand, but due to my concern that we could have queued up for nearly an hour only to end up with a terrible photograph.

"Do not blink. Whatever you do, make sure that you do not blink," I repeatedly told myself. I expected the worst as I was handed back my camera, but I was pleasantly surprised to discover that the photographer had captured a perfect image. It was my favourite picture of the trip, and it remains one of my favourite photos to this day.

We admired the medieval belfry, but we did not enter the understated church as we were not aware of anything interesting inside the building. If we had ventured inside Santa Maria in Cosmedin, we would have discovered that a human skull is on display in a side altar. This allegedly belonged to Saint Valentine. Although the idea of visiting an attraction connected to Saint Valentine in the beautiful city of Rome seems romantic, I am not sure whether Carol would have shared this sentiment if I had taken her to see a human skull! It was probably for the best that our first overseas trip did not involve such an activity.

We could not leave Rome without visiting some of the most celebrated ruins in the world. We had briefly walked past them during our journey to the Colosseum on our first day, so we were familiar with the location. There are ruins of numerous monuments that surround the Roman Forum, which was once the central point of Roman society.

Remarkably, some of the remaining structures date back to the eighth century BC. Whilst we walked amongst the ruins of ancient Rome, it was difficult to comprehend that the buildings that once stood here date back over two thousand years. The knowledge that people would have walked through these grounds on a daily basis all those years ago stirred my imagination.

I tried to picture what it would have been like for people attending processions, public speeches, criminal trials and gladiatorial contests. In truth, it was easier to contemplate such grand events than it was to imagine someone carrying out a routine task such as picking up some food and drink. Some of the ruins were modest, with only small fragments of the original structures remaining, whilst others, such as the Temple of Saturn and the Arch of Septimius Severus, still had imposing sections in place.

As we left the ruins, I asked Carol whether our visit to Rome had met her expectations. Her response mirrored my thoughts on the matter: "Rome has been even more wonderful than I had imagined. It is such a beautiful place with so much history everywhere you look. I have loved every minute of it!"

"We made a good decision to come here on our first trip then," I remarked.

"I think you will find that I chose Rome! You weren't sure whether to go to Rome or Venice!" Carol responded whilst offering a cheeky smile.

"Sorry, I meant to say that you made a good decision."

I was quickly learning how conversations worked between partners: the woman is always right!

We soon found ourselves walking across Ponte Sant'Angelo and admiring the statues of angels that line the bridge. There used to be something more sinister on display, with the bodies of executed criminals placed here as a warning to others.

The construction of the bridge was completed under the orders of our old friend Hadrian. He even had a mausoleum built on the right bank of the Tiber river. The cylindrical Castel Sant'Angelo was later used as a fortress and a castle, before being converted into a museum. Once the tallest building in Rome, it still provides a towering presence at the end of the bridge.

"Fancy a quick trip outside of Italy?" I asked Carol.

Not long after crossing Ponte Sant'Angelo, it was time to temporarily leave Italy behind and pay a visit to the smallest sovereign state in the world...

CHAPTER 5: THE SMALLEST SOVEREIGN STATE IN THE WORLD
VATICAN CITY STATE, GOVERNED BY THE HOLY SEE
APRIL 2012

Crossing the border from Italy into Vatican City was a seamless process. This was not surprising, given the unique nature of this tiny city state. It is enclaved by Italy; in fact, it is surrounded entirely by the city of Rome. It seems highly unusual for a sovereign state to be found within a city that belongs to another country, but the size of Vatican City almost makes this an inevitability.

Its population of around one thousand resides within its forty-four hectares of land, meaning that it is comfortably the smallest sovereign state in the world when measured by either population or geographical area. Interestingly, its labour force is almost five times larger than its population.

Established under the Lateran Treaty of 1929, Vatican City State falls under the jurisdiction of the Holy See. This ultimately comes under the authority of the Catholic Church, which means that some bloke called the Pope is the head of state.

Incidentally, San Marino is one of the few other enclaved sovereign states in the world and is also found within Italy. Perhaps there is something about Italy that makes these small states resist the notion of joining the country that surrounds them, in the manner that a stubborn and determined homeowner refuses to sell their land to a huge property developer.

More importantly, the Holy See is one of only two observer states of the United Nations despite it not fulfilling all the criteria of an independent sovereign state. This meant that I could add another flag to my collection, as I was following the UN's 193 plus 2 model. My haul of four flags in April was hugely satisfying.

"How did it feel to cross the border?" I asked Carol.

"It's not really a border though."

"It is a soft border. We are no longer in Italy, although we are completely within the boundaries of the city of Rome! That is quite cool isn't it?" I enthused.

"I guess. I am just excited about seeing St. Peter's Basilica."

Carol's way of thinking was more in line with what most sensible people will be contemplating as they begin their time in Vatican City. The prospect of visiting one of the most important religious buildings on the planet should surely provide a bigger sense of excitement than stepping foot within the smallest sovereign state in the world. I was clearly in the minority of weirdos.

My obsession with flags did not mean that I was blind to the beauty of the basilica though. Upon entering St. Peter's Square, it was clear why the architecture of this Renaissance church was renowned throughout the world. Several architects, including Bramante, Bernini and Raphael, contributed to the design and construction of the building which was completed in the seventeenth century. The magnificent dome, which is one of the largest in the world, is the central feature of the basilica. This was the most significant contribution of Michelangelo, who began designing it at the age of seventy-one.

For Catholics throughout the world, St. Peter's Basilica is regarded as one of the most important sites associated with their faith. It is said to be the burial place of one of the Twelve Apostles. Unsurprisingly, this is Peter. It has also been the destination for one of the major pilgrim routes for centuries.

Carol and I stood in silence whilst we observed the beauty of the scene in front of us. There was an Egyptian obelisk in the centre and a fountain to the side of it, with semi-circular colonnades flanking the square. Unfortunately, it was late afternoon, so there were many other tourists milling about. Most of them were significantly louder than we were, but this was the least of our concerns.

We could see that there were two enormous queues that seemed to be increasing by the second. A slick American man approached us: "I am just about to start my tour. For thirty Euros you can join our group. One of the lines that you can see is for St. Peter's Basilica, and the other is for the Sistine Chapel. You have to queue up separately for each one, but my tour covers both, and we can skip the line. I start in thirty seconds though."

My instincts in situations like this always tell me to treat everyone as a potential con artist and to disengage as soon as possible.

Therefore, I politely stated: "No thanks."

He trudged off and began addressing the members of his tour group. I managed to hear a brief exchange as we passed his flock.

A lady asked: "What is the order of the itinerary?"

"That's an interesting accent. Where are you from?" he replied.
"Bergen in Norway."
"Cool. My girlfriend is from Bergen. It is a beautiful place."
I turned to Carol and sniggered: "You can guarantee that his girlfriend is not from Bergen. He's an American living in Rome. What are the chances of his girlfriend being from the same city in Norway as the first person who asked a question? He avoided her question and established a friendly connection in the process."

Perhaps I was being harsh on the guy. Maybe his girlfriend really was from Bergen, but hearing this verbal exchange made me feel better about my choice to decline his invitation. I did not feel so pleased when his group bypassed the huge line that we were stood near the back of.

"I am really thirsty. I feel dehydrated," Carol wearily stated.
"We have run out of water. Shall we go back and find a shop?" I suggested.
"No. We've come this far. I'll be OK."
"Are you sure?" I asked.
"I will be fine."

I had a look around the square but there was no sign of any shops to buy a drink from. There were plenty of grand buildings and museums but no convenience stores. I am usually left cursing the presence of a McDonald's or a Starbucks right next to a historical landmark; this was the one occasion when we could have done with such an establishment, yet there was nothing of the sort to be found!

After spending an age standing in line whilst the sun did its best to melt our skin, we finally gained access to St. Peter's Basilica. The dome looked even more impressive from inside the building. Beautiful mosaics were everywhere, including on the dome's interior surface. There are numerous historic works of art located within the basilica, but I was unaware of what they were. I just knew that they were pleasing on the eye.

Bernini's baldachin towers above the high altar, reaching a height of ninety-six feet. Although I marvelled at the bronze canopy, I did not have a clue who it was designed by. Or that it was called a baldachin, or a baldacchino in Italian.

Whilst Michelangelo's *Pietà* is undoubtedly a fine sculpture, I had no idea who had designed this Renaissance marble artwork. If I had looked closer, I would have seen that he had signed the sash that runs across Mary's chest: 'MICHAELA[N]GELUS BONAROTUS FLORENTIN[US] FACIEBA[T],' which roughly translates as 'Michelangelo made this.' Perhaps this was the equivalent of the '[Insert Name] was here' tag of his era. It was the only piece that he ever signed.

"We should find something to drink. Shall we give the roof a miss?" I asked Carol.

"No. I want to go up and see the view. I'm dehydrated but I'll be OK."

I had not seen such determination since I had experienced the bizarre behaviour of a stranger during my walk to work one morning. There had been a 'slow walker' in front of me, so I overtook her and carried on walking along the pavement. She must have taken offence to this for some reason, as she was suddenly transformed into a combative foe. She rushed past me, stepping onto the road in the process of re-establishing her position in front of me. She was now prepared to risk her life in the face of oncoming traffic in order to restore her damaged pride!

Brooklands Road is notably long, so it was not surprising to see her pace eventually slow down. This meant that I had to pass her again, which provoked the same reaction, resulting in a blur of a woman darting past me. At that point, I decided to walk as slowly as possible in order to avoid another weird situation. We must have looked absolutely ridiculous to any passers-by. Mind you, there was a man that jogged backwards along the road each morning, so we would have seemed rather sane in comparison.

"If you are sure you are Ok, we will quickly go up to the top, take some pictures, then come back down."

I had obviously forgotten that we were in the building with the tallest dome in the world, meaning that my statement that we would "quickly go up to the top" was optimistic at best. At least our ascent was broken up by the opportunity to admire the mosaics of the dome from close quarters and to have a brief look at a famous set of statues.

"Do you fancy checking out Jesus and the Apostles?"

It sounded like I had just asked Carol if she wanted to attend a gig that was being headlined by a Christian rock band! The journey became more strenuous after we had examined the statues and mosaics. The next staircase was extremely narrow and winding, which meant that people had to travel slowly in single file. This was hardly what my dehydrated girlfriend needed. Carol somehow managed to avoid passing out and she was rewarded with the spectacular view that she had yearned for.

We had climbed 551 steps to reach the summit, but it was worth it. We were now observing the scene that is displayed on most postcards and online images associated with Vatican City. The statues of the Apostles, the obelisk, and the splendour of St. Peter's Square were all visible below. From this vantage point, I could see why some people say that the semi-circular colonnades symbolise how the Catholic Church is extending its arms out from the basilica and wrapping them around the square in a welcoming embrace.

After taking another five hundred or so steps down a different but equally narrow and winding staircase, we were back at ground level. I asked Carol if she would like to visit the Sistine Chapel, but it appeared that her dehydration had finally defeated her. Given that the queue to enter the chapel was longer than the respective line for the basilica had been, I was not too disappointed when Carol informed me that she was in desperate need of water and that she could not bear the thought of waiting another hour in a queue.

The Sistine Chapel may contain some of the most historic and revered works of art in western civilisation, and it may belong to the Apostolic Palace where the Pope officially resides, but the health of my girlfriend quite rightly came first. It was no good taking the time to behold the beauty of Michelangelo's frescos if it meant that Carol would collapse in the process. *The Last Judgment* would have to wait, both in terms of the fresco itself and our opinion of it. If I had forced Carol to visit the chapel, it may have resulted in the last judgment being handed down on the prospect of our blossoming relationship continuing beyond our trip to Rome!

Subsequently, the Sistine Chapel joined the Pantheon on our list of places to return to during our next visit to the Italian capital. After leaving Vatican City, we replenished our weary bodies with some H2O.

"Perhaps there was not any *acqua minerale* on sale within the tiny sovereign state because they only stock holy water," I pondered.

Carol paid little attention to my woeful joke, as she was more concerned with consuming enough water to avoid passing out.

My next comment piqued her interest though: "I am slightly disappointed that we didn't get to see the Swiss Guards..."

"Swiss?!" Carol interjected.

"Yes, the Swiss Guards have protected Vatican City since the sixteenth century. They were originally mercenaries who were recruited by the Holy See..."

"So, people from Switzerland guard Vatican City?"

"Yes. You must be unmarried, Catholic, and a Swiss male to join. They are the de facto military, which is rather amusing, given that Switzerland is famed for its neutrality."

"You are amused by the strangest of things!"

"I think that you would have been amused by them too if you had seen their ridiculous uniforms. Baggy outfits featuring blue, red, orange and yellow vertical stripes! I'm not sure whether Donatella Versace would approve! Mind you, those fashion shows tend to showcase bizarre costumes."

Our visit to the smallest sovereign state in the world had been brief but wonderful, nonetheless. My wariness to trust others, particularly one

American tour guide, had possibly cost us the opportunity to visit the Sistine Chapel though. Maybe it was for the best, as there is a distinct possibility that Carol would have collapsed through dehydration if she had to spend more time sightseeing in Vatican City. We will just have to admire Michelangelo's artistry during our next visit. You never know, I may even have developed the social confidence to request an audience with the Pope! Perhaps not.

We enjoyed another bottle of Frizzante that evening, before returning to England the following day. I made it home in time to witness United's devastating defeat in the Manchester derby. Not even the prospect of seeing my football team hand control of the Premier League to their local rivals could dampen my spirits. It was clear that travelling was providing me with all the excitement that I needed. I felt as pumped up as the professional wrestler Goldberg as I stared at a list of possible holiday destinations and repeated his catchphrase: "Who's Next?"

CHAPTER 6: THE FLAG THAT GOT AWAY!
EDINBURGH, THE UNITED KINGDOM
MAY 2012

Two years after my first visit to Scotland, I was left disappointed by the result of their independence referendum. This was not because I was particularly eager to see the break-up of the United Kingdom. Something more important was at stake: the collective decision of those north of the border meant that I was unable to add another flag to my collection! If only the Scottish population had considered such consequences before casting their votes!

I had taken a chance by opting for the cheapest mode of transport from Manchester to Edinburgh. My cousin Fiona had informed me that there are bus routes that travel the length and breadth of the United Kingdom on a regular basis. She told me, for example, that she had taken a journey from London to Manchester with Megabus for just £5. It could cost ten times that much to take the train; hence, I developed an interest in exploring the possibility of such routes.

I booked two return tickets to the Scottish capital for around £20. I was ecstatic to have arranged our transport for less money than the retail price of many T-shirts. It was less thrilling to discover that the journey would take around six hours. This was going to be a long drive to the part of the United Kingdom that contains the shortest commercial flight route in the world.

Loganair operates daily flights between the Scottish islands of Westray and Papa Westray that are officially scheduled to last just ninety seconds. In practice, the 1.7-mile journey often takes less than a minute. The shortest flight time ever recorded was forty-seven seconds! There are plans for electric planes to be used for this route from 2021, which should reduce the carbon footprint of these tiny trips. There are already numerous car ferries in operation and the construction of a series of bridges has long been discussed.

Whilst this ludicrously short flight route highlights the environmental concerns caused by humans travelling around the world in the manner that we do, it must be recognised that almost everything about Western society has a negative impact on the planet. In addition to the more obvious issues such as vehicle pollution, the mass-production of meat and the overreliance on single-use plastic, there are many seemingly innocuous activities that have more of an impact on the environment than many of us realise.

I recently read something that left me lost for words: each Google search apparently uses enough energy to power a low energy lightbulb for over one hundred seconds. It also produces 0.2g of carbon dioxide. An article featured in *The Times* in 2009 went further by stating that two Google searches used as much energy as is required to boil a kettle for a cup of tea. This oft-quoted statistic has been broadly derided as a vast overestimation, but it certainly caused people to give some consideration to the subject. I had only previously paid attention to the environmental effect of my chosen method of transportation and the actions taken whilst away from home; now I realise that even planning a trip may have a small impact on our planet.

Mum was not put off by the long bus trip, so she agreed to be my travel companion once again. As we did not have allocated seating, we made sure that we arrived at Shudehill Interchange about half an hour before our early morning departure. The possibility of having to sit next to a stranger on a bus for six hours was horrifying. There were around a dozen people by the relevant bus stand, indicating that many of our fellow travellers did not want to sit next to us either!

We managed to snare a couple of adjoining seats, which removed the possibility of having an extremely loud and chatty stranger trying to make conversation with me for hours on end. Or being sat next to someone who thinks it is a good idea to gorge on eggs, mackerel and stilton for the duration of the journey.

Six hours passed quicker than I had anticipated, perhaps aided by my intermittent napping. Upon arrival at Edinburgh Bus Station, it was apparent that there were a few dodgy characters knocking about. There was a group of youths congregated on the concourse and a few dishevelled individuals stretched out on benches. I immediately concluded, without any evidence to support my harsh judgement, that they were all under the influence of various narcotics. In my eyes, we were in the middle of a scene that belonged in the film *Trainspotting*. Dare I suggest the title of *Busspotting*?

Given that we had travelled to Edinburgh via Megabus, I doubt that anyone is surprised to hear that we had chosen accommodation which charged a much lower price than The Balmoral. At least we got to admire the grand hotel as we walked past. This Victorian building was opened in 1902 and was initially known as the North British Hotel. It was common for railway companies to build hotels near significant stations; in this case, it was the North British Railway Company who were responsible for the creation of the hotel adjacent to Waverley Station.

The clock tower is visible from much of the city centre but I was intrigued by a quirky detail of the landmark rather than its height. Since its creation, the clock has always been set three minutes early, apparently to ensure that people do not miss their train. I felt like I had a connection with the clock, and that we were kindred spirits. After all, I have always set my watch to run a few minutes early in order to avoid being late for anything.

Even though I know that the time is earlier than what my watch is telling me, there is something about seeing the numbers being displayed that makes me panic. If I know that I am getting the seven o'clock train, it is unnerving to see a clock face that tells me that it is currently 7:01; therefore, it kicks me into gear. This tradition continues with the clock tower, although the correct time is displayed on Hogmanay, or New Year's Eve to those who live south of the border.

The Scott Monument was the next landmark that we encountered. My first impression of this 61.11-metre-tall Victorian Gothic tower was not particularly favourable. From a distance, it looked so dark and dirty that it was difficult to appreciate the design features. The merits of cleaning the stonework during the restoration process had been debated in the 1990s but it was eventually decided that this would have damaged the stone.

After approaching the monument for a closer inspection, my appreciation of it grew considerably. A statue of the literary great Sir Walter Scott was situated in the central space between the four columns. I had not studied any Scottish history during my time at university, so I was unaware of whom this individual was. His name did seem familiar, but I was probably getting him mixed up with Walter Smith, who is of course the legendary manager of Rangers Football Club.

The stonework and architectural detail looked more distinctive when observed from close quarters. It is the second tallest monument dedicated to a writer in the world, with only Havana's Jose Marti Monument reaching a greater height. This is a clear indication of how icons of literature are held in high regard within Scotland. The nearby Waverley Station was named after his novel of the same name, and the subsequent series of books that he wrote in a similar style. Scott is regarded by many to be the creator of the modern historical novel.

Other Scottish writers such as Robert Louis Stevenson and Sir Arthur Conan Doyle are celebrated internationally. Indeed, some of the most famous pieces of literature have originated from Scotland, including *Treasure Island, Strange Case of Dr. Jekyll and Mr. Hyde, Peter Pan, The Wind in the Willows* and the *Sherlock Holmes* series.

Robert Burns is perhaps the most revered of them all. The fact that Burns Supper, commonly known as Burns Night, is one of the highlights of the Scottish calendar illustrates this point. It involves the longstanding tradition of reciting the poetry of the eighteenth-century writer whilst enjoying haggis, neeps, tatties and Scotch whisky on his birthday, which falls on the Twenty-Fifth of January. Incidentally, he was the author of the poem "Auld Lang Syne," which is sung in many countries throughout the world at the stroke of midnight on New Year's Eve.

A ten-minute walk led us to our guesthouse. This allowed us to take in some of the sights of Edinburgh and establish our bearings in the process. We strolled along Princes Street, which looked a bit of a mess due to the work that was taking place to install tram lines. There was a long stretch of barriers and fencing that looked rather ugly. This short-term pain seems to have provided long-term gains, as the tram service that connects the city centre to the airport, stopping off at Murrayfield Stadium en route, is efficient and profitable.

I had low expectations upon arrival at our guesthouse. I was unsure whether our 'bed and breakfast' booking included anything other than a bed and a breakfast. I was relieved to discover that our room included central heating and an adequate shower, as well as twin beds. This meant that I avoided the embarrassment of sharing a bed with my mum at the age of twenty-seven.

"It is not bad value for what we paid," I happily stated.

"How much was it?"

"I think it was about £160 for two nights, which is pretty good for Edinburgh."

"So, they use pounds in Scotland? The money is the same as in England then?"

"Well, pound sterling is the currency throughout Great Britain, but they have Scottish pounds here whilst we have English pounds back home. There is no difference, and both can be used either side of the border. They just have different designs."

"That is a bit confusing!" Mum exclaimed.

"I guess it is because the Scots and English would like to honour different historical figures on their monetary notes."

My explanation was not entirely accurate. Scottish banknotes are technically not legal tender anywhere in the United Kingdom, including in Scotland. They are classed as promissory notes, sometimes referred to as a note payable. They are also issued by retail banks rather than a central bank. Either way, my Bank of England banknotes were valid in Scotland. Despite my anxiety causing me to be apprehensive about retailers accepting the money that I handed over, I did not experience any payment issues during our stay north of the border.

After dropping off our luggage in our room, we began our exploration of the Scottish capital. I decided that the highest point in Edinburgh, Arthur's Seat, was the ideal location to get an overview of the area. We joined the Royal Mile at more or less the halfway point, and we were immediately impressed by how clean and presentable it all looked.

"The Royal Mile looks pleasant..." I began.

"Why is it called the Royal Mile?" Mum asked.

"At one end you have Edinburgh Castle and at the other you have Holyrood Palace. Both have Royal connections. The Queen stays in the palace for a week at the beginning of each summer."

"I am guessing that it is a mile between the two points..."

"It's actually a Scots mile between the castle and the palace."

"A Scots mile? Are you joking?" Mum asked.

"No, I'm being serious. A Scots mile is slightly longer than the standard English mile. People have not used that measurement for a long time though."

I had assumed that the Royal Mile consisted of a single road, but it is in fact comprised of a succession of streets that form a thoroughfare. We soon passed a landmark that indicated a dividing point between two sections. The World's End pub is named after the nearby World's End Close, which is an alleyway located where the boundary of the city once stood.

Many years ago, there was a toll to pay for people entering what was then a walled city, which meant that this was as far as the poorer members of society could travel to; hence, it was the world's end for them. High Street had ended, and we were now stood on the Canongate. This name was given due to the route that canons took to Edinburgh, but the rejuvenated section of the Royal Mile is now commonly associated with the Holyrood area.

We were soon stood in front of the Scottish Parliament Building, which is often referred to as Holyrood. The fragmented building is comprised of unusually shaped sections fitted with shiny glass windows and wooden panels. It reminded me of something modern, such as an art museum, rather than a parliamentary building.

I vocalised my initial reaction to Mum: "It looks completely different to what I have become accustomed to seeing from parliamentary buildings across the world."

Mum's thoughts seemed to echo mine: "It is nothing like Westminster in London. That is historic and traditional, but this building is modern and unusual."

"Do you like it though?"

"It is different…but I prefer Westminster. That seems more important and grander."

"I quite like it. I usually prefer more traditional buildings but it's refreshing to see something different. Younger people may be able to from a stronger connection to it. Maybe not though!"

The building has also divided opinion amongst the wider population. The modernist and abstract architectural style has not been well received by some visitors who may already have been frustrated by the fact that it opened three years after it was scheduled to, with an estimated cost that was around ten times higher than initial projections. However, it has been praised by fellow architects and people who hold an interest in that field, to the extent that it won the prestigious Stirling Award in 2005.

It is possible to join a tour inside the building, but we had little interest in doing so. We had the more pressing concern of scaling the highest peak within Edinburgh.

"You always said that you fancied climbing up a volcano, didn't you?" I cheekily asked Mum.

"I definitely did not! Do you think that it is safe?"

"Yes, it is fine. The volcano is extinct… I think."

"Oh, I hope it is."

"I am just kidding. It is definitely extinct. It looks like a gentle climb, as children and pensioners seem to be coping with it."

There are a few different routes to Arthur's Seat, with the one we chose being particularly simple. We began our ascent along a wide and well-kept path, walking amongst people of all ages. I was relieved to discover that we were embarking upon a scenic stroll rather than a treacherous and exhausting adventure. It would have been rather cruel to have made my Mum risk her life by trekking up a dangerous volcano. Especially as she had not yet seen most of the historic landmarks within the Scottish capital.

It took around forty-five minutes to reach the summit, which was not too shabby considering that we periodically stopped to take photographs of our beautiful surroundings. This included taking the time to capture images of the ruins of St. Anthony's Chapel, which are situated on a rocky outcrop above St. Margaret's Loch.

It was fitting that we took photographs here since the history of colour photography is rooted in Scotland. The Scottish physicist James Clerk Maxwell was a pioneer of the three-colour method, with the first permanent colour photograph being taken by Thomas Sutton for Maxwell's demonstration in 1861.

The climb was a little trickier towards the end of the route as the ground was steeper. The grass that covers most of the hill had now given way to rock. It was hardly Ben Nevis though, and it was easy enough for me and my mum to conquer. Having climbed 251 metres above sea level, we were rewarded with a splendid view over Edinburgh, including the distinctive outline of Edinburgh Castle in the distance. Incidentally, that also sits upon an extinct volcano.

"I bet you did not expect to be surrounded by volcanoes this weekend," I remarked.

"Are you trying to scare your poor mum?"

"No. The volcanoes are extinct, and we are not in any danger. I'm fairly confident of that. I hope that I have got my facts right though…"

"You're not filling me with confidence!"

"I am just teasing you. We are safe."

I took lots of photos of a large silver disc that confirmed the height of Arthur's Seat, as well as the longitude and latitude. My intention was to capture an artistic image, but I imagine that it just looked like I was holding a coin in the foreground of the picture.

If we had visited a few days earlier, we could have taken part in a tradition that began over two hundred years ago. Thousands of people once made their way to Arthur's Seat and the surrounding hills on the first morning of May in order to bathe their face in the May dew. The origins of this ritual may be related to the ancient belief that the moisture produced by nature was a sacred entity that was a vital part in making things grow. Harnessing this dew was thought to ensure a good harvest and an abundance of livestock.

At some point, the benefits of the May dew became associated with enhancing one's beauty. The eighteenth-century poet Robert Ferguson referred to how this practice had become especially popular with young women. This tradition was still fairly popular in the middle of the twentieth century, with many people still waking up in the early hours of May Day to bathe their face in the dew. The numbers had dwindled in the decades leading up to the turn of the millennium and I am unsure if there are significant numbers still taking part in this ritual.

For our descent, we took the steeper route down Salisbury Crags that eventually lead us back to our starting point. The sun was setting over the monuments on Calton Hill, and there were a few people laying on the grass in front of the grounds of the Palace of Holyroodhouse. This was a nice scene to take in as we concluded our little trek.

The unmistakable sound of bagpipes was present upon our return to the Royal Mile. The man playing the instrument was clearly dressed to please visiting tourists. He was wearing a tartan kilt and sporran, along with a smart jacket and headwear. He did not have red hair and blue eyes though, so the Scottish stereotypical look was not quite complete.

Not everyone is a fan of this musical instrument, but I like the powerful sound that we have all become accustomed to through popular culture. If this is the Scottish version of busking, then I thoroughly approve. I must confess that I imagine that it would probably feel excruciating to listen to it for an extended period though.

A rowdy group of young English men, seemingly on a stag do, stepped out onto the Royal Mile from one of the intersecting streets. The name of this particular street seemed to have thoroughly amused them, as one of the men shouted: "We've just come from Cockburn Street!"

This drew uncontrollable laughter from the rest of the group, who proceeded to take pictures of the street sign. "Cockburn! The Scottish are mad!"

I was tempted to ruin their fun by informing them that the second 'c' and the 'k' are supposed to be silent. Thankfully, I was aware that this would have been a bad idea and it could have led to me becoming the new target for their tomfoolery. Especially as I was the kind of person who used words such as tomfoolery.

I can only imagine how the leery group of lads would have reacted if they had known that the street was named after Lord Cockburn. Or that he was born in a parish called Cockpen. There used to be a prominent building on the street called Cockburn Hotel, but it was probably for the best that this no longer existed. I just hope that they are not aware that there is a Cockburn Association set up in his honour.

St. Giles Cathedral was the next point of interest that we encountered during our stroll along High Street. The building had a Gothic look to it, but the church has a rather tangled history. It was formed around the twelfth century, with a series of reformations adding to the web of architectural styles. The burning of the church by the English in the fourteenth century may also have impacted its appearance!

Mum and I chose to admire the church's exterior rather than enter the building. There was a large group of tourists stood in front of it, with a guide giving them a summary of what their impending early evening ghost tour would entail. We moved away from the group and ended up stood next to a statue.

"That must be St. Giles," Mum asserted.

I examined the statue before informing her that: "It is actually a statue of Sir Walter Scott. We have already seen two statues created in his honour. They must really like his literature here."

As is the case with many revered authors, Scott was in debt and ill health at the time of his death. His work became more popular, and profitable, after he had passed away. I am currently in good health and fairly prosperous, so that is probably a bad sign for my prospects of becoming a best-selling author!

The church looked as dark and moody as the Scott Monument that we had visited earlier that day. If we had entered the building, we would have seen how the stained-glass windows apparently provide a captivating light which allows one to admire the ornate features of the church's design. Instead, we carried on walking along the Royal Mile until we witnessed a rather bizarre and unsightly custom: a man of advancing years spat on a heart-shaped mosaic on the floor.

"Edinburgh seems such a clean and beautiful place. Why would anyone do that?" I asked Mum.

"I am not sure, but I don't like it."

After watching another person deposit their saliva on the same spot, I consulted my guidebook. I was surprised to learn that people spit on the Heart of Midlothian for good luck. This spot marks the location of the Old Tolbooth, which was the administrative centre of the city, as well as serving as a prison and a site for torture and public executions. Opened at the start of the fifteenth century, the Old Tolbooth remained in place for over four hundred years.

The custom of spitting on the heart seems to have been borne out of disdain for the former prison. I am unsure how this practice eventually became associated with good luck though. I sincerely hope that there have not been any tourists who have been unfortunate enough to attempt to take a selfie by the mosaic just as a passer-by has decided that they needed some good luck!

In any case, this has become embedded in Edinburgh folklore. Sir Walter Scott's novel *The Heart of Midlothian* is regarded by many as his greatest work, and the oldest football club in the Scottish capital also goes by this name. The club's crest is even based on the mosaic found on the Royal Mile. Incidentally, the club commonly known as Hearts, have won the Scottish Cup eight times. It has been claimed that this is the oldest national trophy in world football. Staying on this subject, I believe that the former Liverpool and Rangers player El Hadji Diouf would more than likely approve of the aforementioned spitting custom.

It was not long before we were observing another bizarre tradition. Passers-by seemed inclined to rub the foot of the statue of Scottish historian, economist and writer David Hume. As it turns out, the act of rubbing his big toe had become another strange good luck custom. The people of Edinburgh seem to believe that unsavoury actions such as spitting, and the rubbing of a big toe would bring them good luck. They must think that the people of Wythenshawe are particularly fortunate!

Before embarking on our trip, I had read about a charming tale of how a dog called Bobby had guarded the grave of its recently deceased owner for the final fourteen years of its life. This heartwarming story, however accurate it is, was enough to temporarily draw us away from the main thoroughfare in order to check out a small statue that had been built in his honour.

Upon arrival at the statue located at the corner of Candlemaker Row and George IV Bridge, we were given a clue as to why some believe that the authenticity of the story is questionable. There was a small group of tourists taking pictures of Bobby's statue and the pub behind it was called Greyfriars Bobby's Bar. The commercial gain brought about by tourists charmed by the story has long led to suspicion and cynicism.

It has been questioned whether the police night watchman John Gray really was the dog's owner. It has also been suggested that stray dogs were sometimes found loitering in graveyards and were fed by groundsmen and visitors, to the point where they ended up making a home there. People would then mistakenly believe, perhaps influenced by notions of romanticism, that the dogs were guarding a particular grave. Regardless, I wanted to believe the commonly told tale about Bobby.

We paid a visit to Greyfriars Kirkyard to have a quick look at the graves of Bobby and John Gray before heading back to the Royal Mile. It felt rather strange to be searching for the grave of a dog. We did not have to wait long before we were stood in front of Bobby's resting place, as it is located close to the entrance. After briefly examining both graves, which looked like most others within the grounds, we began walking back to the Royal Mile.

Before we reached Lawnmarket, which was another section of the thoroughfare, we noticed a delightful street to our left. The gentle curve of Victoria Street was pleasing on the eye, which prompted Mum and I to have a closer look. The narrow and tall buildings were painted in an eye-catching array of colours that contrasted beautifully with the old stone architecture belonging to this cobbled street. Most of them contained independent shops, which added to the charm of this wonderful place. The feature that I most enjoyed was the terrace that is situated high above the north side of the street.

The terrace followed the gentle curve of the street, making it the ideal location for a café or a restaurant overlooking one of the most popular areas of the old town. It is no wonder why Victoria Street has featured in so many television shows. Perhaps a more telling indication of its popularity can be garnered from the amount of Instagram posts that feature this street.

We eventually rejoined the Royal Mile before finding somewhere to have dinner on our way back to our guesthouse. We opted for the traditional Scottish restaurant Wagamama.

"What do you think of Edinburgh?" I asked Mum as we prepared for a well-earned sleep.

"It's lovely isn't it? I have really enjoyed today."

"Me too. I think it is a delightful city with wonderful architecture and historic sites. It is busy but nothing like as manic as London. It seems really clean too. And the view from Arthur's Seat was fantastic."

"Yes, it was well worth the walk to the top…even if you failed to mention that we were going to climb a volcano!"

*   *   *

The following morning, our host prepared a breakfast which we consumed with glee. After a warming portion of porridge and a cooked selection of sausages, black pudding and toast, we headed out to explore Edinburgh. We had seen so many of the famous sights during our first day but there were still a few historic landmarks that we were yet to visit.

"Shall we start the day with another walk to the summit of a hill?" I asked Mum.

"OK. You are in charge, so I will go along with what you decide. It's not another volcano is it?"

"I don't think so. It should be an easier walk as it is only about one hundred metres high."

We walked along Princes Street again, which was quieter than it had been the previous day. Most shops were shut because it was Sunday, but the souvenir stores were still welcoming people in. There was a tacky selection of tartan bonnets with red-haired wigs stitched into the material on sale alongside bottles of whisky and boxes of shortbread. Kilts and bagpipes of varying quality were available to purchase too. Scottish flags were on display everywhere we looked, which makes it slightly surprising that the population declined the opportunity to re-establish an independent country a few years later. Not that I am bitter about it!

We strolled past St. Andrew's House, which serves as the headquarters for the Scottish government, on our way to Calton Hill. The proximity to the Scottish Parliament Building and the Palace of Holyroodhouse gave the area a feeling of importance.

There were steps leading to a path, which provided a comfortable and easy walk to the monuments that sit on top of the hill. The Dugald Stewart Monument is a circular temple consisting of nine columns. With the decorative feature on top of the rounded roof of the temple, its shape resembles that of a cafetière. There were not any ground coffee beans inside though. Just a large urn on a podium.

Dugald Stewart was a philosopher and mathematician who gave lectures at Edinburgh University during the period of Scottish Enlightenment in the eighteenth and nineteenth centuries. In truth, I had never heard of him, but his influence can be shown by the number of his pupils who went on to carve their own legacies.

Sir Walter Scott was taught by Stewart, and we had already seen examples of his impact on Scottish history during our brief time in the city. Even the name of the street that the stag party had found so amusing was named after another of his pupils: Henry Thomas Cockburn.

The scene in front of us seemed familiar due to it cropping up in various online searches for 'the best things to see in Edinburgh.' The combination of the striking Dugald Stewart Monument in the foreground and the beautiful image of the city behind it was certainly pleasing on the eye.

A group of American women who appeared to be in their early twenties asked me to take a photograph of them by the monument. They had not only asked a man who had an incomplete grasp of the norms of social interaction but one who was a perfectionist when it came to taking photographs; therefore, they were surprised by my methodical approach. I told them to take a step to the right before I crouched down to find the perfect shot.

"I will take a photo with the monument in the foreground and a view of the castle in the distance," I informed the group.

"OK, whatever" was their collective response.

I could not quite capture the desired image, so I positioned myself as close to the floor as possible, lying flat on my stomach. The group were still holding their pose and their forced smiles, but I could see that they were thinking: 'Just hurry up and take the photo, you weirdo!'

They were probably not bothered about capturing the perfect image or including the castle in the photograph, but I was asked to do a task, so I was going to do it to the best of my ability. Besides, I knew how frustrating it can be when a stranger takes a rubbish photograph of you on holiday. I remained on the floor and took a few more photos. Thank goodness that they were all wearing jeans; otherwise, I may have been accused of trying to look up their skirts.

They thanked me for taking the photographs, but their wariness of me was written all over their faces. They appeared to be gap-year students who were travelling around Europe, which always provokes a feeling of jealousy within me. This free-spirited group were probably enjoying a few months moving from one country to another, whist I was spending two nights in Edinburgh with my mother.

I was grateful that I was able to go on so many trips and I also liked spending time with Mum, but I could not avoid the feeling that I had missed out on the adventures that one experiences when they 'go travelling.' Then again, my fear of social interaction and my shyness were perhaps not compatible with the backpacking lifestyle.

Nelson's Monument was next on the agenda. Reaching a height of thirty-two metres, it apparently offers splendid views of the city. This was not enough to tempt us into climbing the 143 steps that lead to the public viewing gallery though. Instead, we admired the monument from below. It resembled an upturned telescope. It was apparently designed this way due to Vice Admiral Horatio Nelson's association with this particular device. The monument was erected to commemorate Nelson after he was killed during the Battle of Trafalgar in 1805.

Taking into consideration Nelson's Column in Trafalgar Square, it appears that the authorities believed that the best way to honour him was to build a tall monument. Perhaps this was one final dig at his adversary Napoleon Bonaparte, who was said to have been a diminutive figure.

The National Monument of Scotland is a memorial to the Scottish soldiers and sailors who died during the Napoleonic Wars. My initial impression was that the twelve columns were imposing and impressive. It was only after having a quick read of my guidebook that I realised that this was originally only supposed to form part of the monument.

Its design was based on the Parthenon in Athens, but funding dried up three years after construction had begun. It was clear why those in charge had attempted to replicate the historic Greek building, as the elevated position overlooking the city would have created a similarly powerful symbol. However, the project was abandoned with only the façade we were now looking at having been constructed.

Rather than demonstrating the power and importance of Scotland, the unfinished monument was seen as a national disgrace, earning the nicknames of 'Scotland's Folly' and 'The Pride and Poverty of Scotland.' The criticism has softened over time, with people taking a more lighthearted approach. Some people joke that an incomplete structure is the most fitting national monument for the nation. Either way, our fellow tourists seemed impressed. A couple of different groups took it in turns to pose for photographs. Mum and I followed suit before heading back down the hill.

"What did you think of Calton Hill?" I asked Mum.

"The monuments were interesting, and the views were pleasant. The walk was easy too."

"Shall we go to Camera Obscura now?"

"What is that?" Mum enquired.

"Apparently, there is a Victorian camera obscura, whatever that is, which allows you to take a close look around the city. And there are loads of camera illusions and trickery. It is on the Royal Mile."

"OK, you are the boss."

I may not have known much about it, but I had read that Camera Obscura and World of Illusions is a 'must-see' attraction. It turns out that the central feature dates back to the nineteenth century. The Camera Obscura was a precursor for the modern photographic camera, and a spectacular version of this was the star attraction of what was then known as Short's Observatory, Museum of Science and Art.

After reading about its history, I was somewhat surprised by the modern installments that greeted us upon our arrival. The five floors within the building were filled with all sorts of quirky exhibits. Mum and I amused ourselves by taking pictures of each other whilst we were immersed in the world of illusion. One display made it appear that my head was resting on a silver platter. I am sure that there are many people who have demanded to see this image, but I can assure you that it was just a visual trick! Another exhibit provided an image of two versions of me moving in unison; by contrast, this is an image that nobody wants to see!

There were bewildering 'mirror' screens and dazzling lights to walk through, and numerous interactive displays that were informative and interesting. It tied in somewhat with the camera obscura, given that the contraption operates by manipulating the available light and the clever positioning of mirrors.

One of the most popular features was installed a couple of years before our visit. The Vortex Tunnel can have a mind-boggling effect on visitors, yet it operates on a basic principle: making one of our senses contradict another. There is a pathway, complete with handrails, to walk through the tunnel whilst bright and colourful lighting swirls around you in a circular motion. The ground you walk on is stationary, so your sense of touch and sight are in direct conflict.

"Apparently, the brain favours the sense of sight, so people are tricked into thinking that they are moving when they are not," I informed Mum.

"Do you think it will work?" she asked.

"I am not sure. Maybe it would have if they had not told us about how it works. I think we will be too aware of the fact that we are not actually moving."

I was immediately proven wrong. It only took a few seconds in the tunnel for me to admit that I felt disorientated.

"I know that I am not moving, other than when I step forward, yet it feels like we are swirling around!"

"I feel a bit dizzy! It is fun though" Mum replied.

"I am going to concentrate. If I remind myself that we are not actually moving, it should negate the effects of the illusion."

Needless to say, my efforts failed miserably. The nature of the display changed, with the lights moving in a way that made it feel like the room had tilted. It was if someone had heard my proclamation and was determined to undermine me. We both felt even more disorientated than before. This shows how powerful the mind can be but also underscores how it is open to manipulation. The art of illusion has long been embraced as a mesmerising form of entertainment, whether it is performed on a theatre stage, on a cinema screen or by a live magician.

We eventually reached the rooftop terrace. Not only was this the place to find the Camera Obscura, it also provided a superb panorama of the city. Although we had already been blessed with spectacular views of the city from Arthur's Seat and Calton Hill, we were now being afforded a vantage point from within the heart of the old town. We were almost within touching distance of the other buildings and rooftops.

The Camera Obscura, which we had been working our way towards for the previous hour or so, was located within the rooftop chamber. This reminded me of the classic layout of a video game, with players having to work their way up the floors of the building by overcoming increasingly powerful adversaries until they reach the 'big boss' on the top level. I prayed that there was nothing too sinister within the chamber and I hoped that completing our mission would be as satisfying as defeating the final foe in *Street Fighter II* or *Streets of Rage*. Keen video game players will be able to offer a more fitting example.

The chamber was unsurprisingly dark but there were no evil warriors trying to kill us. Instead, a friendly guide welcomed us. She informed us that once a few more people had entered, she would begin demonstrating how the Camera Obscura works.

A minute or so later, she began her talk: "This Victorian contraption harnesses daylight and has similarities to both a pinhole camera and a periscope. This tube here sticks out of the roof and it has a small window to let in light. This reflects off a carefully-positioned mirror, causing the light rays to travel downwards through a set of three lenses until they provide a beautiful image of Edinburgh on the table in front of you."

I was shocked to discover that the image on the table was being produced by the Camera Obscura. I had assumed that it was a fancy screen playing a video sequence. The guide continued to impress everyone in the room: "What you see in front of you are live images of Edinburgh. I will demonstrate how we can focus on specific areas and get a closer view of any passers-by."

She duly changed the positioning of the camera to show us different sections of the old town before zooming in for a closer look at unsuspecting individuals. She chuckled as she stated that: "This guy has absolutely no idea that we are all up here watching him eat his ice cream! We can even manipulate the images. Watch as I place this card over the table to make it appear that we are lifting him up."

This was a clever trick that really did make it look like the man was being elevated above street level. She finished off her talk by reminding us how ground-breaking this technology was: "Remember, this device was created during Victorian times. There were no cinemas or virtual reality back then, so this would have been a magical experience for visitors from that era. There has been the odd tweak here and there, but judging by the expressions on your faces, the same basic technology can still impress people 150 years later."

Mum and I left the premises having thoroughly enjoyed our experience. It had also left us pondering the biggest mystery from our visit: where did the man who we had observed on the Camera Obscura get his ice cream from? We soon saw an ice cream parlour that was heaving with people. This provoked mixed feelings within me. On the one hand, this indicated that the ice cream was most likely of good quality; however, a large crowd of people in a confined area is never appealing. Nevertheless, I plucked up the courage to purchase a couple of ice creams.

We enjoyed our pistachio ice cream before heading to Edinburgh Castle. We were soon approaching the entrance to the complex. There were plenty of steps and steep pathways to climb before we were within the grounds of the castle, which looms over the city from its elevated position 130 metres above sea level. This only added to the feeling that we were about to enter one of the most historic places in Scotland.

"Are you taking me up another volcano?" Mum cautiously asked.

"Kind of. Castle Rock was formed through volcanic activity around 350 million years ago. I think it should be safe now though!"

It is thought that humans have inhabited Castle Rock in one form or another since at least 850 BC, with the current castle being constructed in the twelfth century. Castles signify power and control over the local population and seek to portray strength to anyone thinking of launching an invasion, so being able to see this building from most areas of the city would have meant that it was difficult to escape this symbol of dominance.

It has been claimed that Edinburgh Castle has been one of the most besieged places in the world. It was involved in both Wars of Scottish Independence and the Jacobite Uprising of 1745, as well as being subjected to up to twenty-six sieges during its history.

Incidentally, the Kingdom of Scotland retained its status as an independent country from the Kingdom of England at the conclusion of both Wars of Scottish Independence. Key figures within this struggle, such as Robert the Bruce and William Wallace, have been immortalised through popular culture. The 1995 film *Braveheart* won five Academy Awards, including Best Picture, although it faced some criticism for historical inaccuracies. Its sequel, *Robert the Bruce*, was released in 2019 to much less fanfare.

Inaccuracies aside, my desire to see Scotland regain its independence in 2014 was almost as strong as that of Wallace. I felt like screaming: "You will never take their freedom!" I am the most mild-mannered person that you can imagine though, so if I had ever vocalised my thoughts it would probably have resulted in me saying: "Please vote for independence. I would be ever so grateful. I don't want to offend anyone, so ignore me if you disagree."

Mum and I enjoyed walking around the many areas that were open to the public and observing the intricate details of the various rooms, such as the Great Hall. We learned about the prisoners that were locked up in the castle, which included many Americans who were held during the American War of Independence. As it was a Sunday, we were not treated to the traditional one o'clock firing of the gun but we were able to get a close look at the many cannons that were positioned throughout the complex, including the Argyle Battery.

We heard a few interesting tales about the castle, such as the beer-guzzling elephant that apparently lived onsite, and how the ghost of a young piper can still be heard in the tunnels beneath the castle. However, the most remarkable story was about how the Honours of Scotland, sometimes referred to as the Scottish Crown Jewels, were lost for over one hundred years following the Union of the Kingdom of Scotland and the Kingdom of England. Our old friend Sir Walter Scott was amongst the group of people who rediscovered them in a chest in the sealed Crown Room in 1818.

"These items were lost?" Mum asked with an air of disbelief as we examined the crown, sceptre and sword.

"I guess that the Honours of Scotland held little value to the unified British authorities, as they were just discarded in a chest and forgotten about. I have often left a £5 note in a coat pocket or accidentally dropped a pound coin down the side of a sofa, but I find it hard to imagine losing the Scottish Crown Jewels!"

As we walked past the tall stone walls and over the cobbled path that lead to the Portculls Gate on our way out of the castle, I dared to look at my phone for the first time all afternoon. I had been avoiding the score of the pivotal football match between Manchester City and Newcastle United. The dwindling title hopes of Manchester United hinged on Newcastle being able to deny City a crucial victory in the penultimate game of the season.

I discovered the news that I had feared: City had taken the lead with just twenty minutes of the match remaining. They soon put me out of my misery by adding a second before the final whistle. The title was surely out of reach now. City's final game was at home to relegation-threatened Queens Park Rangers, which was obviously going to be a routine victory for them. At least this meant that the pain of defeat was immediate, and I could accept that it had happened a week in advance.

The footballing gods would not let me off the hook that easily though. They ensured that Queens Park Rangers were somehow winning until the ninety-first minute. Unless you are unfamiliar with English football, you will know that Manchester City scored twice in stoppage time to deliver the most painful blow to the red half of the city. Sport, like life itself, can be cruel.

We had passed through East Princes Street Gardens and admired the Scott Monument on our first day; now it was time to have a look around West Princes Street Gardens. The Ross Fountain has been the central feature of the gardens since it was installed in 1872. The cast-iron fountain was not shining as brightly during our visit as it does now that it has been restored, but I think that its aging appearance complimented the historic castle better than the gleaming turquoise version that currently occupies the gardens.

Increasing levels of tiredness resulted in our decision not to explore many of the garden's landmarks. We did not see the four air-raid shelters nor the Scottish American War Memorial. We were a few years too early to see the statue of Wojtek the Bear, who, bizarrely, was enlisted in the Polish military during the Second World War.

We had an early dinner instead. This may have been our last chance to sample some haggis and whisky, but we opted for Italian cuisine. I regret this choice, as I am yet to taste some of the most famous Scottish dishes. I have not even had a deep-fried Mars Bar. I have had my fair share of Iron Bru though.

∗   ∗   ∗

After another early start, we began our long bus journey home. We had managed to get seats together, which meant that we could discuss our trip with each other rather than a random axe-murderer.

"Did you enjoy our stay in Edinburgh?" I asked Mum.

"It was lovely. It is a fantastic city and I would definitely like to return one day."

"We can go to Loch Ness and look for the monster next time that we visit Scotland."

"Is it real?"

"No. The Loch seems more interesting because of the myth, but it is supposed to be a beautiful sight in its own right."

"Why do people believe the myth?" Mum enquired.

"I think that most people know that the monster does not exist, but they accept that it is a bit of fun. It also helps the local economy due to the tourists that it draws in. Then again, the national animal of Scotland is a Unicorn."

"Unicorns do not exist, do they?"

"No, but they have captured the imagination of countless children. It is another nice myth to believe in I guess."

The journey seemed to drag a bit, as it was a rare occasion in which I was unable to doze off. We had soon run out of sweets, so I was struggling to find ways to pass the time. In the end, I consulted my guidebook for further topics of conversation. I relayed some of the information that I had read: "Scotland is the home of golf and Scotch whisky. It is also been suggested that this is where the '99 Flake' ice cream originated from."

"I wish we had consumed some during our stay."

"A ninety-niner or some whisky?" I asked, knowing that she was referring to the former.

"Ice cream of course! Your mum does not drink whisky. Do you like it?"

"I have never tried it, other than the odd Jack Daniels and Coke. In hindsight, I wish that we had tried some whisky and haggis. We could have seen the penguins too."

"They don't have penguins in Scotland!" Mum exclaimed.

"They have them in Edinburgh zoo, where there is a daily parade. It is a tradition that began after a gate was accidentally left open one day in 1951 and the penguins followed a worker out of the enclosure. It was an amusing sight, so the zoo encouraged this activity to continue."

"That would have been an unexpected sight in Scotland."

"I guess that we should focus on the places that we have visited rather than those which we did not get to see. It was a brilliant couple of days north of the border, and it was lovely to spend some quality time with my Mum as well. We are a good team."

"Yes, we are."

CHAPTER 7: NAKED PEOPLE AND EXPENSIVE FOOD
OSLO, NORWAY
JUNE 2012

"David, do you know that you have been working in this office for five weeks and you have already been on four holidays?!"

My colleague Charlotte may have been in disbelief at how frequently I was jetting off to various European cities but she was a fellow traveller at heart, having backpacked across South-East Asia, Australia and the United States before joining the nine-to-five brigade.

This prompted her to point out another good opportunity for me to venture abroad: "I have seen that Ryanair fly to Oslo and that the prices are ridiculously cheap. You should have a look."

By the following evening, I had booked a short trip to the Norwegian capital with Carol. It was even cheaper than I had expected, as our flights were just £35 each. I had reserved a hotel for about £300 for three nights, which was a reasonable price for a stay in Scandinavia.

Four weeks later, we were preparing to board our flight from Manchester Airport. "Time for a cheap weekend in Norway!" I joked.

The flights may have cost less than a train to London would have, but I was fully aware that Norway frequently sits near the top of the list of countries with the highest cost of living in the world. Upon touching down at Moss Airport, Rygge that Friday night, it became clear why the flights had been so cheap. Low-cost airlines often use smaller airports that are quite a distance from the city that it is marketed as serving.

In this case, the airport was in the municipality of Rygge, which is 10 kilometres away from the smaller city of Moss, but 60 kilometres outside of Oslo. As the vast majority of passengers were intending to visit Oslo, it was somewhat misleading to market this as one of Oslo's airports. The airport no longer operates any commercial flights, with many routes switching to

90

Sandefjord Airport, Torp. As this is 110 kilometres south of Oslo, perhaps I should have been thankful that the airport in Rygge was not any further afield.

Ryanair, Moss Airport and a local transport company had an arrangement that saw a bus service to Oslo city centre depart around twenty minutes after each flight landed. In fairness, this was an efficient and affordable service. Given that the airport was so small that it resembled a bus station, it was easy to locate the departure point directly in front of the main exit.

The journey took about an hour, which meant that we arrived in the city centre shortly before midnight. I felt slightly wary about trying to locate our hotel whilst avoiding any unruly Friday night drunks. I felt added pressure because having been responsible for our flight to a remote airport that was an hour away from Oslo, the last thing that I needed was to test Carol's patience further by leading her on an unpleasant walk late at night.

I was clinging on to the hope that Norway was such an expensive country that nobody could afford to get drunk on a Friday night. I had no such luck. Dragging our hand luggage behind us, we weaved in and out of the tipsy revellers during our five-minute walk to our hotel. I am pleased to report that we survived the ordeal without having any prolonged contact with the intoxicated locals.

The layout of the lobby was unusual. Instead of having a main reception desk, there were a series of touchscreen units being operated by hotel employees. We approached one gentleman and informed him of our reservation.

"Hmm, there is a slight problem with your booking," he informed us.

I braced myself for the worst. Would a "slight problem" mean that we had to sleep on the streets or pay for a room ten times more expensive than we had booked? In the end, it was only a minor inconvenience.

"You have booked a double room for three nights, but we only have a twin room available for tonight. You will have to stay in that, then switch to a double for the last two nights. Is that OK, Sir?" he asked, knowing that we had no option other than to agree to this proposal.

"Yes, that is no problem. We are tired, so we are happy to sleep in any room."

A more ruthless or demanding guest may have argued that they were entitled to a partial refund or a complimentary service; however, I was so mild-mannered that I would have agreed to anything that he said, even if it had meant paying an extra 500 Euros for an undesirable room. As it turns out, there were not any hidden charges and our room was clean and presentable.

"So we flew to an airport which seems closer to Manchester than Oslo, endured what felt like a seven-hour bus journey, had to walk through a bunch of drunks in the middle of the night, and now we have to sleep in separate beds. Do you have any more surprises in store for me?" Carol asked with a devilish look in her eye.

"Erm...err...I don't think so..." I stuttered.

"I am kidding. It is fine. Thank you for arranging the trip. I am looking forward to exploring Oslo tomorrow."

Feeling relieved, we soon took the opportunity to recharge our batteries. Both those belonging to our mobile phones and our bodies.

* * *

A typical Norwegian breakfast consists of open sandwiches, cold cuts, spreads and cheese. I am not sure why I am telling you this, as we made the uninspired decision to stick to cereal and croissants. Nevertheless, we enjoyed our food and it gave us the required energy for the full day of sightseeing that we had planned.

Carol instructed me to slip a few bread rolls and some cheese into a plastic bag and place this in her handbag. I suddenly felt like a criminal. The food in the buffet is only meant for consumption within the restaurant. Although plenty of people take food away, I felt guilty for doing this. After spending the best part of five minutes nervously glancing at my surroundings, I eventually completed the task that I had been assigned. It is a good job that I have no intention of earning a living by illegal means, as I am sure that I would make the least successful criminal in history.

The City Hall, known locally as Oslo Rådhus, was the obvious place to begin. Not only is it the most important administrative building in Oslo, it is also where the Nobel Peace Prize ceremony is held each December. I have a strong interest in human rights, so I understandably held this award in high regard. However, I had never thought about the building in which the prize was handed to the recipient of this accolade.

I was underwhelmed by what I saw. The shape of the building and the red bricks that were used for its construction seemed dull and uninspired. It reminded me of a jobcentre or an old office block in Britain. It was even considered outdated at the time of its official opening in 1950. In fairness, the project had been mooted since the start of the twentieth century, with construction interrupted by the outbreak of the Second World War.

The rectangular shape and uniformed nature of the building, which belongs to the architectural style of functionalism, had few distinguishing features, but the two towers that stand at either end at least made it recognisable from afar. The bright blue sky added some colour to the scene in front of us and provided a nice contrast for our photographs.

I offered my thoughts to Carol: "Some of the most honourable individuals and organisations have been awarded the Nobel Peace Prize in this building. I don't think that the exterior of the building reflects the significance of what has taken place inside."

"Who has been awarded the prize? People like Gandhi?" Carol asked.

"Bizarrely, Gandhi was never awarded the Nobel Peace Prize. I am not sure if it was because the committee viewed things from a European and American perspective, or if they did not want to upset the British. After all, Gandhi was the face of the struggle for Indian independence from Great Britain. Mother Teresa, Nelson Mandela, and Martin Luther King Jr. are famous recipients. Organisations such as UNICEF and the Red Cross have also been honoured in this way."

Incidentally, the Nobel Peace Prize ceremony is the only one of the five Nobel prizes that is held outside of Alfred Nobel's home city of Stockholm. The prizes, which also include chemistry, literature, physics, and physiology or medicine, were set up at the request of Nobel's will, with the first awards being awarded in 1901.

In addition to hosting the aforementioned awards ceremony, the City Hall houses the Munch Room. As much as I would like to tell you that this is a room dedicated to providing packets of Monster Munch to staff and visitors, it is actually where Edvard Munch's painting *Life* is displayed. Munch is a celebrated Norwegian artist who is responsible for *The Scream*, which is one of the most recognisable creations within the world of art.

Although the City Hall's interior is adorned with a vast collection of Norwegian art, we did not venture inside to see for ourselves. We had already made plans to visit the peninsula of Bygdøy, which would likely take up most of our day; therefore, we decided that we did not have the time to explore the Rådhus. Besides, who needs to see celebrated works of art and explore the location of one of the most prestigious award ceremonies in the world, when you can stand outside and look at the functionalist red-brick exterior?

We boarded the ferry to Bygdøy from Aker Brygge, which is located a short distance from the City Hall. We were afforded a view of Akershus Fortress as we sailed away from our departure point. The thirteenth-century medieval castle has served as a military base and a prison during various periods in history.

One of the buildings close to the fortress has housed the office of the Prime Minister of Norway since the government was targeted during the terrorist attacks perpetrated by a far-right extremist in 2011. The majority of the seventy-seven people killed were teenagers attending a summer camp on the nearby island of Utøya.

After a journey that lasted around fifteen minutes, we disembarked and made plans of what we wanted to see and do during our visit. Bygdøy is home to several museums but we did not wish to visit all of them. We wanted to make the most of the pleasant weather rather than spending several hours indoors.

I posed a question to Carol: "Which museum do you fancy visiting? The choices include the Fram Museum, which details the history of Norwegian Polar Exploration, the Norwegian Maritime Museum, the Viking Ship Museum…"

"Definitely the Viking Ship Museum!"

Her response did not surprise me. After all, the Viking era is the most well-known and glamorous, although brutal, period of Nordic history.

"I am happy with that choice. It will be interesting to see some Viking ships. Can we also explore the Norwegian Museum of Cultural History? This includes an open-air museum with a mock old-town."

"OK, that sounds interesting. We will do those two and skip the rest."

We encountered a steep grassy hill on our way to the Viking Ship Museum. Carol challenged me to the top, which was only a few metres above ground level. I showed her no mercy as I left her trailing in my wake! The euphoria of victory proved to be short-lived, as Carol pointed out the problem that we were faced with.

"How are we going to get back down? It's not far to the bottom but it's very steep. We'll probably fall over!"

I vaguely remembered someone once telling me that you are more likely to lose your balance travelling downhill if you move slowly; therefore, I made a bold proclamation: "We will not fall over if we run down the hill."

"Are you sure?" Carol asked with a worried look on her face.

"Yes. We are more likely to fall if we walk down slowly. We'll run so that we keep our balance."

Carol inexplicably put her trust in me, which is something that she immediately regretted. We began running, hand in hand, but I soon lost my balance and fell. This resulted in me dragging Carol down the hill with me. Fortunately, we were both unscathed, aside from the embarrassment. We laughed heartily and embraced in a crumple at the bottom of the hill. Passers-by also laughed. They had good reason to as well. Not only had we made fools of ourselves in public, we also risked serious injury in one of the most expensive countries in the world. Our insurance was so cheap that it barely offered any coverage for mishaps, so we really could have found ourselves in a pickle.

Having almost broken some of my girlfriend's limbs, I decided that we should enter the museum before I caused any more damage. Below a silver half-arch, there was a statue of the Norwegian archaeologist Anne Stine Ingstad and her husband, Helge, who was a renowned explorer. They had discovered the remnants of a settlement in Newfoundland, Canada, which proved that the Vikings had travelled beyond Greenland and made it to North America.

The interior of the museum looked different to what I had expected. The main hall was larger than it had appeared from outside, and it was rather lacking in character. We were soon staring at the *Oseberg* ship, which occupied most of the space within the hall. This is widely acknowledged as one of the best-preserved Viking artefacts in existence.

I was unsure of the level of restoration that had taken place since it was discovered over one hundred years ago, but it was hard not to be impressed when examining an oak ship that had been built in the ninth century. The curled prow was my favourite detail of the vessel, as it was similar to images of Viking ships that I had seen in popular culture.

Interestingly, a replica of the ship was launched from the city of Tønsberg just over two weeks after our stay in Oslo. Following this successful trial, it was taken to open seas in March 2014. The ship apparently performed well, demonstrating that it could indeed have been used by the Vikings to sail across oceans. This was important because there had been a long-running debate as to whether the ship was simply a burial chamber. Human remains had been found in the ship, along with a large collection of grave goods.

We took it in turns to pose for photographs next to the ship.

"What would the Vikings think of my pink jumper?!" I asked Carol.

"They would probably laugh at you, just like I do! You do look cute though!"

"I doubt that the Vikings would think I looked cute. They would probably see me as an embarrassment to mankind!"

We had a look at the other ships in the museum, including the *Gokstad*, which is the largest preserved Viking ship in Norway. It could apparently hold between forty to seventy men. It must have been terrifying to see seventy Vikings disembark on your land. It would be even more frightening to see several of these ships approach your shores.

The *Tune* ship was the final one that is housed in the museum. It was smaller than the others and it was an incomplete structure. The vessels were displayed in rather empty halls that felt bare. The walls were painted white, which along with the daylight that entered through the numerous windows, at least gave the dark ships a distinctive appearance.

We examined numerous artefacts within the museum, including a variety of tools and wood carvings. One of the larger items that we saw was a horse cart that was displayed in a glass box. It was interesting to see these artefacts, as they demonstrated how there was more to the Vikings than the ships that they travelled on and the weapons that they wielded.

The Norwegian Museum of Cultural History, known as the Norsk Folkemuseum, was the next place that we visited. Although there were indoor exhibitions, most people came here to see the open-air museum that showcased Norwegian life from the Middle Ages until the twentieth century. It is one of many that have at some stage claimed to be the oldest open-air museum in the world. Skansen, which I had visited during my stay in Stockholm earlier in the year, was apparently established a few years before the Norsk Folkemuseum.

We began by exploring the 'old town' area, which felt more authentic than I had anticipated. There were times whilst we were walking along the cobbled streets when it did seem like we were in a small Norwegian town in a bygone era. The pastel buildings appeared to be faithful recreations, some of which had been transported from other areas of Norway before being reconstructed and restored in the museum.

There were stores within the 'old town' that visitors could enter. Naturally, Carol chose to have a look inside the wine merchant's shop. Much to her dismay, we were unable to purchase any alcohol! Mind you, given the cost of living in Norway, this was probably for the best!

The vast grounds of the museum were located amongst woodland, which added to the sense that one was escaping the hustle and bustle of modern life. You just had to ignore the road that ran parallel to the edge of the land.

We saw plenty of farm animals grazing in the fields, including black rams, pigs and horses. We even passed a summer dairy farm, although we did not stop for a closer inspection. I enjoyed seeing the buildings that had been relocated from different rural areas in Norway, most of which originated from the eighteenth and nineteenth centuries. The wooden cabins had grass growing on their sloping rooftops, which I found rather charming.

The star attraction of the museum is the Gol Stave Church. Construction of the original building was completed in the early part of the thirteenth century. When a new church was erected in Gol over six hundred years later, the old wooden building was documented and deconstructed before being rebuilt in Bygdøy.

I offered me thoughts to Carol: "The church looks interesting. It reminds me of both a traditional Japanese pagoda and Samurai armour, which is not what I expected from a Norwegian church!"

"It is pretty. I really like it."

We took the obligatory photographs before leaving the museum.

"What else is there to see?" Carol asked me.

I replied with a question of my own: "Do you fancy going to the beach? Looking at the map, it appears that there are a few."

"We're not exactly dressed for it but going to the beach always seems a good idea to me!"

I examined our map before deciding that the beach in Huk was our best bet. We soon saw a sign that pointed us in the right direction. As it was mid-afternoon, we decided that it was finally time to eat the cheese sandwiches that I had smuggled out of the hotel buffet. This was possibly the first time in my life that the act of eating a sandwich had filled me with such guilt!

Following this sinful act, we began walking towards Huk. We were unaware that we would have to travel just under two kilometres. Granted, this may not be a huge distance, but it certainly felt like it was. This may have been because we were unsure of the route or how long it would take to get there. Fortunately, it turned out to be a pleasant walk though what was clearly an affluent area; the huge, attractive houses and expensive-looking cars were an obvious indicator of this.

We eventually reached what appeared to be a large area of woodland. Walking amongst the tall trees and listening to the birds chirping way above our heads, we temporarily forgot about the beach and simply enjoyed our peaceful stroll through the woodland. It was the type of route that seems to bring out the best in people. Passers-by were smiling and saying hello rather than following my lead by warily keeping their distance from each other. This even drew me out of my shell to the extent that I made eye contact and mumbled a greeting to a few of them.

We eventually came to a signpost that indicated that we would have to follow the path to our left if we wanted to visit the regular public beach. Alternatively, we could take the path to our right if we wished to spend some time at the nudist beach.

"So…which beach would you like to go to?" I cheekily asked Carol.

I immediately regretted asking this question. After all, I had only known Carol for less than three months. Maybe she was a secret naturist!

"Let's go to the nudist beach!"

I took a sharp intake of breath whilst I desperately waited to discover if she was joking.

"I am kidding! I am slightly worried that you didn't know that!" she said with a chuckle.

"I was just worried for the people of Bygdøy! The sight of my naked body would be enough to harm their tourist industry for decades to come!"

We were soon stood by the public beach, which was not exactly a long stretch of golden sand. It may not have been as spectacular as a beach in the Caribbean, but it was pleasant, nonetheless. The sight of a thin covering of sand and pebbles in front of the Oslofjord was enhanced by the late-afternoon sun and a solitary tree, which seemed to be crying out to be photographed. We walked along a quiet section of the beach where the only other occupants were some ducks that had ventured ashore.

"I'll take your photo with one," Carol suggested.

This was what I had dreaded. Although I had absolutely no reason to be afraid of a duck, I was wary of getting too close to it. I am unsure if this was because I was fearful of any unexpected movements or whether I was frightened that this particular duck had developed sharp teeth and an appetite for human flesh. Carol found it hilarious that I kept my distance whilst having my picture taken with the duck.

"Are you really scared?"

"It's not that I am scared but..."

The duck charged at me before I could finish my sentence, forcing me to run for safety. At least I had succeeded in having my photograph taken with this dangerous animal before defying the odds by surviving to tell the tale.

Carol was laughing uncontrollably: "You are so cute!"

The Vikings would be even less impressed by me. The pink jumper was bad enough.

Killer ducks aside, it had been a surprisingly peaceful day away from the city centre, but it was now time to head back to the pier for our return journey. We strolled through the woodland without a worry in the world and passed some of the museums on our way to the departure point. As we began the final section of our walk to the pier, I remembered that the final ferry of the day was scheduled to leave sometime in the early evening.

"What's wrong? I can always tell when there is something wrong because you go really quiet. What is it?" Carol asked.

"I am not sure if we have missed the final ferry of the day."

This was enough for Carol to go into full-on panic mode: "What do we do if we have missed the ferry?! Are we stuck here for the night?!"

"Bygdøy is not an island, so we are still connected to Oslo by land. I think that we would have to get a bus. Mind you, we best get a move on."

We ran towards the pier, desperately hoping to avoid the sight of the final ferry of the day leaving us behind. Fortunately, we saw a queue of people and a ferry approaching the pier. A nearby sign displayed the timetable, which confirmed that we were indeed boarding the final ferry of the day. We had been lucky.

Following a smooth ferry journey and subsequent walk to the hotel room, we took the opportunity to unwind for a couple of hours before heading back out for our evening meal. We had not made any dinner plans, so we ended up walking around looking for an enticing restaurant. Most of them seemed to specialise in seafood, which did not appeal to us at the time.

"They must like their seafood. I don't particularly fancy it. Is that what we can expect from Norwegian food?" Carol asked me.

"I have read that Norwegian specialities include fermented fish and sheep's head."

"Yuk!" Carol exclaimed with a disgusted look on her face.

We eventually stumbled upon a steakhouse, which Carol immediately decided would be a good choice: "It is nearly ten o'clock. This will do."

The sight of the chef stood outside the main entrance smoking and the other staff looking like they were itching to clear the tables and close the restaurant for the night was not enough to deter us. After sitting down in one of the many empty booths, we examined our surroundings. The steakhouse had the usual wooden décor, but our attention was immediately seized by the giant moose head that was situated high above my left shoulder.

"It looks like you!" Carol sniggered.

"To be fair, it's more handsome than me."

"Is that what's on the menu tonight?"

"Possibly! Moose and reindeer meat are delicacies in Norway."

"What have we let ourselves in for?" Carol asked with an obvious sense of dread.

We were relieved to discover that the menu was comprised of the usual beef dishes that one expects to be served with in a steakhouse. Carol ordered a sirloin steak whilst I opted to have a stacked burger. We thoroughly enjoyed our meals, prompting us to order an apple pie for dessert. Due to our hunger and being in 'holiday mode,' we had not paid much attention to the pricelist.

We had only paid for our ferry journeys and a couple of museum entrance fees earlier that day. Everything had seemed reasonably priced considering that we were in a country with a reputation for being ludicrously expensive. Our bill arrived, which meant that it was time for the first big test of our budget.

The total came to over 1,300 Norwegian Krone. I pulled out my phone to calculate how much this was in Pound Sterling. Given that this sounded like a huge figure, I was dreading the result. It turns out that our meal had cost over £100. This would be regarded as being extremely expensive for a burger, steak, apple pie and a couple of diet Cokes in England. We were in Norway though.

The price of our meal may have been even higher than we had expected but we were given a bigger surprise upon leaving the restaurant. It was nearly midnight, yet the sky was almost as bright as it had been in the early evening. We were not far enough north to be experiencing the 'midnight sun' but it was still startling to be able to walk around in natural light at this hour.

*   *   *

Engebret Café was the first port of call the following morning. This was not because we were still hungry after our breakfast at the hotel; rather, it was due to its interesting history. It is the oldest restaurant in continuous operation in Oslo, having served Norwegian home-cooking since 1857 and welcoming famous artists over the years, including Edvard Munch.

We again declined the opportunity to enter a place associated with Munch, which was more to do with the expensive prices rather than any ill-feeling towards him. I took a photograph of the café and the statue of Norwegian stage actor Johannes Brun that was in front of it.

I lead us on a route that would take us through central Oslo, passing several landmarks on our way to Vigeland Sculpture Park. We briefly stopped to admire the seventeenth-century Oslo Cathedral, which was not particularly grand in appearance. The brickwork appeared to have a pale-yellow colour and the tower had a green copper top, which is commonplace in much of Northern Europe. It looked more like an ordinary church than a cathedral, but I was pleased enough to have ticked off another notable tourist attraction.

The easy-to-pronounce Stortingsbygningen, which has been the home of the Norwegian Parliament since 1866, was the next point of interest that we encountered. The yellow brick building was designed by the Swedish architect Emil Victor Langlet after it was deemed that the initial proposal looked too much like a church. The semi-circular central section, which had a Norwegian flag flying above it, juts out of the H-shaped main body of the building. Apparently, Langlet wanted the shape to "resemble outstretched arms to welcome the representatives of the people, or with them the entire nation." There are large granite lion sculptures by the start of the two ramps that lead to the main entrance from either side.

Surprisingly, the statues outside of the Norwegian Parliament were carved by a convicted murderer! Gulbrand Eriksen Mørstad had been making counterfeit money with Knut Olson Offerdalen before he killed his partner in crime. Although he was initially given a death sentence, this was later reduced to life in prison. Whilst incarcerated in Akershus Fortress, he was recruited by the artist Christopher Borch and he eventually contributed to the creation of the lion sculptures. He was subsequently pardoned by the government "for services to the Norwegian Parliament," before spending his latter years in the United States of America.

There was a strange statue of a human head on a pedestal in front of the Stortingsbygningen. I was unsure why this was there, but Carol suggested that I pose for a photograph with it. I stared at the giant head, almost nose-to-nose, with a blank expression to match that of the statue.

"He looks livelier than you!" Carol giggled.

"I am usually pretty good at staring competitions, but this is one contest that I cannot win," I conceded.

"I think you need to put your glasses on. His eyes are closed!"

"As much as I would like to claim victory, I think his eyes are just about open."

Following this inconclusive result, I led Carol to the next prestigious building. The National Theatre is one of the most important venues for performing arts in Norway. The names of Ibsen, Holberg and Bjørnson were prominently displayed above the main entrance, indicating that they had made huge contributions to the history of the arts.

There were statues of esteemed playwrights Ludvig Holberg and Henrik Ibsen standing proudly in front of the building, which led me to question why Bjørnstjerne Martinius Bjørnson had not received such an honour. After all, he was the first Norwegian recipient of the Nobel Prize in Literature and he wrote the lyrics to the Norwegian national anthem, "Ja, vi elsker dette landet," which translates as "Yes, we love this country." Perhaps his name was deemed to have been too difficult to spell or too long to engrave onto a statue!

Given that we still had lots of tourist attractions to visit, I did not dwell on this thought for too long. We purchased a couple of bottles of water from a small shop and continued our walk along Karl Johans gate towards the Royal Palace. Our route took us through the fifty-four acres of the Palace Park before we reached the Palace Square.

The square is the country's main parade ground, and the symbolic meeting place for the King and the Norwegian people. Important events in the country's history have been marked here, including celebrations of royal marriages and birthdays. The Royal Family often wave from their balconies during parades that mark significant events such as Constitution Day.

The scaffolding on the neo-classical Palace detracted from the grandeur somewhat, but it was still possible to imagine what this open space would look like during national celebrations. As is often the case, an equestrian statue on a pedestal occupied the central point of the square. This particular statue honoured King Charles John, who ruled Sweden and Norway during the nineteenth century. He previously held the position of Prince of Pontecorvo, which was a Principality in Italy. Not bad going for a man who was born in France.

101

We opened our bottles before each taking a big gulp of water. Carol immediately spat hers out and had a look of disgust written all over her face. What could have been so unpleasant to have provoked this reaction? Had her water been contaminated?

Carol informed me what horror had occurred: "I must have picked up a bottle of sparkling water by mistake!"

"Is that all?! I thought that something serious had happened!"

"It has! Sparkling water is horrible!"

We placed our bottles on the floor whilst we took some photographs of the palace.

"The changing of the guard does not take place for a few hours, so we should probably move on. Are you happy to walk to Vigeland Sculpture Park? It looks like it will be a fair distance. Is that OK with you?" I asked Carol.

"Yeah, that is fine with me. I have enjoyed walking through the city so far. It has an open feel to it and the air feels fresh and clean."

"I know what you mean. The air does feel cleaner and less polluted in Scandinavia. The air quality in this part of Europe is apparently amongst the best in the developed world."

We left the palace behind and began our long walk towards the sculpture park. The sloping streets were lined with trees rather than skyscrapers, which made for a nice change from most capital cities throughout the world. Midway through our thirty-minute walk, I offered Carol some of my water.

"We can swap bottles if you like. I don't mind sparkling water."

"Oh. I must have accidentally left mine behind at the palace."

"Hmm…you *accidentally* left it behind?"

"I honestly forgot that it was there."

"I wonder if King Harald V is currently enjoying your sparkling water with his caviar?"

The route to the main area of the sculpture park was lined with some of the 212 bronze and granite statues that were designed by Gustav Vigeland. Although I have been referring to Vigeland Sculpture Park, the sculptures are officially located within the Vigeland installation in Frogner Park.

A series of naked figures greeted us on a bridge that we crossed. Thankfully, I am referring to statues rather than real human beings! They depicted a variety of ages and genders, arranged in all manner of positions. Carol posed with one, mimicking what appeared to be a couple of athletic figures who had their hands raised to the sky.

The Angry Boy is probably the most popular sculpture. As the name suggests, it features a little boy having a tantrum. His face is screwed up, his fists are clenched, and he is in the process of stamping his foot on the ground. He is naked, of course.

I braced myself for the inevitable comment and Carol did not disappoint: "He looks like you when a team scores against Man United!"

"I am unable to recall any occasion on which I was naked whilst watching a United game!"

"Well, apart from that, he is your twin!"

"I hope that you don't really think that I look like a little boy!"

"I am just kidding of course. Or am I?! Ha!"

The sculptures that we had seen were just a taste of what was to come. *The Fountain* showcases a group of naked people holding up a water feature whilst surrounded by other naked humans intertwined with a series of trees. *The Monolith* is the park's centrepiece. The seventeen-metre column consists of 121, you guessed it, naked figures clinging on to each other.

"It looks like a giant willy!" was Carol's cultured verdict.

"You could have compared me to this one rather than the angry little naked boy!"

The Wheel of Life at the far end of the park highlights one of the main themes that Vigeland seems to have focused on. A group of naked people of different ages and genders are holding on to each other to form a circle of human life.

The sculptures throughout the park depict varies stages of life from cradle to the grave. There are lots of examples of the familial aspect to human existence, including *Old Man Holding Little Boy in His Hand.* Many of the sculptures are rather strange though. For example, *Man Chasing Four Geniuses* features a man swatting away four demonic babies. The self-explanatory *Heap of Dead Bodies* is even more unnerving, as is *Man Throwing Woman Over His Head.*

We discussed the merits of the park during our walk back to the heart of the city. I began by stating: "That was an enjoyable but surreal experience."

"It was weird! We had fun though," Carol replied.

"We may find it a bit strange but Vigeland was obviously a celebrated artist. He even designed the Nobel Peace Prize medal."

"Are there any naked people on the medal?!"

"I don't think so! Shall we have some lunch before it gets too late?" I asked.

"Yes, let's get something quick and cheap. Of course, we could have had another free lunch if you had been willing to take some bread rolls from breakfast."

"I could not have gone through that again!"

"You are such a wimp! Anyway, let's get something to eat. We don't want to be eating too late, otherwise we won't be hungry for dinner tonight."

McDonald's fitted the criteria for a quick meal. We were in Norway, so a cheap lunch was not likely even in this establishment, but it would surely be more affordable than Engebret Café. This would prove to be a good indicator of how expensive things are in Norway. The Big Mac Index, published by *The Economist* since 1986, is a light-hearted way of testing the extent to which market exchange rates result in the varying cost of goods in different countries.

I am unable to recall what Carol ordered but I clearly remember my large Big Mac meal costing the equivalent of more than £10. This seemed to fall in line with the pricing that we had encountered at the steakhouse the previous evening. I did not know this at the time, but it also confirmed the figures for 2012 which ranked Norway alongside Switzerland as having the most expensive Big Macs on the planet. To put into context the difference between economies throughout the world, you could have bought thirty burgers in India for every seven in Norway that year.

Having consumed our expensive burgers, we continued our day's sightseeing by visiting Akershus Fortress. Apparently, this was the place to earn a pardon for murder; not that I was planning on committing any crimes during our remaining time in Oslo! The castle was built in the final decade of the thirteenth century following an attack on the city that showed that the existing defences were insufficient. It appears to have been a successful project, as the fortress has survived all subsequent sieges. It was, however, surrendered to the Nazis during the Second World War.

Carol and I walked along the cobbled pathways and under the arches that led to the castle. We could not resist posing for photographs by the tiny guardhouse and pretending to fire the many cannons that were on display. The clouds began to obscure the bright blue sky as we explored the citadel before admiring Akershus Church and the castle walls.

Carol and I declined the opportunity to visit the Norwegian Armed Forces Museum or the Norwegian Resistance Museum. We had instead elected to spend our time outside, taking a moment to have a look out across the bay from our elevated position. The two towers belonging to the City Hall were the most prominent landmarks on display. The building was growing on me.

We made sure that we had dinner earlier than we had done on the previous evening; however, we still struggled to find a restaurant that appealed to us. Perhaps this was because our taste buds were not as sophisticated as they are now, or we just did not fancy any traditional Norwegian seafood. Either way, we eventually made the decision to stick with what we knew by returning to the steakhouse that we had previously dined in. Given that we knew how much a meal would cost there, maybe we incorrectly believed that we were taking part in a gameshow in which we had to get rid of all our money as quickly as possible. Or we were the central characters in a recreation of the film *Brewster's Millions*.

To be fair, we thoroughly enjoyed our steaks and desserts. We even treated ourselves to a couple of pints of Ringnes Pilsner. If our aim had been to accumulate an even higher bill, alcohol was the ideal choice. Alcoholic beverages in Norway are taxed at a higher rate than anywhere else in Europe due to the government's desire to curb alcoholism. Statistics show that this has not succeeded, given that alcohol consumption remains as high as ever.

The bill was even pricier than it had been on the previous evening, and we soon realised that we did not have enough money to pay it. Fortunately, Carol had brought her debit card. I am not sure what we would have done without it. This highlighted how expensive things are in Norway and made me realise just how cheap our flights had been.

I laid out my thoughts to Carol: "Our return flights costed a total of £70, but we have spent over £200 on two evening meals in Oslo! And we have not exactly dined in a restaurant with three Michelin stars."

"That is ridiculous! We have travelled hundreds of miles in an airplane for a fraction of the price of a few steaks!"

"From what I have read, flying was much more expensive in the 1980s. Most people would have to save up for a flight, and you were regarded as being well-off if you could travel once a year. I guess that is why our dads still wear their shirts and suit jackets on the days that they fly. Despite being a relatively low-earner, I have been abroad four times in the last couple of months. I almost feel like praising Ryanair. Almost."

We took the opportunity to go for one last walk around the city before retiring to our hotel room. The sleek and modern Oslo Opera House was one of the most obvious landmarks that we had not yet visited, so we made sure that we stopped by for a quick look whilst we still had the chance. Although construction had only been completed four years earlier, it had already become one of the most iconic buildings in Scandinavia.

The exterior of the building, which was positioned by the waterfront, mostly consisted of marble and white granite. The sharp angles and large glass panels give it a distinctive yet somewhat minimalistic look. We took the opportunity to ascend the angular walkway to the roof, which acts as a viewing platform where visitors can admire the city and part of the Oslofjord.

Carol and I enjoyed this viewpoint, especially as there was a feeling of peace and tranquillity due to the lack of fellow tourists. The silence was soon broken by a comment from Carol that I would go on to remind her about for years to come: "I think I can see the Northern Lights!"

She soon realised that she had mistaken the artificial lighting emanating from some buildings across the waterfront for the *Aurora Borealis*. This natural phenomenon can of course be seen from Norway, but it is usually witnessed in more northern areas of the country and where artificial lighting is less common. Her expression indicated that she was bracing herself for an onslaught of mickey-taking, but I just looked at her and we shared a laugh. It has become an ongoing joke between us. Either one of us will often say something along the lines of, 'Look, it is the Northern Lights,' whenever we see any artificial lighting at night.

We took it in turns to pose next to the statue of Kirsten Flagstad that is situated near the Opera House. Unsurprisingly, Flagstad was a Norwegian opera singer who is widely regarded as one of the greatest singers of the twentieth century.

We were oblivious to a more unusual installation in the water. *She Lies*, which is a phrase that I am sure is uttered by misogynists throughout the world, is a stainless steel and glass sculpture that was created by Italian artist Monica Bonvicini. Based on Caspar David Freidrich's painting *The Sea of Ice*, it appears to float on a concrete platform that is tethered to the harbour floor. The sculpture turns on its axis in line with the tide and the wind, reminding viewers of the ever-changing force of nature.

Carol and I walked to the bus station to make sure that we were confident where to head to the following morning. As a result of the lighting attached to the station tower, the sky had a red tinge to it. This presented the first opportunity to gently tease Carol about her earlier faux pas: "Are we looking at the Northern Lights?!"

Our final night in Oslo was concluded by watching *Dirty Dancing: Havana Nights* in our room. Whilst most people quite rightly view this 2004 film as an unnecessary and below-par sequel, Carol has a long-standing obsession with anything to do with Cuba. Incidentally, the film began life as a serious political screenplay that was based on the real-life account of an American woman who was romantically involved with a Cuban revolutionary. Eventually, the filmmakers abandoned virtually every aspect of the original story and morphed it into a sequel for the 1987 blockbuster *Dirty Dancing*. The corny and predictable film was at least made enjoyable by the Cuban theme and beautiful scenery. It may have been filmed in Puerto Rico, but we could at least pretend it was Cuba.

"I have had a wonderful time. How about you?" I asked Carol.

"It has been amazing. I'm already looking forward to our next trip, wherever that may be."

"I have an empty wallet but a head full of happy memories."

CHAPTER 8: A TITANIC WEEKEND
BELFAST AND GIANT'S CAUSEWAY, THE UNITED KINGDOM
JULY 2012

My next overseas trip had been organised as a birthday present for Mum. I had managed to book some easyJet flights to Belfast that departed from Manchester at six o'clock in the morning on Saturday and would see us return on Sunday evening.

"We are flying to Béal Feirste," I declared to Mum whilst we stood in the queue for our departure gate at Manchester Airport. In order to avoid embarrassing myself in front of our fellow passengers, I had whispered this as quietly as possible.

"Is that your attempt to use an Irish accent?" Mum asked.

"No, that was the original Irish name for Belfast. It roughly translates as 'mouth of the sand-bank ford,' I believe."

An hour later, we were touching down at Belfast International Airport. The bus to the city centre took around half that time, which once again highlighted how air travel had been transformed into a quick and accessible form of transportation that felt as ordinary as travelling by land.

One of the first sights that we saw after arriving in the city centre was a mural dedicated to the legendary footballer George Best. Arguably Belfast's most famous son, Best is best known for his sporting and non-sporting exploits in my home city of Manchester. He won the European Cup with Manchester United in 1968 and he was the recipient of the prestigious Ballon d'Or award that year. He is regarded as one of the first footballers to become a true celebrity. Despite the many off-field problems that followed him until his death in 2005, he is fondly remembered in both cities.

Rightly or wrongly, the sight of murals on brick walls in Belfast conjured up images in my mind of the turbulent history of this region. After all, there is still plenty of street art depicting the violence that accompanied the Troubles. If we had visited a few decades earlier, we would have found ourselves in one of the most dangerous cities in Europe. Whilst it would be unwise for me to go into too much detail about the events of that dark period of history, Northern Ireland has clearly been blighted by sectarian and political tension.

The island of Ireland was predominantly a Catholic country, but the influx of Scottish migrants and English colonists saw an increased presence of the Protestant faith. The partition of Ireland and the subsequent establishment of a country that was independent from the United Kingdom happened in various stages, such as the creation of the Irish Free State in 1922 and the official declaration of the Republic of Ireland in 1949.

Northern Ireland remained part of the United Kingdom but there was simmering tension between sections of the population who held strong views regarding its constitutional status. A simplistic explanation is that Unionists, who were mostly Protestants, wanted Northern Ireland to remain as part of the United Kingdom, whilst Irish Nationalists, who were mostly Catholics, hoped for Irish reunification. Of course, the situation is more nuanced than this.

After decades of violence, which claimed the lives of more than 3,500 people, the Good Friday Agreement of 1998 provided the platform for peace. This resulted in a devolved system of government in Northern Ireland that could establish its own laws and regulations. For example, strict abortion and same-sex marriage laws differed greatly from the rest of the United Kingdom until they were amended in 2019.

There is always a worry that the violence could return, with the marching season providing potential flashpoints. The largest parades occur on the Twelfth of July, so I was relieved to have arrived in Belfast nine days after this date. The potential re-establishment of a hard border with the Republic of Ireland as a result of the United Kingdom leaving the European Union, which is a scenario that was not considered likely at the time of our trip in 2012, is another concern for those hoping to avoid further tension within the Emerald Isle.

I tried to remove any thoughts of the violent history of this region from my mind and chose to focus on the important matter of finding somewhere to have breakfast. We decided to locate our accommodation on Hope Street before satisfying our hunger. After tracking down the Days Hotel, we found a café on the nearby Great Victoria Street. It was the type of establishment that is commonly referred to as a 'greasy spoon.' We were playing it safe rather than making a political statement by opting for a couple of full English breakfasts instead of an Ulster fry, which was almost identical apart from the addition of black pudding, potato bread and soda bread.

"Did you enjoy that breakfast?" I asked Mum.

"It wasn't great but at least it was filling. It was very salty though!"

109

I agreed with her assessment, but I always chuckle to myself when Mum states that a meal was too salty. She was correct on this occasion, but she would have said the same even if we had consumed food that had not contained a trace of salt.

Since we were unable to check in to our hotel until mid-afternoon, we would have to carry our backpacks whilst we explored the city. We began by checking out a couple of famous landmarks that were located on the same street as the café in which we had dined. The Crown Liquor Saloon is one of the city's most well-known pubs and is now a Grade A Listed Building. The decorative tiling gave the Victorian saloon a distinctive look, and we were reminded of its rich history by the sign that proudly stated that it was established in 1849. As I did not fancy going on an all-day 'bender' with my mum, we did not step inside for a closer look. If we had done so, we would have been able to admire the stained-glass windows, more elaborate tiling and wooden décor of the pub's interior.

The Europa Hotel was an imposing presence on the opposite side of the street. Since its opening in 1971, it has become the place to stay if you are a famous face visiting the city. World leaders such as U.S. President Bill Clinton and First Lady Hilary Clinton, journalists such as Sir Trevor McDonald, and a whole host of celebrities including Julia Roberts, have stayed in this esteemed building.

It is best known, however, for holding the unwanted title of 'The most bombed hotel in the world.' Incredibly, it was subjected to thirty-six bomb attacks throughout the Troubles. During those difficult years, there was a permanent notice attached to each room door warning guests that they may be required to evacuate the hotel at any time. Remarkably, there were not any fatalities as a result of the bombings.

I conveyed my thoughts to Mum: "It feels like a normal city. People are going about their business and it feels safe. It is hard to imagine that this would have been so different just a few decades ago. The hotel in front of us was bombed as recently as 1993."

"I am glad that the city is safer now. Not just for us but for the locals."

"I am younger than you, so it is perhaps different for me, but I find it hard to get my head around the fact that a region within the United Kingdom was so dangerous as recently as the 1990s."

The Grand Opera House, which is situated next door to the hotel, suffered extensive damage during the 1991 and 1993 bombings. It is apparently an example of the Oriental style of theatre architecture, but I thought that the facade reminded me of a Victorian train station. Unfortunately, we did not get the opportunity to admire the opulent auditorium. Notable artists to have performed at the Opera House include a young Luciano Pavarotti in 1963, whilst former U.S. President General

Dwight D. Eisenhower is an example of one of the famous people who have watched a show here.

Belfast City Hall was the next landmark that we visited. There were numerous statues, including one of Queen Victoria, within the grounds of this Baroque Revival building. The copper dome that crowns the Portland stone exterior is one of the most recognisable sights in the city.

We had a quick look at the *Titanic* Memorial Garden that had been opened three months before our visit to commemorate the centenary of the disaster. The centrepiece of the garden is the *Titanic* Memorial, which honours the lives lost as a result of the sinking of the RMS *Titanic* in 1912. The memorial seemed to be an artistic interpretation of the disaster, with a female figure holding a wreath over a deceased sailor and a couple of mermaids who were clinging on to him. The disaster will forever be intertwined with the history of Belfast, which is where the ship was built. We would discover more about this during our trip.

The City Hall was formerly known as the White Linen Hall, which highlights how the city was once a hugely important part of the linen industry. Belfast briefly became more populous than Dublin towards the end of the nineteenth century, gaining city status in the process. The Linen Quarter also includes the Linen Library Hall and a former Victorian linen warehouse that houses the oldest library in Belfast.

We walked along Victoria Street, only stopping to have a brief glance at the Royal Courts of Belfast and the Victoria Square shopping centre, on our way to the Albert Memorial Clock. This was constructed in the 1860s as a memorial to Queen Victoria's late husband, Prince Albert. The clock tower is one of the city's most well-known landmarks and it is another example of a structure that suffered bomb damage during the Troubles.

I crouched down and took a series of photographs of the clock tower and the nearby Queen's Square Fountains. I changed the angle of my camera, unaware that it was the tower that was not straight. The sandstone tower had developed a slight lean due to be being built on soft, marshy land. Although it is not as pronounced as that of the Leaning Tower of Pisa, it has been embraced and it is now regarded as part of its charm. A common phrase uttered by locals is that: 'Old Albert not only has the time; he also has the inclination.'

I had read that the clock tower was once a notorious haunt for prostitutes who would seek out visiting sailors that arrived at the nearby docks. I tried to make light of this by telling Mum that we should probably leave before people got the wrong idea.

"What do you mean?" Mum asked.

"I'm not sure," I responded whilst immediately regretting my previous comment. A conversation with my mum about prostitution was not something that I particularly relished.

"What idea would people get?"

"I just mean that we should move on rather than hanging around here all day."

I desperately hoped for a change of subject and, unlikely as it sounds, my wish was granted by a giant fish. I can assure you that my sanity remained intact! *The Big Fish* is a ceramic mosaic sculpture that is ten metres in length. Created by the delightfully named John Kindness, it has been well-received by the citizens of Belfast since its installation in 1999.

"That's unusual!" I proclaimed.

"Why is there a big fish there?" Mum asked.

"I have no idea. Maybe it was too big for someone to carry home."

Upon closer inspection, it was evident that the ceramic tiles of the fish were adorned with images and text that related to the history of Belfast, some of which was in the form of newspaper headlines. We posed for photographs next to the fish, which is sometimes referred to as the 'Salmon of Knowledge,' before crossing the River Lagan.

After ascending the spiral access ramps of the Lagan Weir's pedestrian footbridge, we made our way to the Titanic Quarter on the other side. Incidentally, the footbridge has been replaced by a newer model since our visit. The distinctive shape of the Titanic Belfast building and two huge yellow cranes dominated the skyline. The twin shipbuilding gantry cranes, named after the biblical figures of Samson and Goliath, were constructed in the late 1960s and 1970s. Situated within the Harland & Wolff shipyard, they have since become unlikely landmarks of Belfast that symbolise the city's industrial past and its hope for the future. The larger of the two cranes stands at 348 feet tall, with each being able to lift loads of up to 840 tonnes.

Their names certainly seemed appropriate, which prompted Mum's quick-witted joke: "David, I don't think that Goliath will be happy that you are approaching!"

Mum had beaten me to the punch, and I was struggling to come up with a quip of my own. My feeble effort of: "I am not sure if Samson would approve of my lack of hair," was the best that I could come up with. I attempted to step up the pace in order to avoid dwelling on my pathetic excuse of a joke.

We passed the Odyssey Complex, which included what was then known as the Odyssey Arena, on our way to the Titanic Belfast. The world's largest Titanic tourist attraction had only been open for just under four months, which suggested that we had chosen a good time to visit the city. The design of the monument is intended to reflect the shipbuilding history of Belfast, with its angular form mimicking the appearance of ship prows. Standing at thirty-eight metres tall, the building is the same height as the RMS *Titanic*'s hull. The exterior has a shiny appearance due to the aluminium shards that adorn most of it.

My initial impression of the building mirrored the unfortunate observation that has been made countless times: "I hate to say it, but it looks like an iceberg."

"It does! Is that intentional?"

"Surely not. I cannot imagine that the designers would want to focus on the cause of the ship's demise rather than its construction and heritage."

It has been suggested by some that the design of the building deliberately incorporated the shape of an iceberg and the White Star Line logo of the shipping company that owned the *Titanic*, but this seems less likely than the simpler explanation of a ship's prow facing in each direction.

Despite the sinking of the ship occurring more than one hundred years ago, it remains in the global consciousness, with my generation perhaps owing this to the 1997 film *Titanic*. The scene involving Leonardo DiCaprio and Kate Winslet 'flying' on the ship's bow is one of the most recognisable sequences in cinematic history, but the film also reminded younger viewers that over 1,500 people died during its fateful maiden voyage from Southampton to New York.

We found the perfect angle to take some photographs that captured both the cut-out Titanic sign and the huge building behind it, before approaching the visitor centre. Rowan Gillespie's *Titanica* sculpture, which features a diving female figure with her arms outstretched on either side whilst balancing on a slender base, stands in front of the main entrance.

The atrium was a large open area that provided an indication of the scale of the tourist attraction. It was interesting to learn more about the story of the *Titanic*. We were shown some short films and photo galleries that were accompanied by information about Belfast during the time of the ship's construction, the launch of the vessel and the reaction to the disaster. Sections of steel scaffolding and large-scale models demonstrated the dimensions of the ship, as well as providing some insight into how it was made.

As with any exhibition relating to the loss of life, enabling a human connection is of utmost importance. We read about how the passengers encompassed numerous sections of society, including wealthy individuals wishing to be associated with the prestige of this voyage, families hoping to start a new life in the United States of America, and travelling workers who lived wherever they could hang their hat. Tragically, the majority of the passengers and crew would perish just a few days later. The photographs and film footage of such people boarding the ship allowed visitors to attribute human faces to the grim statistics.

The visitor centre overlooks the slipways where the *Titanic* and its sister ship *Olympic* were built and eventually launched before heading to Southampton. This is a powerful way of illustrating the history of the ship's construction. The original concrete ramps and embedded tracks remain in place, with visitors now able to walk along a life-size plan of the ships' decks and read the names of the victims of the disaster that are inscribed on the memorial panels.

The Thompson Graving Dock was the last place where the *Titanic* sat on dry land before setting sail. This remains largely intact and it is probably the best place to gain a picture of the scale of the ship. What looks like a ship-sized hole in the ground was where this infamous vessel docked whilst its propellers were fitted, and its hull was painted.

The adjacent pump-house now contains a visitor centre and a café, but the old brick building and the chains that were sprawled across the floor in front of it retained an authentic look, which reinforced the feeling that we were standing in an historic area.

Following an educational and emotional visit, we left the Titanic Quarter and crossed back over the River Lagan. St. Anne's Cathedral, which was completed in 1904, was the next landmark that we visited. The Romanesque building was not the largest cathedral that I had ever seen but it was certainly aesthetically pleasing. The main façade looked a little bit like a mixture of a French church and a Disney castle. I do have notably poor eyesight and our trip to Belfast took place over eight years ago, so my assessment is probably way off the mark.

A surprising feature was the *Spire of Hope*, which reminded me of *The Spire of Dublin*, except this forty-metre structure protrudes from the cathedral roof. Love it or hate it, the spire has certainly become a talking point amongst locals since its installation in 2007.

We walked through the Cathedral Quarter, passing the former headquarters of the Ulster Bank, which has now been converted into the five-star Merchant Hotel. This nineteenth-century building is embellished with gold and diamonds, including the largest chandelier in Northern Ireland, making it the ideal place for wealthy clientele to spend extravagant sums of money. The hotel has received awards for the 'World's Best Hotel Bar' and the 'World's Best Cocktail Bar.'

I cast an envious glance in the building's direction, knowing that such honours were not likely to have been bestowed upon the Days Hotel. In any case, it was time to find out how much disparity in grandeur there was between the two establishments. Our budget hotel, which has since been taken over by Holiday Inn, did at least have the distinction of being one of the largest within Belfast.

Our room was basic but of decent enough quality to spend a single night in. We only popped into the room to drop off our rucksacks before heading back out to explore more of the city, but it was long enough to figure out the type of guests that the hotel appealed to. A rowdy group of revellers were making a lot of noise next door. Unfortunately for us, the walls were thin. Considering that we could hear such a racket during the late afternoon, our chances of having a peaceful night's sleep seemed slim.

As we left the hotel, we were given another idea of what lay in store for us later that evening. A limo stopped at the traffic lights whilst we prepared to cross the road. The window slowly descended, unleashing the booming sound of LMFAO's "Sexy and I Know It." Some rather intoxicated drunk women began singing this to us and the group of pedestrians we were stood with, blissfully unaware of the irony.

We boarded a bus to Belfast Castle from Upper Queen Street. It took less than half an hour to reach Cave Hill Country Park, which is where the castle is located. Cave Hill reminded me of Arthur's Seat in Edinburgh, which we had visited a couple of months earlier. It rises to a height of 1,207 feet, and it is home to three caves and a fort.

"Are you ready to start our climb up the hill?" I asked Mum.

"Yes, I look forward to it."

"Let's do this!"

We began our steady ascent, frequently stopping to take photographs of the beautiful scenery before we reached the castle grounds. The current version of the castle was built in the nineteenth century, using the Scottish Baronial style of architecture. Whilst walking around the gardens in front of the castle, we agreed that the bus journey and walk up the hill was worth it.

The winding staircase and the garden's colourful flowers are picturesque, which makes it no surprise that the sandstone castle is a popular wedding venue. I thought that it looked like a pretty country home rather than a defensive fortification. We were not sure if the castle was open to the public but as it was getting late in the day, we decided to continue climbing up the hill in order to take in the views out to sea and over the city of Belfast. Although we did not reach the summit, we were able to admire the view of the rocky outcrop that has been nicknamed 'Napoleon's Nose' due to an apparent likeness to the former Emperor of the French.

"Do you think that it looks like Napoleon?" I asked Mum.

"No! Do you?"

"It is supposed to look like a silhouette of him lying down and looking up to the sky, but I don't see it. I have read that it was also the inspiration for Jonathan Swift's *Gulliver's Travels* due to its likeness to a sleeping giant safeguarding the city. I prefer this comparison."

It was a beautiful place to enjoy the peace and tranquillity. I just wished that we could have spent more time there. I have read that it is possible to see as far as Scotland and the Isle of Man on a clear day, but I was content to have been blessed with the views that we had been afforded.

Unfortunately, it has been the scene of various tragic events. During the Second World War, a bomb exploded near the castle grounds during a Germain raid. In a separate incident during the same global conflict, ten people died after an American jet crashed into Cave Hill amongst heavy fog. Apparently, this partly inspired Richard Attenborough's final film, *Closing the Ring.*

After returning to street level, we waited for the bus back to the city centre. Just as the vehicle arrived, I noticed that we were standing on the wrong side of the road. Despite knowing that the bus was heading in the opposite direction to where we needed to travel to, I went through the motions of asking the driver whether it would take us back to the city centre. The bus had already stopped for us, and only us, so I felt that I at least had to engage with the driver.

"Does this go to the city?" I mumbled.

"No. You need the stand that says, 'towards the city centre,' on the opposite side of the road."

Stung by this sarcastic response, I regretted the fact that I had decided against the idea of pretending to be Chinese tourists who did not understand English very well. If I had said, "This bus, go city," I probably would have received a kinder response. Then again, this may have backfired if the driver was xenophobic. I waited for the bus, and all the cars behind it, to travel out of sight before making the walk of shame across to the bus stop on the other side of the road.

We were soon back in the city centre searching for an eatery to dine in. We ended up in a Chinese restaurant, in which we were served by a white guy who was dressed as if he could not decide whether he was willing to commit to wearing Oriental attire or just stick to plain black clothing. With his build and haircut, he resembled a white version of the 'Supreme Leader of North Korea' Kim Jong-un. It is likely that I had made this comparison because I had just read that Kim had been promoted to the rank of Marshall of North Korea in the Korean People's Army rather than a genuine similarity in appearance.

We enjoyed our meal even though it was not authentic Chinese food. With our hunger satisfied, we headed back to our hotel. As I had expected, we were denied the chance of a good night's sleep by our noisy neighbours and a steady stream of drunken partygoers who were returning to their rooms throughout the night.

* * *

I decided to try some potato bread and soda bread during our last breakfast of the trip. Sadly, I ruined any chance of being able to taste the flavours of these Northern Irish offerings by drowning them in baked beans. After consuming a hearty breakfast, we checked out of the hotel. I had arranged for a tour of Giant's Causeway that would occupy our entire day before we flew back to Manchester. This went against all my risk-averse instincts, as it would mean that we would not have much time between the end of the tour and when we were required to be at the airport.

Something else that felt unusual was entering a youth hostel with my mother, but this was what we needed to do in order to confirm our places on the tour. Our booking confirmation stated that we needed to collect our tickets from Belfast International Youth Hostel. My less than pleasant experience in a hostel in Barcelona the previous year left me feeling slightly apprehensive as I entered the building. I am not sure what horrors I expected to uncover but we managed to retrieve our tickets from the front desk without being spat at or decapitated.

It took less than half an hour for our coach to reach the first scheduled stop at Carrickfergus Castle. Considering that it has a history dating back to the twelfth century, the medieval castle has been well preserved. Before becoming a tourist attraction, it accommodated royalty and featured in several wars. It was used as a garrison during the First World War, as an air raid shelter in the Second World War, and it came under fire during the Napoleonic Wars.

More unexpectedly, a small battle that was connected to the American War of Independence took place in the surrounding harbour. The famed American naval commander John Paul Jones oversaw a successful attempt to capture HMS *Drake* from the British in 1778. The history of the United States is obviously linked to Britain, but I was still surprised to learn about how events in these waters influenced the fate of those on the other side of the Atlantic.

Our guide detailed the castle's wartime history before stating that: "The last witchcraft trial to take place in Ireland was held in Carrickfergus in 1711. Eight women were found guilty and were jailed for one year. Apparently, a woman called Mary Dunbar was exhibiting signs of demonic possession, for which she blamed eight women who she claimed were witches. The women were set upon by an angry mob, with one of them losing an eye in the process. The Islandmagee Witch Trial did not involve any physical evidence, so you have to feel sympathy for these poor ladies."

"Mum, you will have to make sure that you don't do anything to make the locals think that you are a witch," I joked.

"Why do you say that? Do you think that I am a witch?"

"No, I just mean...erm..."

"I am kidding. I am sure that you don't think I am a witch."

"Of course not. The people of Carrickfergus did not think that those women were witches either though."

"So why did they find them guilty?" Mum asked.

"Historically, people have made unfounded accusations in order to eliminate their rivals or people who they do not like. Allegations of witchcraft were an early form of this; hence, the term 'witch hunt' is commonly used to describe such allegations."

"It is so strange that this used to happen."

"It still happens in some parts of the world. People are sometimes killed or assaulted by angry mobs in places such as India or Africa after being accused of being witches, or for doing something else forbidden. It is just an excuse for violence, of course."

Even more bizarrely, in 2017 there were a series of attacks in Malawi against people who were accused of being vampires. Rumours of bloodsucking activity, which took advantage of long-held beliefs surrounding mythical events, led to the accused being set on fire or stoned by lynch mobs.

Upon stepping off the coach, it was immediately clear why this location had been chosen for the castle. Situated on a rocky promontory surrounded by sea, the strategic advantages were obvious. We climbed down some of the rocks and took some photographs before inspecting a bronze statue outside of the castle.

Standing at five feet and three inches tall, it is apparently a life-size replica of King William III, which has prompted many people to joke that he must have been a short man and to state that they felt tall whilst stood by the statue. Considering that I am only marginally taller than the statue, I was in no position to pass such comment! The statue may be doing him a disservice, as he was thought to have been three inches taller than this. Nevertheless, he was not the most imposing figure and he was asthmatic. I nodded my head as a show of appreciation for my fellow asthmatic short man.

The arrival of the protestant Dutchman, and the subsequent defeat of the catholic deposed King James II in 1690, was a significant historical event that helped shape the future of the region. More importantly, it showed that not every man from the Netherlands is eight feet tall.

A long and scenic coastal drive provided us with beautiful views of the Glens of Antrim. The nine valleys belonging to County Antrim were the type of natural beauty that I had always associated with Ireland. It was a shame that we did not have much time to truly explore the region but at least we were being shown a glimpse of its magnificence.

Our tour guide used this opportunity to talk about one of the most well-known mythical creatures in Irish folklore. The Leprechaun has become synonymous with the Emerald Isle, but its depiction has changed considerably over the years. They initially appeared to be more sinister in nature, often attempting to play tricks on unsuspecting humans. The first known reference to Leprechauns describes how the King of Ulster woke up on a beach to find three of them dragging him into the sea. After he captured them, he was granted three wishes in return for their release.

As they have since been capitalised on by souvenir sellers and by the tourist industry in general, they are now commonly portrayed as jovial drunks who are more likely to perform a jig for you rather than attempt any menacing behaviour at your expense. Their lack of height has been a consistent feature though; at less than three feet tall, they make King William III and me seem tall. Well, almost.

Our guide changed the subject a little: "We have beautiful scenery here in Northern Ireland, don't you think?"

We all vocalised our agreement by collectively mumbling, "Yes," followed by some variation of, "very beautiful," or "stunning."

Our politeness resulted in us behaving as if we were in a trance. The scenery was indeed beautiful but even if it were hideous, we would have agreed with him. The psychology of a tour group can be strange, as we surrender our capacity for independent thought after putting our collective trust in the guide.

He continued to provide information to the submissive group: "C.S. Lewis was enthralled by our amazing landscape. They say that it inspired him to write *The Chronicles of Narnia* series. I take it that you have all heard of the stories, including *The Lion, the Witch and the Wardrobe?*"

Again, we all mumbled a positive response in unison. We disembarked at the iconic Carrick-a-Rede Rope Bridge. It is thought that salmon fishermen have been building bridges from the mainland to the miniscule island of Carrickarede for around 300 years, with the current incarnation having been installed in 2008.

We followed our guide like lemmings to the edge of a cliff. I hoped that we were indeed being led to the bridge rather than being taken on the type of mass suicide mission that is often misattributed to the aforementioned rodents. We slowly descended the steps that led to the bridge whilst I weighed up how sturdy and safe it looked. Having to walk twenty metres across the wooden planks that were being supported by wire ropes was a daunting prospect, especially after looking down at the sea thirty metres below.

The sign informing us that there were only eight people allowed on the bridge at any one time was both reassuring and worrying. It was good to see that safety measures had been put in place, but it also highlighted how the bridge could only support a certain weight before becoming unsafe. The limit on the numbers permitted to cross at least meant that we would have the room to take photographs of each other. This would require summoning the courage to step onto the rope bridge though.

Given that I was a fit and healthy man in his twenties, I did the noble thing by letting Mum cross the bridge first. Her hesitant initial steps and her tight grip on the ropes clearly indicated that she was as wary as I was.

"You can do it," were the words of encouragement that I offered from my position of safety.

After seeing Mum overcoming her fear, it was my turn to face the music. Placing my first step on the rope bridge was a strange sensation. The wooden planks felt fairly solid under my foot but there was a bit of lateral movement that was unnerving. Incidentally, the phrase 'lateral movement' always makes me think of the television show *Tipping Point*. I am unable to say these words without imagining Ben Shephard providing a play-by-play account of a couple of counters moving a millimetre to the side whilst another mind-numbing slow-motion replay of the 'action' is shown to the viewers. Anyway, we all know that it is impossible to win any prizes from this type of machine outside of the ITV television studios. The only thing that you are likely to gain from playing such a machine in an amusement park or an arcade is an overwhelming sense of frustration.

A few steps later, I felt surer of myself. Our surroundings were magnificent. The view of grass-covered cliff-tops, the blue sky and the vast sea below would not look out of place on a postcard. It was unsettling to look down though. Mum cautiously took her hands off the ropes whilst she posed for a photograph. Her uneasiness was written all over her face, but I think that I managed to fool any onlookers that I was as cool as a cucumber when it was my turn to be photographed. We successfully crossed the bridge and spent a few minutes taking in the stunning coastal landscape from the island before joining the queue to return to the mainland. It was less of an ordeal the second time around, which meant that I could truly appreciate the experience.

We drove past Giant's Causeway in order to make a quick stop by Dunlace Castle. My worrisome mind started to panic that something would happen that would result in us not being able to see the main attraction of the tour. An even bigger concern was the fact that we seemed to be a little behind schedule. We did not have much leeway in terms of the amount of time that we would be left with to reach the airport following the tour's conclusion. Our guide attempted to reassure me: "We will get you back in time…even if this means that the driver has to put his foot down."

This hardly put my mind at rest. I not only had to fret about the possibility of missing our flight, but now I also had to worry about our driver recklessly taking us over the edge of a cliff.

Dunlace Castle has a spectacular setting on a rocky outcrop, with a steep drop on either side. The ruins of the medieval castle can be reached via a bridge from the mainland, but we did not have time for a closer inspection. As this was not a scheduled stop on our tour, we were just grateful to be able to admire it from afar.

Our guide provided us with some interesting information: "Legend states that the part of the building which housed the kitchen fell into the sea in the seventeenth century. Only a kitchen boy survived. They say that the screams of the doomed staff can be heard during stormy nights. Like most legends, there is little truth to the story. The kitchen was still intact in the eighteenth, perhaps nineteenth century. However, the north wall of the residence building did fall into the sea during the eighteenth century."

It was time to visit Giant's Causeway. This is what we had booked the tour for, so it was a relief to finally arrive at the UNESCO World Heritage Site. It is one of the most popular tourist attractions in Northern Ireland, with over a million annual visitors in recent years. The award-winning visitor centre had only opened a fortnight beforehand, indicating that the 'luck of the Irish' was once again on our side.

The building's architecture was clearly inspired by the landscape. Its exterior was adorned with dark pillars that had a similar appearance to the basalt columns of Giant's Causeway. The visitor centre was designed to blend into its natural surroundings, with grass having been planted on the roof of the single-storey earth-defended structure.

We were handed an audio system and headphones, which were intended to provide information as we made our way around the centre. I immediately discarded mine, as I preferred to read the information that was on display.

According to legend, the Irish giant Finn McCool threw chunks of land into the sea in order to build a pathway to battle his Scottish rival, Benandonner. He apparently retreated after realising that he was no match for his foe. Finn's wife came up with a clever plan: she disguised him as a baby, which made Benandonner think that his rival must be enormous, considering that this was the size of his offspring. The Scottish giant promptly fled back to his homeland, destroying the path behind him.

Alternatively, the scientific explanation points to volcanic activity around sixty million years ago. The 40,000 interlocking basalt columns were formed after the lava cooled and contracted. Although this was more plausible than the story about the giants, it is understandable why people choose to keep alive the legend of Finn McCool.

"Do you like the story about the giants? Do you believe it?" Mum asked.

"No but it is quite cool. You could even say McCool."

After my joke fell flat on its face, I felt like scarpering away as quickly as Benandonner did when seeing Finn dressed as a baby. Once we stepped outside, we concurred that Giant's Causeway is a wonderful sight to behold. Most of the columns appeared to be hexagonal in shape and varied in height. They were scattered far across the land and seemed to lead out to the sea, with the tallest columns situated by the water. Some of them must have been at least twelve metres high, which created a dramatic landscape for the waves to crash into.

The skies were now ominously dark, which made me worry about our tight schedule once more. Given that we could not leave without the rest of the group, I told myself to make the most of our visit to this breathtaking natural phenomenon.

One of my favourite photographs that I took captured the silhouette of a couple who were stood upon the tallest columns by the sea. Following our return to England, I had this image printed onto a canvas that I hung up in the flat that I lived in at the time. I have often wondered who they were. They obviously had no idea that the outline of their figures was on display in my home and I had no clue as to where in the world they came from. Maybe this served as a fitting symbol for my failure to make connections with those who I encounter.

We were late setting off on our return journey to Belfast city centre and our guide now sounded less confident of being able to get us back in time: "I think that you should be OK."

Our scenario was hardly as dramatic as those in which Northern Irish actor Liam Neeson found himself in during the *Taken* film series, but I felt a rush of adrenaline as the coach raced back to our original departure point. Thankfully, we made it back early enough to catch another bus to the airport in time for our flight back to Manchester. We even ended up with about ninety minutes to spare, which indicates how I had been unnecessarily worrying about this all day. Our brief trip to Northern Ireland had been thoroughly enjoyable and I was pleased that we had managed to see so much in such a short period of time.

"Did you enjoy your birthday trip?" I asked Mum.

"Yes, it was lovely. I always like spending time with my sons, but it was even more special to explore Northern Ireland with you."

I was happy to hear that Mum had enjoyed the trip and that we still had a mutual love of travelling. It appeared that Mum shared my sentiment that I would much sooner spend money on creating memories with loved ones rather than on material things. After all, our joyful memories are what we will cling onto and cherish during our latter years.

CHAPTER 9: THE GATEWAY TO A DESERTED ISLAND
FARO, PORTUGAL
AUGUST 2012

"You don't need to take your debit card. You have your Euros. It is just another thing to worry about. I can look after it for you whilst you are away."

Mum's suggestion seemed to make sense; therefore, I handed my card to her at the drop-off point at Manchester Airport. I had arranged to meet Carol at the main entrance of Terminal 3 ahead of our three-night trip to Faro, and Mum had kindly provided a lift from my workplace after I had finished Friday's shift.

I only realised my error after we had been presented with our bill in an Italian restaurant in the departures lounge. Carol often says that she can tell that something is wrong because I go extremely quiet, even by my standards.

"What's wrong?" she asked.

"I gave my debit card to Mum. I have just realised that I do not have the means to pay for this meal. Even worse than that, I have arranged to pay for our accommodation by card upon arrival."

Given that I was unaware of whether Carol had brought any money or debit cards with her, I took a deep breath. Her response would not only dictate whether we were able to pay for our stay in the Algarve, but it could also result in us having to exchange our Euros back into British Pounds in order to pay for our meal.

"It's OK, I can pay with my card."

A feeling of relief surged through my body, which was immediately followed by one of intense embarrassment.

"So, let me get this right," Carol began. "You gave me a surprise present of a trip to Portugal but now you have conveniently forgotten your debit card, which means that I have to pay for our accommodation as well as this meal? Hmm..."

"Well, yes...erm...but..." I squirmed.

A chuckling Carol put me out of my misery: "It's OK, I am only kidding. I am thankful for our trip."

"I am glad that you have brought your card. We would have been snookered without it. I will reimburse you as soon as we get back though."

Our waitress returned to our table in time to hear the end of my previous sentence; thus, completing this embarrassing episode.

We arrived in Faro late on Friday night. A short taxi ride took us to our accommodation, where we checked in with the elderly lady who was renting out her apartment.

"Will you be paying by card?" she asked me.

Carol interjected: "He left his debit card at home on purpose so that I will have to use my mine instead!"

"OK," the bemused looking lady replied.

Our apartment was basic, but it appeared to be clean enough. There were no unsightly stains and the electrical sockets looked just about safe. We even had a small balcony. After a midnight feast of Pringles, which are a reliable snack for travellers due to their robust packaging, we decided to get some much-needed sleep.

*　*　*

We woke up to a glorious blue sky and an intense heat. It was not yet nine in the morning, but we were already being treated to the type of weather that one associates with the Algarve. Carol and I had been on a couple of city breaks but this was our first taste of a summer holiday, albeit a condensed one. We had two full days to explore the regional capital, so we decided to grab a quick bite to eat before heading out.

After filling our stomachs with bread rolls and stale croissants, we were presented with our first glimpse of the city. It was becoming clear why most tourists who arrive in Faro immediately move on to the trendier resorts in places such as Albufeira. Although it was pleasant enough in appearance, it had the feel of a sleepy coastal village that one would expect to encounter en route to a major city.

The Igreja do Carmo was the first significant landmark that we encountered. This eighteenth-century church, with its Baroque façade and twin bell towers, was a relatively small version of the religious buildings that are commonplace throughout Latin America. These churches are usually referred to as colonial buildings, owing to the fact that the Portuguese and Spanish constructed them in the colonies that they established throughout the world. It is said that the construction of this church was financed by the gold that was plundered from the Portuguese colony of Brazil.

The Portuguese Empire, which captured land in places such as China, India, Africa and across the Americas, existed from the start of the fifteenth century and only officially ended in December 1999 with the handover of Macao. Whilst the practice of slavery dates back as far as can be documented, the Portuguese are believed to be the first to transport slaves in large numbers from Africa to Europe and the Americas.

The Spanish and British later followed suit, with an estimated 25 million Africans forcibly removed from their homeland and into a life of misery. The African continent was robbed of its resources, both in terms of its people and its valuable materials, whilst the European nations became richer. The demographic makeup of the Americas was grossly distorted in the process, including the eradication of the indigenous people of the Caribbean, known as the Taíno. This once again highlights how European nations enslaved other parts of the world and created empires that endured long after the horrors of the Second World War had occurred.

With the issue of colonialism set to one side, we approached the church for a closer inspection. The whitewashed building has an immaculate yet understated appearance. Whilst there is nothing too extravagant about its façade, I thought that it was prettier than most religious buildings that I had previously seen. The lavish interior, with its gilded woodwork and stain-glass windows, was completed a century and a half before the exterior was finished. Judging by its opulent decorative features, it seems that some of the Brazilian gold may have ended up inside the church!

The Capela dos Ossos, or 'Chapel of Bones,' is the rather macabre reason why tourists visit the church. The walls are covered by the skulls and bones of over one thousand Carmelite monks. This is intended to highlight the brevity of human existence and the importance of having a life of virtue. It is a rather sombre and surreal experience to be staring at the remains of so many human beings.

"I wonder what kind of life each of these people had," I pondered. "They were all monks, but they will have had their own experiences and friendships. They probably had no idea that their bones would become a tourist attraction hundreds of years later."

"Maybe our bones will end up in a chapel in Wigan one day!" Carol suggested.

We did not want to spend too much time dwelling on the bones of perished monks; after all, we were on holiday in the sunny Algarve. Instead, we decided to have a wander through the old town before heading to the beach.

Our route took us through the Arco da Vila, which is one of the gates leading into the old town. In addition to providing a point of entry, this structure has become a tourist attraction. The origins of the walled city of Faro may go back as far as the eighth century BC, but the neoclassical gateway was redesigned in 1812. Carol and I enthusiastically took photographs whilst admiring the belfry and a statue above the archway. We worked out that it depicted a religious figure within Catholicism, but we were unaware that this was Saint Thomas Aquinas. He is regarded as one of the Catholic Church's greatest philosophers.

The religious theme continued upon our entry to the old town. The most significant building that we encountered was Sé Catedral de Faro, which is unsurprisingly known as Faro Cathedral within the English language. Consecrated in the thirteenth century, it has been subjected to various invasions and earthquakes over the course of its history. Whilst much of the building has been reconstructed, the Gothic main entrance and bell tower remain in place. Church bells are often positioned within a tower in a manner that obscures their view from the public; therefore, it was refreshing to be able to clearly see the shape of each exposed bell against the bright blue sky.

"I think we can climb to the top. Shall we do that?" I asked Carol.

"Yes, that would be nice. Will you ring the bells?"

"I'll compose a melody for you," I declared whilst sincerely hoping that Carol would not hold me to that promise.

After paying a few Euros to enter the complex, we were greeted by a small courtyard that was surrounded by a few small buildings, including the cathedral. We soon discovered that one of the buildings was another chapel of bones.

"What is it with bones in Faro?!" I asked.

"I think we'll give that a miss!" Carol decided.

We had a quick look at the tiny Chapel of St. Michael before moving on to the cathedral. The interior was unspectacular for the most part, although some of its chapels were richly decorated. The blue and white glazed tiles belonging to Chapel of Nossa Senhora do Rosário were my favourite feature.

As it is only a small cathedral, the walk to the top of the bell tower involved just sixty-eight steps. I would not have complained if the journey had been more arduous because the view over the old town and the lagoon proved to be so rewarding. We could not see much sign of wildlife from our viewpoint, but a wide range of birds visit the Ria Formosa Natural Park during their annual winter migration from Europe to Africa. Around 20,000 birds are thought to visit the lagoon network each winter. The area is also home to numerous rare species, such as the chameleon, the seahorse, and the delightfully named Portuguese Water Dog.

We inspected the bells from close quarters, and I am pleased to say that Carol did not make me ring them. Instead, we asked a stranger to take our photograph. I say we, but I really mean that it was Carol who asked. Being as socially inept as I was, I would not have dreamt of asking a favour from someone that I did not know.

After descending the bell tower, we continued our walk through the old town. It was charming but tiny. Some of the streets featured the pretty tiled patterns that Portugal is known for; however, there was something else that caught our eye. A large dollop of dog excrement had been left on a street leading to another gate by the marina. For the remainder of our trip, we used the term 'poo street' as a point of reference when trying to navigate our way through the old town.

We walked around the small but delightful marina, occasionally posing for photographs next to the understated boats. There was no sign of any yachts, which underlined how the fashionable and wealthy crowd tended to move on to the surrounding resorts rather than staying in Faro.

There are some sections of the historic walls that surround the old town still in place. We inspected the accompanying information that detailed the history of the city. This included King Alfonso III of Portugal capturing Faro in 1249. It had been one of the last strongholds of the Moors in the Algarve. The city also suffered significant damage after being sacked by English privateers in the sixteenth century, before being devastated by an earthquake and a tsunami during the eighteenth century.

We were surprised to see a selection of exercise equipment by the walls. Other than in television shows featuring Venice Beach in California, I had never previously seen gym equipment being placed outside for the public to use free-of-charge. Carol tried out the rudimentary cross-trainer whilst I took her photograph.

"You should have a go!" Carol suggested, knowing that I would hate the thought of tourists taking photographs of me exercising.

"Maybe another time! I think we should grab something to eat and head to the beach."

Thankfully, the prospect of consuming some food and sunbathing on a beach was enough for Carol to agree to move on. I noticed that it was later than I had realised, so we bought some sandwiches and crisps to take with us. The bus to Praia de Faro took us back in the direction of the airport.

Upon arrival, we exited the vehicle and stepped onto the first stretch of sand that we encountered. We felt somewhat underwhelmed. The beach was small and crowded, and the sand was rather dark and unattractive. Still, we were happy to relax in the sun for the remainder of the afternoon. Whilst

Carol tried to doze off, I contemplated something that has always astounded me: "I find it scarcely believable that sand such as what we are lying on is used to make glass."

"Is that how glass is made? Really?" Carol asked out of politeness.

"Glass is made by heating sand to extreme temperatures and then letting it cool. The Egyptians and Syrians are thought to have made glass as early as 3600 BC," I explained as I lifted some grains of sand. "It is astonishing that this can become glass, and that ancient civilisations figured how to make it."

I turned to Carol, but she was fast asleep. That was not the first time that someone had nodded off whilst I rambled on about something, and it would not be the last!

We were unaware that you can find more attractive and less crowded sections of the beach if you take the time to walk a little further from the bus drop-off point. In any case, I joined Carol in dozing in the sun for a few hours.

The view of the beach and the sea that we were blessed with whilst we waited for the return bus journey was better than we had been afforded during our time on the sand. The sight of old men fishing off the bridge whilst the sun set behind them was unexpectedly pleasant.

We enjoyed a brief nap after arriving back at our accommodation, then made ourselves presentable for dinner. There was a knock on our door whilst I was in the shower.

"There's someone knocking on our door!" Carol shouted, with more than a hint of panic.

Obviously, I could not open the door, so it was left to Carol.

"Sorry to disturb you, but I think your shower is leaking. I was on the floor below and there is some water coming through the ceiling. Maybe I can fix it for you?"

I desperately hoped that this stranger meant that he could fix it after I had finished my shower rather than at this precise moment. A bigger concern of mine was obtaining confirmation that this mystery voice belonged to a member of staff, as opposed to a random person who had walked in off the street. The man left and Carol informed me that he was indeed an employee and that he would fix the shower whilst we were out for dinner.

It was later than we had anticipated, so we picked the first acceptable-looking restaurant in the old town. Although the pizza and pasta that we ate was nice, it felt a bit of a shame not to be sampling traditional Portuguese food. A bottle of wine later, such concerns had long gone! We were a couple of lightweights who were tipsy and enjoying a short summer holiday. After stumbling through the narrow streets, we eventually found ourselves back at our accommodation.

"I have enjoyed our day. Faro seems a lovely place. I am a happy David."

"You are a drunk David!"

"Yes, I am! Goodnight my dear!"

* * *

After our merry night on the town, we took the opportunity to sleep in until mid-morning. We had another basic breakfast before strolling through the old town to the marina. Via poo street, of course. We were soon collared by one of the numerous people offering boat trips.

"Would you like to spend the day on Ilha Deserta? For twenty Euros you can take our return ferry to the island. Would you like to go?" the lady asked.

"What is the island like?" Carol enquired.

"As you may have guessed, the name means 'Deserted Island.' It is an uninhabited island with beautiful beaches. It is like paradise!"

"We'll take two tickets. When does the next ferry leave?" I asked.

"Great decision! You will love it! The next ferry departs in forty-five minutes. Here are your tickets. Have a lovely day!"

We decided to have an early lunch at a small restaurant by the marina whilst we waited for the ferry. I ordered a hotdog and Carol opted for a cheeseburger. She also provided me with a basic Spanish lesson. Where better to learn Spanish than in…Portugal.

"Do you know how to say hotdog in Spanish?" she asked.

I shook my head.

"*Perro caliente*. Perro means dog and caliente means hot."

"How do you say cheeseburger?"

"*Hamburguesa con queso*. That translates as hamburger with cheese."

"Do you know how to order them in Portuguese?" I asked.

"No."

"Well, that was useful!"

In case any of you are interested, which I find extremely doubtful, the Portuguese translations for our food choices are *cachorro quente* and *hamburguer de queijo*. Anyway, we enjoyed our junk food before making our way to the ferry departure point.

We were treated to a pleasant view of the walled old town as we sailed away from the marina. It took less than twenty minutes to reach Ilha Deserta. Also known as Ilha da Barreta, it is the least developed of the three islands that surround the Ria Formosa National Park. It is seven kilometres long and its widest point measures at just six hundred metres.

Most of our fellow tourists pitched up by the sun loungers and parasols that were located within the first hundred yards or so from our point of arrival. Wary of the lesson that we had learned the previous day, we carried on walking along the beach. Five minutes later, there was nobody else in sight. Now it really did feel like we were on a deserted island.

"This is the most beautiful beach that I have ever seen," I declared.

"I can't believe how quiet it is. It is not often that you can have a beach all to yourself. Well, at least as far as our eyes can see."

I had assumed that the lady who sold us our ferry tickets had been exaggerating, but it did indeed feel like paradise. The sand was golden, the sky was a bright shade of blue, and the sea was calm and glistening under the searing sun. And we had it all to ourselves!

Our afternoon consisted of sunbathing, swimming in the sea and generally having fun on the sand. I am not talking about anything inappropriate; rather, I am referring to such innocent activities as writing our names in the sand and taking a photograph of the reflection of Carol in my sunglasses. We also made the most of the lack of fellow tourists by running up and down the beach like Rocky Balboa and Apollo Creed.

It had been one of the most blissful days of my life, and it had given me a taste of what Summer holidays were like. I began to imagine how wonderful it would be to experience a fortnight on a tropical island. All good things must come to an end though. We were afforded another picturesque view of the old town during our return ferry, this time enhanced by a beautiful sunset.

Carol and I indulged in another pre-dinner nap and a leak-free shower before heading out to the old town in search of an evening meal. We sampled some of the region's food, in the form of cured meat, olives, cheese and roast pig. And another bottle of wine. Given that a parade slowly made its way past the restaurant terrace, the people of Faro must have been aware that it was the last night of our trip. They really should not have gone to so much trouble!

The wine added to my merriment enough for me to declare that it had been one of the best days of my life. Our long weekend in Faro had exceeded all of my expectations.

*   *   *

The following morning, we had time to take one last stroll around Faro before our flight home. This involved inspecting statues of King Alfonso III and Francisco Gomes de Avelar, who was the Bishop of Faro. We also stopped by an obelisk dedicated to local diplomat Ferreira d'Almeida. Most importantly of all, we posed for photographs next to the 'I Love Faro' sign. The tourist experience was now complete.

CHAPTER 10: THE MOST DENSELY POPULATED REGION ON EARTH
MACAO, SPECIAL ADMINISTRATIVE REGION OF THE PEOPLE'S REPUBLIC OF CHINA
NOVEMBER 2012

Mum and Uncle Wai Lun had organised a two-week stay for us in Hong Kong, along with Auntie Josephine and my cousin Fiona. The dying embers of my obsession with mixed martial arts had led me to arrange a trip to Macao in order to watch a UFC show during our time in Asia. Incidentally, the alternative Portuguese spelling of Macau is often used, which hints at its previous existence under colonial rule. The territory was first leased to the Portuguese in 1557, and it was only returned to China in 1999. Like Hong Kong, it is a Special Administrative Region of China, with a slightly more relaxed approach to government and economics than in mainland China.

The journey from Manchester to Hong Kong, via Munich, took about fifteen hours. It was nine o'clock in the evening when we landed at Hong Kong International Airport, so Mum and I were happy to head straight to our accommodation for some much-needed sleep. Uncle Wai Lun greeted us at the airport, from where we took a taxi back to the apartment that the five of us were sharing. We crossed the Tsing Ma Bridge, which is one of the world's longest suspension bridges, on our way to our accommodation in Sheung Wan.

*   *   *

Mum's old school friend, who we refer to as Uncle Sydney, and his wife, Rosalie, accompanied the two of us on our trip to Macao. They were familiar with the area from previous visits and it was a good excuse to spend some time with Mum's friends. It did not take us long to walk from our apartment to the Hong Kong-Macau Ferry Terminal. At least the name reassured me that we were in the right place.

We stopped to take photographs of the Western Market, which is a red brick colonial building that stood out amongst the sea of office towers and residential complexes. With a history going back to the mid-nineteenth century, it is the oldest surviving market building in Hong Kong. The ferry terminal is connected to an MTR station and the Shun Tak Centre, where we had a late breakfast consisting of congee.

Our journey took around an hour, which Rosalie and I spent playing *Candy Crush*. As I had assumed that it was a game for young people who were addicted to their phones, I was surprised to discover that she was over one hundred levels ahead of me! In any case, our indoor seating was comfortable enough and the time passed quickly.

An alternative way of travelling between Hong Kong, Macao and mainland China was opened in 2018. The Hong Kong-Zhuhai-Macau Bridge is a network consisting of three cable-stayed bridges, an undersea tunnel, and four artificial islands. This ambitious project, which cost the equivalent of over £14 billion, resulted in China achieving the record of having the longest sea crossing in the world.

Upon arrival at the Macao ferry terminal, the four of us made our way towards passport control. Mum realised that I would not be able to join the same queue as the others, as I did not possess a Hong Kong identity card. It was only when I got to the front of the 'other passports' queue that I realised that I needed to fill out a landing card. This meant that I had to go to the back of the queue where the cards were available to pick up and complete.

I looked around and noticed that the others had already gone through. Fifteen minutes later, I had still not reached my previous position at the front of the queue. Mum had probably started to panic that I had been detained by the authorities at this point. Suddenly, Uncle Sydney appeared by the side of the passport control desk. I am not sure if it was because he was a retired Hong Kong anti-corruption police officer, or simply because he asked politely, but I was now being summoned to the front of the queue. I could feel the disapproving looks of the people that I was bypassing, but I was relieved when I was waved through by the border control officer.

I was ready to explore Macao, but Uncle Sydney and Rosalie were ready for lunch. We dined in a reasonable-looking restaurant, but I was not hungry enough to eat much more than a bowl of rice, some steamed vegetables and a few cuts of roast pork. The others seemed to have more of an appetite than I had, which resulted in us spending over an hour in the restaurant.

I was itching to get out and begin our sightseeing, especially as I was aware of the limited time at our disposal. *UFC on Fuel TV: Franklin vs. Le* was taking place that evening, which meant that we only had a few spare hours that day, as well as the following morning and afternoon. As we had eaten in the Taipa area, which is home to a mixture of colonial buildings and residential housing amongst its winding pathways, at least we could start the sightseeing without further delay.

The Taipa House Museum is one of the most well-known collections of colonial buildings in Macao. The restored pastel green structures are considered a fair representation of the accommodation that was available for wealthy Portuguese families in the first half of the twentieth century. The large veranda of one of the houses reminded me of how homes in the Deep South of the United States of America are depicted on television. Mum and I posed for photographs in a pedicab that had been made available for this purpose. This traditional mode of transport is no longer in extensive use these days due to the fast-paced life in Macao. I think the 'high-rollers' prefer to turn up to the casinos in Lamborghinis anyway.

After our brief visit to the aforementioned houses, we stopped by the Our Lady of Carmo Church, which had been completed in 1885. There was a large wooden cross in the square in front of the church, which served as a handy prop to use in my photographs. More importantly, it was an indicator of the influence of the Portuguese on the local population's religious beliefs. The Catholic faith became one of the most common religions during colonial rule, but Buddhism and Chinese folk religions have since become more widespread.

We moved on to an area dedicated to the biggest religion of them all: dirty, filthy money. The Cotai Strip is home to a string of large casinos and hotels similar to what can be found in Las Vegas. I was surprised to discover that Macao, not Las Vegas, is the gambling capital of the world. The revenue from this industry is larger here than anywhere else on the planet.

Macao is the only region of China in which casinos are permitted by law. This is one of the reasons why the Chinese government have been relatively relaxed about the Special Administrative Region status that Macao holds. Like Hong Kong, it has been a huge source of revenue for China due to it authorising activities that have been banned in the mainland. Problems only arise when citizens voice their disapproval of the government. China just about managed this balancing act for the best part of two decades, but the recent protests in Hong Kong are an indication of serious trouble ahead.

We were probably the only tourists in town who had no intention of gambling. By the end of the weekend, I had achieved an unlikely double of abstaining from placing a single bet during my visits to Las Vegas and Macao. Some years later, I would go on to complete a remarkable hat-trick in Monte Carlo. In case you have not figured it out yet, I hardly lead a rock 'n' roll lifestyle!

Uncle Sydney and Rosalie had booked a two-night stay for us all in the rather extravagant Galaxy Macau hotel. Mum and I dropped off our luggage in our large and luxurious room.

"We're lucky that they have arranged the accommodation," Mum stated.

"Definitely. We would have been in a Travelodge if it had been left to me! Although I doubt that there are any of those on the Cotai Strip!"

Upon meeting up with Uncle Sydney and Rosalie again, we thanked them before heading out. Our exit route took us through a room that contained a huge Santa figure and an assortment of Christmas decorations. This traditional character that I associated with Western culture felt a little out of place in a modern hotel-casino complex in China. After examining this unexpected scene, we moved on to The Venetian Macao.

Like its sister resort in Las Vegas, it contains a hotel and a casino. In fact, it is the largest casino in the world. I took some photographs of the exterior of the dazzling resort, which was guaranteed to make an impression due to its enormous size. To put this into context, there are only six buildings in the entire world that are larger when measured by floor area.

It was similar to the Las Vegas resort that I visited in 2009, with both featuring artificial networks of canals running through them. It felt strange to see gondolas filled with tourists sailing past whilst inside a building. To add to this surreal moment, there was a fake blue sky above us. The section we were in was filled with bridges, lampposts and balconies. This would no doubt be a picturesque scene if we were actually in Venice, but it seemed rather odd in this setting. The four of us strolled alongside the artificial canals and took some photographs before the others said their goodbyes. I was due to watch the UFC show within the Cotai Arena that belongs to The Venetian resort, whereas the others planned to have dinner in a nearby restaurant.

Whilst waiting in the queue for the arena, I spotted the Japanese mixed martial artist Yoshihiro Akiyama. I could not resist asking for a photograph with the man they call 'Sexyama.' As he was gracious enough to grant my request, I refrained from giving him a big hug. The show, which saw Cung Le defeat Rich Franklin in the main event, lasted around five hours. By this stage, attending live events had become a rather drawn-out and tiresome affair. Indeed, my interest in the sport itself was on the wane.

I experienced something even more tedious after the show: the process of being assigned a taxi by the staff outside the main entrance of the resort. I was in a long queue, but this was not the sole reason why I had to wait over two hours. Taxis were driving to the main entrance and dropping off passengers, only to then speed off without picking anyone else up. Perhaps they were reticent to welcome any drunkards, but it was more likely that they were aware that most of us would only rack up a cheap fare, given that we were staying a short distance from our current location.

Eventually, the more vocal members of the queue kicked up enough of a fuss to ensure that the hotel staff flagged down every taxi and made them accept our custom, regardless of how far we had to travel. Without this intervention, I would probably still be in the queue all these years later! My taxi journey only took a few minutes. In truth, I probably could have walked to the hotel and back a dozen times whilst I waited in the queue. I was just too much of a coward to walk around in an unfamiliar location late at night. No wonder why the taxi drivers were trying to avoid us.

I was aware that Mum was fast asleep, so I tried to be as quiet as possible when entering our hotel room. I would say that this reminded me of creeping back into the family home after a drunken night during my teenage years, but that only occurred in the alternative reality in which I actually had a social life. Eating a takeaway from the legendary King Wah Chinese chip shop in Timperley whilst watching WWE, *Buffy the Vampire Slayer*, or whatever else was on television was the type of Friday night that I was accustomed to during my youth.

*　　*　　*

Our second day in Macao was spent away from the Cotai Strip. We took a taxi across the Sai Van Bridge, which connects Taipa Island to the Macao Peninsular, before heading to the fifteenth-century A-Ma Temple. Upon arrival, we walked through one of the Buddhist temple's gates and had a look at the intricate archways, stone lions and carvings. I posed in front of a decorative wall, which resembled a giant porthole, before having a walk through the grounds. The multitude of incense cones that were in and around the temple certainly provided a powerful strike to our senses.

Incidentally, it is believed that Macao gained its name from the temple. Upon their arrival, the Portuguese were said to have asked the locals for the name of the area. This verbal exchange fell victim to the language barrier, with the natives responding with the name of the temple rather than the region. 'A-Maa-gok' was interpreted as 'Macau,' which was then applied to the entire region that the Portuguese colonised.

We moved on to the nearby Our Lady of Penha Chapel, which is located at the top of Penha Hill. If we needed a further reminder of the European influence on Macao, then this beautifully reconstructed seventeenth-century church provided it. We were afforded a clear view of Macau Tower from our vantage point. Standing at 1,109 feet tall, it is one of the most recognisable structures in Macao.

I gave me verdict to the others: "It looks exactly how I would expect a city's showpiece tower to look like; basically, a giant pole with a sphere near the top, which no doubt contains all of the usual visitor attractions. Oh, and an antenna right at the top to add a bit more height. It still looks impressive though!"

The tower, which was opened in 2001, does indeed house many standard tourist attractions, such as an observation deck and a shopping centre. It also has a revolving restaurant and an outdoor 'Sky Walk.' If that is not enough to satisfy the needs of adrenaline junkies, it offers a bungee jumping facility. The Guinness World Record for the world's highest bungee jump from a building was achieved here a few years prior to our visit. I was not tempted to match this feat.

Like much of Macao, the tower was the brainchild of the recently deceased Hong Kong billionaire Stanley Ho. He had been so impressed by a visit to the Sky Tower in Auckland that he decided to have his own one built in Macao. I guess that is what billionaires do! It is probably the equivalent of someone with average wealth purchasing a nice pair of shoes after they have spotted them on someone walking down the street!

The next landmark that we passed was another legacy of Stanley Ho's influence on Macao. One of his companies began building the Casino Lisboa complex in the late 1960s. The capacity was significantly expanded in 1991, with the most eye-catching building added just a few years prior to our visit. Aside from the Macau Tower, the Grand Lisboa is the tallest building in Macao, with its unusual shape said to embody the spirit of the Special Administrative Region. I thought that the 24-carat gold-coated glass building looked like a flame, but it was apparently designed to represent the open petals of a lotus flower.

If we had entered the complex, we would have encountered 800 gaming tables and 1,000 slot machines in the casino at the foot of the tower. I have read that the interior of the building, which features an abundance of gold leaf and dazzling lighting, is as extravagant as its external appearance. It also houses *The Star of Stanley Ho*, which is a 218-carat diamond. Of course.

We quickly moved on to another of Macao's most distinctive landmarks. In complete contrast with the Grand Lisboa, the seventeenth-century Ruins of Saint Paul's, along with the rest of the historic centre of Macao, are a UNESCO World Heritage Site. Although little more than the beautiful granite façade remains, it was once one of the largest Catholic churches in Asia. The original complex, which was built by the Jesuits and dedicated to Saint Paul the Apostle, also included St. Paul's College.

We walked up the sixty-eight stone steps to the façade at the top of the hill, passing a series of pink and red flowers en route. I admired the biblical statues belonging to the ornate ruins, which would not have looked out of place next to the Duomo in Milan, before concluding that it was astonishing that the façade was still standing. Prior to excavation work carried out in the 1990s, it had been debated whether the ruins should be demolished due to their structural instability. It was rather strange to be staring at this beautiful façade that had nothing behind it; most of the church had been destroyed by a fire during a typhoon in 1835.

Our next port of call was at another historic site. The seventeenth-century Forteleza do Monte is a former military fort situated at the top of Mount Hill. It is now home to the Museum of Macau, which we declined to enter due to time constraints. I took a photograph of one of the fort's cannons from an angle that made it look like it was taking aim at the Grand Lisboa.

"Do you think I can strike the Lisboa from here?" I jokingly asked Mum.

"Stanley Ho would not be happy!" she replied.

"It feels rather symbolic: something that is hundreds of years old pointed at an ostentatious monstrosity, seemingly ready to destroy it."

"If you say so," Mum chuckled.

I resisted the urge to fire the cannon.

Our remaining time in Macao saw the four of us navigate the busy streets of the commercial centre. The area was heaving with people, which should not have come as a surprise considering that Macao is the most densely populated region on Earth. To provide some perspective on how crowded it is, one only needs to compare the population density figure with the respective number for London. There are just over 14,000 people per square mile in the capital city of the United Kingdom; remarkably, the relative figure for Macao is just under 55,000! The busy streets of London do not seem so hectic now!

The narrow streets were lined with modest restaurants, souvenir stalls and bakeries. We indulged in some egg custard tarts, which brought back some fond childhood memories. Mum always made sure that she bought some of these sweet treats for my brother and me whenever we were in a Chinese restaurant or when she had been shopping in Manchester's Chinatown. I had always assumed that they were of Chinese origin, but they were actually imported by Macao's Portuguese colonists. Their popularity eventually spread to other regions such as Hong Kong.

I was glad that we did not spend too long trying to push our way past the sea of people that had filled the network of streets. When we eventually reached the open space of Senado Square, the feeling of relief was palpable. My mind felt like it had been tricked though. On first inspection, one could easily believe that they were standing in a square somewhere in Western

Europe. There was a wave-patterned mosaic of coloured stones beneath our feet and the surrounding buildings had been constructed in a European style. The fountain in the centre of this public space seemed rather ordinary; however, the fact that many locals refer to the square as 'The Fountain' hints at the significance of this addition. During colonial rule, the Portuguese authorities built a bronze statue in honour of Vicente Nicolau de Mesquita. He was responsible for the deaths of many Qing Chinese soldiers, which led to resentment amongst the local population. There has recently been a global discussion about the validity of statues that honour controversial historical figures, but half a century ago the Chinese population of Macao took matters into their own hands.

The statue was torn down during political protests and rioting that occurred in 1966 following a police crackdown on demonstrations against the issues of corruption and colonial rule. This became known as the '12-3 Incident,' due to the event happening on the Third of December. The colonial government relinquished some of their control following the protests and a fountain was erected in the spot where the statue once stood.

We noticed that there were a couple of teenage girls walking around the square whilst holding up signs that read: 'Free Hugs.'

"Would you like a free hug?" Mum asked.

It almost felt like Mum was acting as a pimp for a watered-down physical service that was being offered by these girls. If this had happened in 2020, everybody would have run a mile! The signs would probably have been interpreted as: 'Would you like to contract COVID-19?' Looking back, it certainly makes you realise how we have all become so used to social distancing that a simple thing like a hug seems fraught with danger.

Before leaving Macao, we paid a visit to the graveyard where Uncle Sydney's grandmother rests. He continued the tradition of offering money and gifts to pass on to those in the afterlife. This is done by burning the items in question. As burning real money is regarded as an action that will bring bad luck in many Asian cultures, not to mention that it is unaffordable to all but the richest members of society, most people burn packets of joss paper instead.

Uncle Sydney burned some joss paper, in addition to other paper gifts that symbolised a wide range of items such as tea, food, and clothing. This gesture is intended to provide a comfortable existence for loved ones in the afterlife. Some people will go as far as burning paper representations of cars, TVs and smartphones. I wonder if this means that some dead people have a better phone than I do!

After a straightforward ferry journey back to Hong Kong, we said our goodbyes to Sydney and Rosalie before returning to our apartment. It had been a most pleasant trip to Macao, but it was time to shift our focus back to the other Special Administrative Region of China.

"I am excited by the thought of seeing more of Hong Kong," I stated.

"Yes, I am looking forward to showing you more of its attractions."

With fond memories of Macao already banked and the prospect of exploring Hong Kong on my mind, I went to sleep with a sense of contentment.

CHAPTER 11: CONTRASTING FORTUNES
HONG KONG, SPECIAL ADMINISTRATIVE REGION OF THE PEOPLE'S REPUBLIC OF CHINA
NOVEMBER 2012

My mother's side of the family are from Hong Kong whilst my father's clan are from Great Britain, which has always left me feeling slightly awkward in relation to this former British colony. The history of the region reveals much about the unsavoury nature of colonialism and how the legacy of this era can stir up a range of emotions.

The demand for Chinese commodities such as silk, tea and porcelain in the eighteenth century far outweighed the goods that Britain sold to China. To counter this trade imbalance, the British authorities permitted merchants to sell opium from Bengal. The Qing Dynasty, who ruled much of what is now regarded as mainland China, had banned the trade of this drug and ordered the seizure of any opium transported into the country. They were unable to stop all the incoming drug trade, however, with smugglers managing to sell enough opium to reverse the trade surplus. This had the knock-on effect of severely damaging the Chinese silver trade and increasing the number of opium addicts in the country. The British refused the Chinese request to halt this illegal trade, which eventually led to military conflict between the two countries.

Hong Kong was ceded to Britain after the Chinese were defeated in the First Opium War, whilst Kowloon was added to the British colony after the Second Opium War. Britain acquired a ninety-nine-year lease of the New Territories in 1898. Barring a four-year spell of Japanese occupation during the Second World War, Hong Kong and the expanded territory remained under British control until it was handed back to China in 1997.

I had visited Hong Kong as a young child before the handover, but I am unable to remember much about this. I have a vague recollection of landing at the now-defunct Kai Tak Airport, which was regarded as one of the most

145

difficult and dangerous airports for pilots to land aircraft. The runway was surrounded by water on all sides and planes had to fly at a low altitude, appearing to pass close by to skyscrapers before making a sharp right-hand turn preceding the final approach. Only experienced pilots were permitted to land at the airport that had gained the nickname of the 'Kai Tak Heart Attack.' Perhaps it was for the best that I was too young to have been aware of the unique nature of the airport approach!

Aged fourteen, I had travelled to Hong Kong with my mum and my seventeen-year-old brother in 1999, but I paid little attention to any changes which had occurred following the handover. John and I had shaved all our hair off prior to the trip, which meant that we resembled a younger version of the Mitchell brothers. Although it is doubtful that the people of Hong Kong were familiar with *EastEnders*, they would, nevertheless, have been bemused by our strange appearance.

This would be my first trip to Hong Kong as an adult, although I was again travelling with my mum. I was interested in seeing if the tense history between China and the United Kingdom would be evident during the trip. From a personal point of view, my feelings were muddied even further by my disapproval of many actions of the Chinese government. China's human rights record is appalling, and the suppression of free speech is worrying.

This has been a divisive issue for the people of Hong Kong, who find themselves in a different situation to those in mainland China. It is a Special Administrative Region that operates under the principle of 'One Country, Two Systems.' Hong Kong citizens enjoy much greater freedom than the people of mainland China, but not as much as those who live within Western democratic countries.

Mum's generation tend to take the view that they should be grateful for the freedoms that they enjoy, but the younger members of Hong Kong society often take a more confrontational stance against the authorities from Beijing. They have had a taste of freedom and have been teased with the idea of democracy; therefore, they are not willing to relinquish any of their rights. Tension flared up a couple of years after our trip in 2012, with democracy activists acutely aware that the fifty years of partial freedoms guaranteed by the Sino-British Joint Declaration are due to expire in 2047.

Following a good night's sleep, we woke up and had some breakfast. My hazy memories of an earlier trip to Hong Kong include my Grandad, who we would refer to as 'Gung Gung,' returning from his daily morning walk and tai chi session with a treat from McDonald's. Grandad and Grandma both died prior to my teenage years, so my recollections from our trips to Hong Kong are my strongest link to their memory. Grandad ran a shoe factory, and he was enthusiastic about his craft. He was not a hugely successful businessman, but Mum often refers to his passion for his work. I remember him having a calm and kind personality, even if I am unable to recall many specific conversations that I had with him.

Likewise, I cannot remember much about Grandma. I know that she used to enjoy spending hours playing mahjong and chatting to her close friend, who we referred to as Yee Paw. Mum had informed me that we were going to meet Yee Paw at some point in the trip, so this was going to be another way of keeping Grandma's memory alive.

There was no McDonald's on this occasion, but Auntie Jo brought a breakfast consisting of pastries and congee up to the apartment. We were tired after our trip to Macao, so we decided to have an easy-going day. Mum, Auntie Jo and I boarded one of the vehicles belonging to the Hong Kong Tramways. This was a cheap and effective way of seeing some of the city whilst gaining our bearings.

We had always referred to these narrow-gauge double-decker electric trams as 'ding-ding' and I had fond memories of riding these vehicles during previous trips to Hong Kong. One can travel the length of Hong Kong Island for the equivalent of 20 pence whilst soaking in the sights of everyday city life from the top deck. The trams, which are a legacy of British rule, have been operating since 1904. We boarded one of the vehicles and made our way to the back of the top deck. With the windows open, I could almost shake hands with the people who were sat in any tram that pulled up behind us whenever we were stationary.

After our thoroughly enjoyable 'ding-ding' ride, which transported us through popular regions such as the business district of Admiralty and the shopping haven of Causeway Bay, we had lunch in an ordinary-looking restaurant. Having grown up in a European country, the seating arrangements seemed odd to me. We were ushered into the first available seats, despite this meaning that we were sharing a table with strangers. This is the norm in Hong Kong, with people accepting that it is inevitable that restaurants are going to be so busy that this is the only practical solution in everyday dining establishments such as this one.

Although it felt slightly unusual, my uneasiness soon wore off after our food was brought to the table. We enjoyed a nice meal consisting of stir-fried vegetables and shredded pork. The more surprising element was that Mum ordered a pot of 'English' tea rather than the typical Chinese green leaf alternative. The most unexpected aspect was that the tea was served with condensed milk.

"Is it normal to have condensed milk with tea in Hong Kong?" I asked Mum.

"Dairy products have never been a big part of the diet in Hong Kong. We usually have green tea, but if we do have English tea, then we would use condensed milk. It is cheap and easy to store."

147

Indeed, the absence of dairy products in the traditional Chinese diet is reflected by the fact that many Chinese people are lactose intolerant. Condensed milk does not contain as much liquid as traditional variations of the product, meaning that the tea does not become as diluted. As Hong Kong citizens are used to strong tea, it is understandable that they would approve of this.

I tried some of the tea with condensed milk and I was pleasantly surprised by how it tasted. It had an unusually sweet flavour, but I found it pleasant. I am not sure whether I would choose to drink this on a regular basis though.

"The addition of milk to tea is rather strange anyway. The two items don't really go together but British people seem to love it!" Mum commented.

I had been thinking like a British person, of course. Tea originates from Asia and it is not traditionally served with milk. However, the British were unable to stomach the bitter flavour of tea that was imported from across the Empire without adding something sweet like milk or sugar. It has been suggested that milk also served the purpose of stopping delicate cups from cracking. Either way, the Brits began consuming so much of if that the drink came to be seen as quintessentially British. People even say, 'As British as a cup of tea,' despite the fact that it has been imported from Asia. Other food and drink recipes have been bizarrely adjusted to suit British tastes, such as watered-down curries like the 'Tikka Masala.'

The bill came to just a few dozen Hong Kong Dollars, which is the equivalent of a few British Pounds. This highlighted how food, aside from in luxurious restaurants, is cheap in Hong Kong. Many other commodities are also relatively inexpensive, including electronic products. My brother and I have fond memories of shopping for video games during previous trips. We were able to bring back a stack of games for a fraction of the price that we would have been charged in England.

However, not everything is cheap in Hong Kong. In complete contrast to food and transport, property prices are astronomically high. Hong Kong is one of the most densely populated places on Earth, which has resulted in costly land prices. To the extent that Hong Kong has the most expensive housing market on Earth. The average house price is the equivalent of around one million British Pounds. The limited number of houses are out of the question for most people, with most of the population residing in apartments within tower blocks.

Limited space for property and high costs have led to many apartments being partitioned and rented out by landlords. Mum and her siblings spent some of their childhood in an apartment that was shared with a couple of other families. They all had their separate sections within the apartment, which Mum says was ingeniously divided in a vertical manner, but there were some communal areas.

The situation has become even more extreme in recent times with some landlords dividing properties into lots of small areas that are little more than the size of a bed. Some people are practically living in cages, with some describing them as 'coffin cubicles.' Poorer Hong Kong citizens are unable to afford anything more than this, which results in a sad scenario of someone having to sleep in and store all of their possessions in an area barely bigger than a bed. This is the more extreme end of the spectrum, of course, but it is a growing problem within Hong Kong.

There is an even grimmer reality surrounding the lack of affordable housing. The number of homeless people in Hong Kong has been on the rise in the last decade, with an increasing number resorting to sleeping in 24-hour fast food restaurants such as McDonald's. This is not a problem exclusive to Hong Kong, with the worldwide phenomenon of people sleeping in this type of establishment leading to the coining of the term 'McRefugees.'

This issue was thrust into the spotlight in Hong Kong in 2015 when CCTV footage emerged of a homeless person lying dead within a McDonald's restaurant in Kowloon for hours whilst oblivious diners satisfied their hunger. Hundreds of 'McRefugees' in Hong Kong lost their temporary shelters when the global franchise was forced to close its restaurants due to the outbreak of COVID-19.

If the cost of a Hong Kong home seems high, then the prices of parking spaces will undoubtedly shock you. During our trip, I was astonished to see a report on the daily news broadcast that detailed how a Hong Kong parking space had been sold for the equivalent of over £500,000. The record figure rose to the equivalent of nearly £800,000 in 2019, which is more than the price of many homes. With land at a premium, there are hardly any parking spaces amongst the plethora of skyscrapers; thus, rich businessmen tend to pay ridiculous prices for any centrally located spaces that become available. This is not a problem for most Hong Kong citizens who rely on public transport rather than driving their own vehicles.

It was time for Mum, Auntie Jo and I to try another form of public transport. We began walking to the closest Mass Transit Railway, or MTR station. It had been enjoyable to observe the chaos of this busy metropolis from the comfort of the 'ding-ding' tram, but it was not quite as pleasant to walk amongst the heaving crowds.

I was thankful that the weather was more tolerable than it had been during our previous trip in July 1999. It had been unbearably hot, to the extent that we would walk in and out of every shop we came across, just so that we could receive a cold blast from the air conditioning. The more moderate weather on this occasion allowed me to wear a pair of jeans and a T-shirt without feeling uncomfortable.

The efficiency of the public transport system was clear to see, even amongst the mass of fellow passengers. Auntie Jo handed us a couple of pre-loaded Octopus cards. Launched six years before Londoners were presented with the Oyster card, these contactless cards have a much broader capability than their British equivalent. Initially launched as a payment method for the MTR, their functionality has since been expanded to include most forms of public transport. One can seamlessly transition from the MTR, which includes both heavy and light rail, to a bus or a ferry. Even some taxi operators accept this form of payment.

We scanned our cards and passed through the ticket checkpoints before I noticed something that made the Octopus cards seem even more impressive: I saw a commuter use his card to purchase some confectionary from a vending machine.

"Octopus cards be used to buy goods?" I asked Auntie Jo.

"Yes, you can buy things in shops as well as vending machines. And not just shops within the transport stations. Supermarkets, car parks and fast-food restaurants all accept payment by Octopus."

"That is impressive. These cards are useful then. You can load the card with a decent amount of money and use it for pretty much everything by the sound of it," I declared.

"It is best not to top it up with a huge amount though, as you don't want to lose it if it has lots of value stored," Auntie Jo replied.

"You can also use the cards for non-payment purposes, such as accessing buildings, and it can serve as a basic form of identification," Mum interjected.

The average daily value of transactions made using Octopus cards is the equivalent of just under £20 million, which underlines how widespread their use is.

We descended the escalators and waited for the train to arrive. Although the platform was crowded, there seemed to be an efficient system in place. There were glass screens separating the passengers from the tracks, with doors that would slide open once the train had arrived. There were even markings demonstrating where people should stand whilst they let passengers alight before boarding the vehicle.

During our journey, I had a look at the map of the network. Many of the station names appeared in English, which reflects the territory's colonial past. Stations names such as Prince Edward, Diamond Hill and Quarry Bay would not sound out of place in a British city. The station serving the Happy Valley Racecourse was another legacy of British rule. The racecourse, built in 1845, was initially aimed at the British occupiers of

Hong Kong, but horse racing became popular with Chinese residents. Or at least, gambling on horse racing became popular.

There are only a small number of authorised gambling outlets in Hong Kong, with betting via bookmakers illegal. This has allowed the government-approved outlets to establish a monopoly within the gambling sector. As the authorities reap the benefits through taxation, they are undoubtedly pleased that Hong Kong is the somewhat surprising location of the largest horse racing gambling revenue in the world.

"I didn't know that there was a Disneyland in Hong Kong," I remarked as I studied the map.

"Yes, we have one," Auntie Jo replied. She currently resides in England, but she clearly still regarded herself as a Hong Kong citizen.

We alighted at Wan Chai MTR station before making the short walk to Hong Kong Convention and Exhibition Centre. Built on reclaimed land in the 1980s and 1990s, it is one of the most recognisable complexes by Victoria Harbour. Its waterside location and shape reminded me somewhat of Sydney Opera House, only with much more glass. As the name suggests, it is used for numerous functions throughout the year, including many involving international trade. Despite Hong Kong belonging to the Communist regime of China, the region has remained a key location for business conducted between countries from around the world.

We were not too concerned about this as we walked through the complex before making our way over to Golden Bauhinia Square. Unsurprisingly, there is a giant statue of a golden bauhinia in the centre of the square. Sometimes referred to as the Hong Kong orchid tree, the bauhinia x blakeana produces purple flowers that are often compared to butterflies. To underline how strong the association is between the bauhinia and the region, the shape of the flower features on the flag of Hong Kong.

The handover ceremonies were held in this square in 1997, with the six-metre-high statue becoming an important image for the status of Hong Kong following its return to China. There is a daily flag-raising ceremony held here, which is accompanied by the playing of the national anthem. After observing the scene, which included the city skyline and both the Hong Kong and China flags flying high behind the gilded statue, it was easy to see how this location was symbolically important for the Chinese authorities.

Later that evening, we caught sight of another building that is regarded as symbolic. The Bank of China Tower was constructed in the years preceding the handover, with its sharp-edged design leading some to believe that the Chinese authorities wanted to make a statement.

"It looks like a huge knife, as if they wanted to say that Hong Kong belongs to the powerful country of China," Mum commented.

"Many Chinese people think that this is a sign of bad luck due to its similarity to a knife," Auntie Jo added.

We spent the final part of our evening in the International Finance Centre complex. This consists of two skyscrapers, a mall, and a Four Seasons hotel. The second tower, known as 2IFC, is the second tallest building in Hong Kong. With the tower's subtle lighting, it looked spectacular against the blanket of darkness above the city.

Auntie Jo took us to a restaurant that was entirely dedicated to serving desserts. It had gone ten o'clock at night, but it was packed with people enjoying a sweet treat. We enjoyed a collection of cakes and custard desserts before heading back to our apartment.

*   *   *

The following day, we had lunch with Uncle Dickie, who is my mum's brother, and his family in a nice restaurant. There was a variety of interesting-looking dishes on offer, but my shyness meant that I was reluctant to manoeuvre the glass turntable in order to reach them. I believe that English-speaking people sometimes refer to this contraption as a 'Lazy Susan.' It has been claimed that Thomas Jefferson invented this device for his daughter Susan. It is unknown whether this story has any factual merit, but it is probably the most interesting version regarding its conception.

Whilst nobody else hesitated to move the desired food towards them, I sat there like a lost little boy who was waiting for his mother to put some food on his plate. Mum duly obliged.

"What are these dishes?" I asked her.

"This one is duck's tongue, and that one is chicken feet," she replied.

I almost wished that I had just eaten the food without enquiring. I began picking at the duck's tongue with my chopsticks, but I was finding it difficult to locate anything edible.

"With the bone running through it, and a lack of anything I can eat, it hardly seems worthwhile," I commented.

"Come on, you are Chinese. We used to say that we will eat anything that moves! Seriously though, a lot of families were poor, so we would make sure that no food went to waste," Mum advised.

I found both dishes difficult to eat, as there was no meat, or anything of substance on them. I had to gnaw at them and suck any trace of goodness from the bones. It almost felt like I was performing a French kiss with the remains of a duck and indulging in a foot fetish with a slaughtered chicken. There was not any particular taste to either the duck's tongue or the chicken feet, so it was not an unpleasant experience; it was just a lot of work with such little reward at the end of it. The dishes remain popular amongst affluent citizens, perhaps due to a feeling of nostalgia.

I enjoyed some of the more familiar offerings, such as stir-fried vegetables, chicken and shredded pork. Having already become intimate with the duck's tongue, I was rewarded with a taste of its flesh. My cousin Bert noticed that I was wearing my tightest T-shirt.

"Not bad. Could be better," he said as he gripped my bicep. The smirk on his face indicated that he was winding me up, but I still felt emasculated.

Mum, Uncle Wai Lun and Uncle Dickie took part in the traditional post-meal activity of fighting over the bill. Whilst many English people politely offer to pay before secretly being relieved that one of their dining partners has decided that they will pay for everyone, Chinese people tend to almost feel insulted if they are not the one who wins this battle. These fierce encounters can last several minutes, with the winner earning the glory of footing an expensive bill.

Uncle Dickie and his wife, Candy, emerged victorious on this occasion. We all made our way back to their home after the meal. Upon arrival, I was shocked to discover that they lived in a large house away from the city centre. Not only that, but Bert had a matching house next door. Given the housing market in Hong Kong, I pondered whether they had recently won the lottery.

Mum chatted in Cantonese with her siblings, before informing me that Bert had carried out some successful business connected to the management of artists within the music industry. One of the bands that he is involved with, C AllStar, have risen from humble beginnings busking on the streets of Mong Kok to become Canto-pop stars. We assumed that Bert's dealings in the music industry had paid for both houses. Either that or he was Hong Kong's equivalent of Pablo Escobar.

Another of my cousins, Kelly, and her boyfriend, Kyle, kindly gave me a tour of Uncle Dickie's home. Kyle and I quickly found common ground in the form of our support for Manchester United. He had spent some time studying in Australia, but I was unable to detect any hint of a *Crocodile Dundee* accent.

"You are lucky that you live in Manchester. Do you go to many games?" Kyle asked.

"I only go to a few matches each season. It can be expensive," I replied.

I made the decision not to reveal that I had been unable to summon the strength to attend a match at Old Trafford since I had witnessed United throw away a two-goal lead to draw 4-4 against Everton in an encounter that had effectively cost them the previous season's title. At least the team was still competing for major honours back then. That seems like a lifetime ago.

In contrast to the impressive houses that we had just visited, Mum took me to the area in Mongkok where she had spent her formative years. During previous trips to Hong Kong, my brother and I had taken great delight in searching for our desired video games in the electronics store within a small shopping centre near the old family home.

We had returned from Hong Kong in 1999 with a SEGA Dreamcast, months before it was available in the United Kingdom. At the beginning of the following school year, I suddenly received lots of invitations to parties for the first time. In truth, it was the Dreamcast that had received the offers, as bringing the console seemed to be a condition of my attendance. I declined the invitations in any case, instead choosing to stay at home and watch TV with my parents. Oh, how thrilling my teenage years were!

Mum and I had a look around the shopping centre, which comprised of just a few stores, and reminisced about how excited John and I had been to visit here in the past. It was clear to see that this was a modest area where residents were not particularly wealthy. It was a further reminder of how lucky we were to have been blessed with a comfortable life back in the United Kingdom. It also made me appreciate the less crowded setting that I was used to.

Our next destination was an expensive showpiece building in West Kowloon that was designed to signal Hong Kong's standing in the world. The International Commerce Centre is the tallest building in the Special Administrative Region. The original design had to be adjusted due to regulations which state that buildings are not allowed to be taller than the surrounding mountains, which illustrates the scale of ambition involved.

Uncle Wai Lun, Auntie Jo, Fiona, Mum and I entered the lift that would take us to the Sky100 observatory deck.

"I guess that it is on the one-hundredth floor?!" I sarcastically asked the others.

"Well, it is officially on the one-hundredth floor, but the floor count may be different to what you expect due to tetraphobia," Uncle Wai Lun answered.

I had little idea of what this term meant, but I quickly worked out that it was not a fear of the classic video game *Tetris*. Instead, this refers to an aversion to the number four that is prevalent in many Asian countries. The phobia can be explained by the fact that the word meaning 'four' sounds like the word for 'death' in several Asian languages, including Chinese. After being informed of this by my uncle, I had a look at the lift buttons. Every number ending in four had been omitted, which seemed to confirm the information that I had just been given.

Like most showpiece skyscrapers nowadays, there was a high-speed lift that was marketed as a selling-point of the building. The lift took us to the

Sky100 indoor observatory deck in just sixty seconds. We were impressed by the splendid 360-degree view over Victoria Harbour and the cityscape of Hong Kong on the other side of the water. There was less smog than I had anticipated, which meant that the surrounding buildings were easy to distinguish. We were more or less directly facing the IFC towers and the Bank of China Tower.

Mum and I had dinner at Yee Paw's apartment that evening. As I mentioned earlier, she was my Grandmother's best friend, so Mum felt a strong connection to her. As is the case with many Hong Kong families, there were multiple generations living in the same apartment. A difficult housing market and a strong sense of family loyalty results in many Hong Kong citizens not only living with their parents, but also their grandparents and great grandparents. The concept of filial piety, which generally equates to being good to one's parents, is a central element of Confucianism that is commonplace in Chinese society.

Yee Paw's grandson chatted to me about English Premier League football, which underscored how it is one of the nation's most successful exports. Wherever you are in the world, there is a good chance that people will be enthusiastic about the league. He told me that he had recently flown to London to watch an Arsenal match. He had only spent two nights in England before flying back.

"It was a great price and I was so happy to attend a live game!" he enthused.

"I can understand. I have done the same with MMA events around the world. I have just been to the UFC show in Macao," I replied.

"Cool, I bet that was good. You like football and MMA then?"

"Yeah, but I am not as passionate about either sport anymore. I think I have watched too much over the years!"

It was nice to see Mum reminisce about her memories of her mother whilst catching up with Yee Paw. We enjoyed some tasty homecooked food before returning to our apartment.

*   *   *

Mum was feeling a little unwell the following morning, complaining of a sore throat and suspecting that she may be about to develop a cough or a cold. I was surprised to see her put on a face covering when we left our apartment. Like most Westerners, I had always assumed that they were worn for protective purposes; however, Mum informed me that there is a more altruistic reason for sporting a mask.

"In Hong Kong, we wear them when we think that we may be displaying symptoms of influenza or similar illnesses. This became more prevalent after the SARS outbreak a few years ago, but we tend to wear them even if we just have a common cold"

"I always thought that so many East Asian people wore them because they were worried about catching an illness. I feel bad for thinking that there were lots of hypochondriacs about when they are actually being considerate to others."

"Don't worry, most people think that. We also wear them when there is heavy smog. This provides some protection, although not much, from the pollution."

This conversation seems more relevant in 2020 than it did at the time. COVID-19 has caused Westerners to educate themselves about the use of face coverings in relation to infections. Asians who wore them were receiving verbal abuse during the early stages of the pandemic, but countries from around the world have now embraced the wearing of masks following advice from the World Health Organization.

We made our way to Wong Tai Sin Temple after breakfast. This shrine is incredibly popular amongst locals and tourists alike, perhaps due to its promise of answering one's prayers: 'What you request is what you get.'

It is primarily a Taoist temple, but it also houses Confucian and Buddhist literature. Wong Tai Sin was a fourth-century monk who became a deity. He remained obscure until the Taoist priest Leung Renyan arrived in Hong Kong with a sacred portrait of Wong Tai Sin in 1915. He opened an herbal medicine shop and installed an altar with the portrait at the back of the store. Customers soon began praying at the altar and sought guidance from the Great Immortal Wong.

A few years after Leung's shop was destroyed by a fire, he collaborated with fellow Taoists to construct a new shrine near Kowloon City Pier. The Second World War resulted in an influx of refugees from mainland China. Many of them settled near the temple, which welcomed new arrivals. Its popularity continued to increase during the subsequent decades, eventually becoming the revered site that it is today.

Mum and I walked through the archway that marks the main entrance to the temple. This was grey, but we were soon encountering the red and yellow colours that have become synonymous with much of Chinese culture.

We walked through the pleasantly named Good Wish Gardens and examined the Nine Dragon Wall. There are many statues throughout the complex, most of which include the usual fare of lions and dragons, but my favourite one resembled Yoda from *Star Wars*. I stood and watched numerous people kneeling to pray under a series of red and gold paper lanterns that were being suspended above them. I imagine that they all firmly believed that their requests would be granted. I would say that I hope that they were, but maybe I should not just in case they wished for the destruction of life on planet Earth.

We paid a visit to Nathan Road in the late afternoon. This is the main thoroughfare in Kowloon, and it serves as another reminder of Hong Kong's colonial past. Lieutenant-Colonel Sir Matthew Nathan was a British soldier who served as Governor of a variety of regions scattered across the globe, including Hong Kong, Queensland and Sierra Leone.

The road, which runs for over two miles, is lined with restaurants and shops. As we began walking towards Tsim Sha Tsui, I noticed the absence of pubs and bars that one frequently encounters in most countries around the world.

"Are there not many pubs in Hong Kong?" I asked Mum.

"Chinese people tend to drink with a meal rather than going out just to consume alcohol. There are lots of expats, so there are some areas such as Lan Kwai Fong which have bars that cater for their drinking culture."

The next thing I noticed came as a bigger surprise to me: all of the scaffolding that I had seen in Hong Kong had been made from bamboo. It was a little unnerving to see this material attached to modern skyscrapers. My Western brain was telling me that this was surely unsafe.

"Is it normal for scaffolding to me made from bamboo here?" I asked.

"Yes, it is what we use in Hong Kong. Bamboo has been used for hundreds of years. It is cheaper and lighter to transport. Plus, it is less dangerous if there are any problems and it falls down."

I still struggled to comprehend how a futuristic building made from metal and glass that almost touches the sky could have bamboo scaffolding. I eventually conceded that this traditional method must be effective if it is still being used today.

Mum and I were now in Tsim Sha Tsui, which is an area that is popular with tourists. The high-end shops and restaurants seemed to confirm this. Mum pointed towards one of the more striking buildings: "The Peninsular Hotel is famous and luxurious. Wealthy people indulge in high tea within this colonial building."

As we were not rich, we ended up having some Chinese fast food instead. For some reason, it felt strange to order plates of vegetables and steamed buns from a display board like those found in McDonald's or Burger King. The food was of decent quality and it seemed to truly represent Cantonese cuisine rather than the takeaways back in England.

Mum had brought me to this area to show me 'A Symphony of Lights.' The world's largest permanent light and sound show occurs by Victoria Harbour every evening at eight o'clock. As we had some time to kill before the show, we decided to explore the surrounding attractions.

The Hong Kong Cultural Centre resembled a large beige horseshoe. In fairness, the angled walls, unusual staircases and walkways were more impressive upon closer inspection. I took photos of the imposing exterior, but we only entered the building in order to use the toilet. The spacious lobby did not provide many clues as to the purpose of the centre, so Mum informed me that it is used for concerts, opera shows, ballet, theatre productions and art exhibitions.

I was more interested in the Former Kowloon-Canton Railway Clock Tower that is located outside of the cultural centre. The red brick and granite tower, which reaches a height of forty-four metres, is a protected monument. It was completed in 1915, and as the name suggests, it once belonged to the terminus of the Kowloon-Canton Railway. Kowloon Station was relocated in 1974 and the Hong Kong Cultural Centre replaced it by the end of the following decade.

It appeared that I was not the only one who was admiring the Clock Tower; a white sculpture depicted a young boy looking up and pointing at it. This was part of Danny Yung's *Tian Tian Xiang Shang* exhibition. 'Tian Tian Xiang Shang' is a Chinese proverb that means 'study well and climb higher every day.' Yung created a series of conceptual comics in the 1970s based around this proverb, which portrayed Tian Tian as a curious boy who constantly questions everything. There have been exhibitions featuring the Tian Tian figurines in various locations across the world. The pointing little boy certainly enhanced my photographs anyway. Thankfully, there were no boys pointing at me whilst I used the toilet inside the centre.

As darkness descended, we began walking along the Avenue of Stars by the Victoria Harbour waterfront. This is the equivalent of the Hollywood Walk of Fame, instead honouring successful individuals associated with the Hong Kong film industry. *Infernal Affairs* was one of the most successful films to come out of Hong Kong since the handover. It spawned two sequels and the Martin Scorsese remake *The Departed*. I prefer the original version.

I recognised several names that have become well known in Hollywood, including Chow Yun-Fat, John Woo and Jackie Chan. There was a small crowd gathered around the square belonging to Lee Jun-Fan. He found global fame as Bruce Lee, of course. The martial arts pioneer featured in several hugely successful American films in the early 1970s before his sudden and mysterious death in 1973.

There was also a statue of Bruce Lee mimicking one of his famous martial arts stances by the waterfront. Like most other tourists, I took numerous photographs of this against the backdrop of the harbour. I was one of the few who did not feel an urge to pose alongside the statue. Or if I did, this was buried deep beneath my shyness and social anxiety.

As we waited for the light show to begin, Mum and I discussed our surroundings. "Victoria Harbour seems to be a popular place in Hong Kong. There are lots of tourists, boats, restaurants and important buildings," I commented.

"Yes, I think the British viewed it as strategically important. Since then, it has become a tourist attraction. They keep building on either side."

"It looks like they are running out of space though."

"Well, they will probably just reclaim more land."

"Really?" I asked.

"Yes. There have been many land reclamations in Hong Kong due to the lack of space. Both the British and Chinese authorities have raised the seabed and pumped water out of areas of the ocean that they have isolated. Some of the land around the harbour was not here until human intervention."

'A Symphony of Lights' began right on cue at eight o'clock. There are over forty buildings that participate in the light show, either by being lit up in a variety of bright colours or by projecting lasers into the night sky. The impressive show involves five themes that celebrate the spirit of Hong Kong.

The first couple of themes, 'Awakening' and 'Energy,' comprised of lots of laser lights, but it was not particularly clear what was being represented. Apparently, this was supposed to pay homage to the growth and vibrant nature of Hong Kong.

The show improved by the third stage. 'Heritage' featured the traditional lucky red and gold colours and the sound of Chinese musical instruments blaring out over the harbour. 'Partnership' saw an increase in the level of symbolism; laser beams were projected from both sides of the harbour, connecting in the middle to signify a unified partnership.

The colourful final scene, 'Celebration,' was intended to portray a bright future for Hong Kong. In truth, I did not pay much attention to the symbolic significance of it all, but I enjoyed the dazzling show, nevertheless. It was a nice moment to share with Mum in the place where she spent her formative years.

*   *   *

We spent the following day on Lantau Island, which is the home of traditional fishing villages and numerous tourist attractions. It is also the largest island in Hong Kong, and almost twice the size of Hong Kong Island. Due to the lack of available land in the metropolis, it is no surprise that the authorities have constructed various projects on Lantau Island. The main purpose of our trip was to visit the island's most notable landmark, which is the giant Tian Tian Buddha statue.

Uncle Sydney, Rosalie, Mum and I travelled to the island via a ferry from Central Pier. Judging by how busy the ten piers were, this form of transport was obviously still heavily used in the region. We boarded our vessel and found some indoor seating. It was at this point that Mum decided to tell me about a recent tragedy: "There was a big accident last month. Two ferries collided, killing dozens of people, including children."

"Thanks for telling me that! Now I am feeling nervous!"

"It will be OK. There are thousands of these journeys every year and very few accidents have occurred."

The incident that Mum had been referring to was the collision between *Sea Smooth* and *Lamma IV* on the National Day of the People's Republic of China on the First of October in 2012. Thirty-nine people died and a further ninety-two were injured, making it the deadliest maritime disaster in Hong Kong for forty years. The captains of the vessels were both imprisoned for their part in the tragedy, with the skipper of *Sea Smooth* facing fierce criticism for leaving the scene of the accident.

Thankfully, our journey was smooth and uneventful. Having arrived on Lantau Island about an hour after our departure, we immediately headed to the traditional fishing village of Tai O. The houses in this area were built upon stilts above tidal flats, which makes it popular amongst tourists. I took a series of photographs of these unique buildings and the numerous boats that were navigating the channel between them.

The village may be photogenic, but the modest restaurants can seem less appealing to Western visitors. The establishment in which we dined at was little more than a tin shack serving food that had been prepared by a two-person team. They appeared to be a married couple who were relying on the income supplied by hungry tourists to support their basic needs. It was clear that this was not a wealthy village, and that its residents most likely lived in poor conditions. Despite my reservations about the hygiene standards of the restaurant, we consumed a tasty meal of seafood and vegetables before moving on to our next destination.

A rather uncomfortable bus journey took us to within sight of the giant Buddha statue in Ngong Ping. The serene-looking Buddha seemed to project a calming presence to those below its position upon a hilltop. I was fascinated by a series of warrior statues that lined the path leading to the Buddha and the main gate of the Po Lin Monastery. The others patiently waited whilst I took countless photographs of different combinations of statues, the gate and the Buddha. All against the backdrop of the picturesque hills.

Before visiting the Buddha, we paid a quick visit to the monastery. Various colourful shrines, statues, flowers and lanterns can be found within the largest Buddhist monastery in Hong Kong. We may have spent longer there if we had visited a couple of years later, as the Grand Hall of Ten Thousand Buddhas was built in 2014. We certainly would have if we had decided to count all of the statues of Buddha.

Despite having already eaten in Tai O, we had some more food within the monastery's vegetarian restaurant. We were not particularly hungry, but this is regarded as a good place to sample the typical food that a monk consumes. We shared a small portion of vegetables and tofu, which was tastier than I had expected. The teenage version of me would have been horrified by the prospect of eating so many vegetables. Tofu would have been enough to send me over the edge!

As we climbed the 268 steps leading to the Buddha, it became clear just how big the statue was. Reaching a height of thirty-four metres, and comprised of over two hundred bronze pieces, it is the second largest outdoor sitting Buddha in the world. Ascending the steps was an arduous task in the uncomfortable heat, but the sight of Buddha provided the necessary motivation. Perhaps I need to project a similarly impressive image on the wall in front of the cross trainer in my local gym the next time that I am flagging.

We were finally able to relax and admire the statue after we had reached the top of the stairway. I noticed that the right hand of Buddha was raised with his palm facing outwards, whilst his left hand was resting on his lap. I did not know the symbolic value of this, but apparently the former represents the removal of affliction, whilst the latter is a sign of generosity. Regardless, the statue evoked a calming presence. The Buddha rests upon a lotus and a base that is modelled on the Altar of Heaven.

Having travelled this far and endured the difficult climb to the top, I was surprised to find myself more interested in the six smaller statues that surround the base of the Buddha, seemingly presenting him with gifts. 'The Offering of the Six Devas' includes flowers, fruit, incense, music, ointment and a lamp. The offerings are intended to represent the 'Six Perfections' of generosity, meditation, morality, wisdom, zeal and patience. I imagine that most children would not be too thrilled to receive these gifts on Christmas Day though!

I found the six dutiful statues to be fascinating, and I probably ended up taking more photographs of them than of the main attraction. The hills once again provided a stunning backdrop to the pictures. I had the pick of the bunch printed onto a canvas and I recently made it my Facebook cover photo. The people who built the Tian Tian Buddha statue in the early 1990s would not have had a clue that part of their creation would feature in something as significant as my social media profile in 2020!

We briefly explored the exhibitions within the three-floor base platform underneath the statue before making our way back down the steps. The others decided that we should take the cable car down to Tung Chung, which was a twenty-five-minute journey that provided us with breathtaking views of the natural landscape. With the sun setting over Buddha, it was the best cable car ride that I had ever experienced, and it was the perfect way to end a fantastic day on Lantau Island.

Before being treated to a homecooked dinner at Uncle Sydney and Rosalie's apartment in the New Territories, we popped into a local supermarket. Whilst the others bought some food that would form part of that night's meal, Mum and I filled our basket with dried seafood. As Mum was spending an extra fortnight in Hong Kong, she asked me to take home the goods in my suitcase.

"You are not really supposed to take seafood back into the UK, but you will be fine," Mum stated.

"OK, I guess," I sheepishly replied. My heart was now filled with dread. I instantly began to imagine various scenarios that involved me being arrested for smuggling illegal goods into the country. I felt unable to refuse my mother's request even though the thought of the proposal was making me feel sick. I calmed down by telling myself that I would not have to deal with this problem for several days.

I initially thought that Uncle Sydney and Rosalie's household was, like many in Hong Kong, multi-generational. Their youngest son, Victor, his wife, Jo, and their young child, Hoven, seemed to have their own living space within the apartment. I had been given a tour of the place and there was a room containing a cot for Hoven; therefore, I assumed that the three of them lived with Uncle Sydney and Rosalie.

I was shocked when I was told the living arrangements of our friends. Hoven lived there with his grandparents but Victor and Jo lived in their own apartment. They both worked full-time, whilst Uncle Sydney and Rosalie were retired, which meant that they could look after him during the day. Victor and Jo came to visit Hoven after work each evening and stayed for dinner. With Hoven fast asleep, they went back to their own apartment ready for work the following morning. This would be considered bizarre to people in England, but I guess it was a practical arrangement.

Like many families in Hong Kong, Uncle Sydney and Rosalie employed a live-in maid who helped to look after Hoven as well as cleaning their apartment. There are more than 300,000 domestic helpers in Hong Kong, with around half of them, like Uncle Sydney and Rosalie's maid, coming from the Philippines. Ninety-nine per cent of such workers are female, which was also the case in this situation.

There has been much scrutiny over the treatment of domestic helpers in Hong Kong, particularly over their low pay. They are not eligible for the minimum wage and are often paid significantly less than the rest of the population. A bigger concern has been their vulnerability to human rights abuse, with Indonesian and Filipino women occasionally subjected to violence, intimidation or the withholding of wages. At least I knew that Uncle Sydney and Rosalie would treat their maid with kindness and understanding.

This was another aspect of their family set-up that would seem strange to people in the United Kingdom, but it was very much the norm here. I felt uncomfortable with the thought of someone working in a foreign country and serving a fairly wealthy family six days a week so that they could earn enough money to provide a basic living for their family back home. However, this was part of life in Hong Kong, where it was viewed by many as necessary in order to function in such a busy and crowded region.

Whilst we played with Hoven before dinner, Victor and Jo told us about an upcoming interview that their young son was scheduled to attend. Considering that the young lad was only two years old, this came as another surprise to me. I wondered what type of interview a two-year-old could have lined up. It turns out that it was part of an assessment for a school for gifted children.

"How does someone judge a two-year-old's ability and potential?" I asked.

"They can form a picture of children who have developed ahead of schedule in terms of intellect and skill. We are very nervous about this, as it could have a big impact on his future," Jo informed us.

I thought that it was ridiculous that a two-year-old could be faced with an interview that could potentially have a bearing on their future. After returning to Manchester, I found out that Hoven did not get selected for the school. The sky has not fallen in and he seems to be doing OK though.

Victor and Jo left soon after we had all enjoyed a nice meal. It felt strange that they left Hoven before we did, but I understood that they needed a good night's sleep before working the following day. Victor was a train driver, so he needed to be feeling alert during his shift. I took some photographs of the cityscape that was lit up underneath the night sky before we said our goodbyes and returned to our apartment.

*   *   *

We met up with Uncle Sydney and Rosalie again the following morning. Repulse Bay was our destination this time. I sincerely hoped that the area was nicer than the name suggested. None of the others knew about the origin of the name, so I Googled it during our bus journey.

I informed the others of my findings: "Not even Google can definitively tell me why it is called Repulse Bay. One of the possible explanations is that the pirates who preyed on merchant ships were forced back, or repulsed, by the Royal Navy. Nobody is sure though."

The intense brightness of the sun caused me to squint as soon as we disembarked at Repulse Bay. We walked onto the beach, which was full of tourists taking photographs. This was undoubtedly a beautiful place, but it was not the type of scenery that I had associated with this part of the world. It turns out that it is one of the most expensive and luxurious areas in Hong Kong. The beach had been artificially extended, and grand buildings were erected in order to attract high-end clientele. It seemed to have worked, as the likes of Marlon Brando and Ernest Hemingway had stayed at the Repulse Bay Hotel at some point.

The absurd Hong Kong housing market is even crazier in Repulse Bay, with some properties being sold recently for the equivalent of over £100 million. Fortunately, Mum and I were not on the lookout for an affordable holiday home there. Despite being in an upmarket area, we soon came across a rather crude joke within the shopping centre. We were casually browsing the vast T-shirt collection of one store when Uncle Sydney started chuckling to himself.

"You will not understand why this T-shirt is funny!" Uncle Sydney proclaimed.

He was right. I had no idea why the slogan 'Delay No More' would be deemed humorous.

"Why is it funny?" I asked.

Uncle Sydney took great delight in informing me: "The English words 'Delay No More' sound almost identical to the Cantonese for 'F**k Your Mother!' It has become an inside joke for Hong Kong people. Westerners could wear that T-shirt, oblivious to the fact that they are insulting people that they encounter!"

Mum and I left Uncle Sydney and Rosalie before visiting the Hong Kong Museum of History in the afternoon. This was one of the few places in Hong Kong that Mum had not previously explored, so she was keen to see what she could learn about the place where she was born. The permanent exhibition was called 'The Hong Kong Story.' The first couple of sections focused on the natural environment and the prehistoric history of the region. This did not particularly interest us, as it resembled a generic exhibition on the early years of the planet.

We found the next two sections, which focused on the various dynasties that ruled in pre-colonial times and folk culture, to be more enjoyable. In addition to information relating to traditional Chinese architecture, there was a life-size replica of a fishing junk. This type of sailing boat has been used in China since the second century, and due to their narrow and flat design, they have proven to be an effective way of navigating the shallow waters that surround Hong Kong. The sails incorporated bamboo spines, once again underlining the usefulness of this material. The masts were often a crimson colour due to the earlier models being dipped in tannins in order to strengthen them. The crimson masts still feature in the tourist junk ships that cater to tourists in Victoria Harbour.

The most fascinating display featured a recreation of the activities of the Cheung Chau Bun Festival. The centrepiece of the festival involves sixty-feet bamboo towers covered with buns in front of Pak Tai Temple. The tradition involves young men climbing up the towers and attempting to snatch food that has been offered to the lonely spirits. The buns provide good fortune for one's family, with those nearer the top being the most coveted. During one of these races in 1978, more than one hundred people were injured after a tower collapsed. Nowadays, carefully managed exhibition events take place instead, often involving plastic buns.

We were stood in front of a replica of a bun mountain in the museum, which I thought was a fantastic sight to behold.

"Shall we race?" Mum asked.

I hoped that she was joking, as any attempt to climb the display would surely result in injury or arrest.

"We will give it a miss this time. I find this festival to be really interesting though," I replied.

After gaining a better understanding of the suffering endured during the Opium Wars in the next section, we were then faced with the most impressive display in the museum. Within the section that highlighted the growth of the city during the colonial era, there was a full-scale replica street that visitors could walk along. This featured a variety of buildings that would have been commonplace during this period of history. A bank, a post office, a teahouse and a tailor's shop were all recreated. The subtle lighting of the streetlamps helped one picture themselves walking down such a passage in a bygone era. I always enjoy museum exhibits of this nature, as they allow the visitor to build a better picture of the subject in question.

We soon encountered another life-size exhibit that interested me, this time in the form of a replica 'ding-ding' tram. Despite having recently travelled on the real thing, I could not resist the opportunity to climb aboard and have my photograph taken.

The next section focused on the Japanese occupation of Hong Kong during the Second World War. This part of the museum was designed to resemble the appearance of an air-raid shelter, in order to illustrate the sense of fear and the suffering that occurred during the Japanese assault. The occupation lasted three years and eight months, which is a statistic that is ingrained in the collective memory of Hong Kong. Indeed, local people simply refer to this period as 'Three Years and Eight Months.' Technically, Hong Kong passed back and forth between two foreign occupations, but the Imperial Japanese invaders caused a much greater degree of misery than the British.

The British surrendered to the Japanese on the Twenty-Fifth of December in 1941, which became to be known as 'Black Christmas.' This was rubber-stamped the following day at the Peninsula Hotel, which was where the Japanese established their administrative centre and military headquarters. When we had walked past the hotel a few days earlier, I had no idea that this grand building was once a place to be feared.

Life was tough for the people of Hong Kong during this period. As well as the usual atrocities of war, which included the execution of an estimated 10,000 civilians and the mass rape of local women, the forced deportation of the unemployed and the undesirable led to a population decline of around one million. The economy was devastated, and food was severely rationed, which added to the hardship.

Mainland China and Korea had been occupied prior to the start of the war, which resulted in resentment towards the Japanese in both countries. Japan has been criticised for not facing up to its mistakes in the same way that Germany has, with ill-feeling resurfacing in recent years due to an increase in revisionist Japanese history that portrays a nationalistic tone. The issue of 'comfort women' has been contentious within Asia. This practice involved women from numerous countries that the Imperial Japanese regime had conquered being forced into the life of a sex slave.

There has been a fierce debate regarding the number of women who were taken, the level of brutality involved and the degree of compensation due. Various rulings have been made over the years, including a 2015 agreement between the leaders of Japan and South Korea to settle the dispute. Although this involved compensation for elderly women who had once been forced to serve as 'comfort women,' the broader significance of the deal was that Japan issued another apology and South Korea agreed to refrain from criticising Japan regarding this issue.

The hostility between these countries exists more within the older generation who lived through this era or were raised in the post-war years. Younger people are more likely to take the view that we must move on from the mistakes of the past.

The final section of the exhibition highlighted Hong Kong's return to China and its development into a modern metropolis. This detailed the economic growth of the region and the construction of the skyscrapers and impressive projects that have come to fruition in recent decades.

With our understanding of Hong Kong's history enhanced, it was time to satisfy our hunger. We again met with Uncle Sydney and Rosalie, but this time we were joined by their other son, Kevin, and some friends. We dined in a restaurant that specialised in communal hotpots. This practice involves a skillet of broth resting on a flame, usually a portable stove in the centre of the table.

A wide range of food is laid out, with diners adding items to the broth as they please. If you fancy eating some fish, this can be placed into the broth to cook for a few minutes whilst others do the same with their desired food, whether it be beef, vegetables or whatever else is on offer. This can go on for hours until everyone has enjoyed a delicious meal.

Being an introvert, I sat there quietly whilst the others began placing their food in the hotpot. Mum recognised my hesitancy and began to help me out by placing items into the broth that she knew I liked.

"Do you still need your Mum to feed you?! You need to be a man!" Uncle Sydney said with a chuckle.

"I am on schedule to become an adult by the year 2020," I joked. The jury is still out on that subject.

I am unsure of the cost of the meal, but all diners were free to drink as much as they desired at no additional expense. There were buckets of ice filled with an assortment of beverages. Whilst everyone else drank several bottles of beer, I sank a few cans of Sprite and Grape-flavoured Fanta.

"You were not joking about still being a child, were you?!" Uncle Sydney said with laughter.

This was confirmed once again following the conclusion of the meal. Mum and I were saying our goodbyes and preparing to take a bus back to our apartment when Uncle Sydney pointed out that it would be wise to go to the toilet before leaving the restaurant.

"I will be fine," I stated, despite being aware that I needed to relieve myself.

"It may take about an hour before you get back to your apartment. Are you sure?" he asked.

I shrugged my shoulders. It took some further encouragement from the others before I agreed to go to the toilet. I realised how foolish I had been during the bus journey, which seemed to take an eternity. I also considered the worrying fact that at twenty-seven years old I still needed to be told to go to the toilet.

*　　*　　*

The main item on the following day's agenda was a trip to Lamma Island. Fiona had met up with some friends whilst Mum, Uncle Wai Lun, Auntie Jo and I made our way to Central Pier. Upon arrival, we discovered that we would have to wait around thirty minutes for the next ferry. We sat down outside and bought some drinks and ice cream to cool us down; however, the heat proved too much for Auntie Jo. She informed us that she would return to the apartment and relax whilst we spent the day on the island.

This was where Chow Yun-Fat grew up, but I held little hope of bumping into the movie star during our day trip. After experiencing another smooth journey that took around thirty minutes, it was time to explore the island. Our surroundings told us that traditional fishing villages were a key part of its history, whilst the rolling green hills indicated that this was a place of natural beauty.

People come to Lamma Island to escape the concrete jungle of Hong Kong. There are beaches, hills and hiking trails that provide a change of pace from the hustle and bustle of city life. The number of cyclists who had already raced past us were an indication of one of the biggest differences between Lamma Island and Hong Kong Island. Fire trucks, ambulances and small vehicles used to transport goods through the villages are the only automobiles permitted on the island. This regulation, combined with the fact that buildings are only allowed to have three storeys, has resulted in a tranquil environment containing an abundance of natural beauty.

After walking around this peaceful island for a couple of hours, we had lunch in one of the numerous seafood restaurants on the island. It was the type of modest establishment that I had become accustomed to. White plastic chairs and disposable paper tablecloths had become synonymous with mealtimes. Despite the basic appearance of the restaurant, the food was once again delicious.

We would indulge in more seafood later that evening back on Hong Kong Island. Joined by Uncle Sydney and Rosalie, who had recommended an upmarket eatery, we paid a brief visit to an aquarium opposite the restaurant before dinner. As they chatted with the shop owners in Cantonese, of which I only have an extremely limited understanding, the others seemed more interested in the fish than I had anticipated. It felt a bit strange to be discussing the purchase of these water-based pets prior to us dining at a seafood restaurant.

I was even more alarmed forty minutes later when the food was being brought to our table in the restaurant.

"Do you recognise that crab?" a smiling Uncle Sydney asked.

It was starting to dawn on me what had transpired.

"How about that one?" he asked whilst pointing at the fish that seemed to be staring straight at me.

Yep, that confirmed it. We had not visited an aquarium at all! The place that housed the fish must have belonged to the restaurant. They had been swimming around without a care in the world, oblivious to the fact that people like us were casually deliberating which ones would end up in our tummies.

I was unsure of how I felt about this. It is fairly common for customers to pick which fish to eat in beachfront restaurants in the Mediterranean, but something about this seemed particularly cruel. Perhaps I should not have been so squeamish; after all, our detachment from the food that we consume has made us forget about the cold reality of eating meat or fish. Humans have had to hunt animals in order to feed themselves for centuries. Nowadays, our food is mass-produced, with the slaughter taking place out of sight. We just open a nicely presented package and cook it without contemplating the fact that what we are eating was once part of a living creature.

In any case, I was able to forget about this and enjoy another tasty meal. I imagine that the bill was much higher than it had been for lunch on Lamma Island, but I did not get a chance to tot up the damage. Uncle Sydney had won the fierce battle for the right to pay on this occasion.

*   *   *

We spent most of the following day at Victoria Peak, which is one of Hong Kong's most popular tourist attractions. Before starting our journey to what is usually referred to as The Peak, we made a detour in order to ride an escalator. I can assure you that we had not lost our sanity; I just wanted to experience the world's longest outdoor covered escalator system.

We made use of our Octopus cards by taking the MTR to the bustling Central district, from where we could travel 800 metres to the residential Mid-Levels Neighbourhood. Opened in the early 1990s, the system was intended to ease congestion at street level and offer an easier route up and down the hilly terrain. In addition to offering a useful service to commuters, it has since become a quirky tourist attraction. It is estimated that between 60,000 and 80,000 people use the escalator system each day. It is free to ride, which was the most important thing for a cheapskate like me.

"Let's do this!" I enthusiastically said to Mum as we began our journey. It did not take long for the novelty to wear off and for me to realise that we had travelled here simply to stand on a crowded escalator for twenty minutes. About a minute into our journey, I discovered that this was not one continuous escalator, but a series of them that form a connected route above street level. I felt cheated! My disappointment increased after I noticed the absence of an escalator travelling in the opposite direction.

"How are we going to get back down?" I asked Mum.

She pointed to the staircase and said: "We will walk."

This soul-destroying news made me question the wisdom of my plan. The prospect of standing still for twenty minutes whilst the escalator slowly transported us to the highest point, and then immediately walking back down was absurd.

"People can get off at various points along the route, so we don't have to travel the whole way up," Mum suggested.

Channelling my warrior spirit, I declared: "We've come this far, we cannot turn back now."

Incidentally, the escalators travel downwards prior to ten o'clock in the morning, as most commuters are heading towards the Central district. We inched our way past the bars of Lan Kwai Fong and Jamia Mosque during our riveting, adrenaline-pumping journey. There must have been around twenty escalators, but it felt like a thousand by the time we had reached the top. We had conquered the world's longest outdoor covered escalator system! Maybe one day I will be recounting such glorious moments to younger family members.

The journey back down the staircase was much quicker, albeit tougher on our joints. It was a short walk to one of the Peak Tram stations. We had gone up an escalator then immediately walked back down the stairs; now we were going to catch a tram that would take us beyond the Mid-Levels to Victoria Peak. At least I was gaining a better understanding of what it must feel like to be a yo-yo.

I had noticed that there seemed to be Filipinas and Indonesian women everywhere we had passed since we left our apartment, which had not been the case on any other day.

"Is there a special event within the migrant community happening today?" I asked Mum.

"No, it is like this every Sunday."

"Why?"

"The maids in Hong Kong are usually immigrants, with most coming from Indonesia and the Philippines. They have a hard life, working six days a week. Most of them have Sundays off, so they congregate with their friends," Mum explained.

I pondered what life must be like for these domestic helpers. Not only do they work more or less every hour of the day for six days a week, but Hong Kong law states that they must live with their employer. At least most of us can escape our boss each evening and weekend; imagine living in a small room in their house!

With their families still in their home country, Sundays are the only opportunity to see their friends and have some fun. However, when you are paid less than the minimum wage, from which you send most of your money back to your family, and you do not have your own home, you have little choice but to gather in public spaces. Consequently, 300,000 of these women spend most of the week hidden away in their employers' apartments; on Sundays, however, they can be seen wherever you look.

The sight of so many of them sat on cardboard or blankets on any available space, including along the pavement, was a shock to my system. It felt like they represented an intermediate level between the homeless and the rest of Hong Kong society. Most seemed to be accepting of their situation, as they used this time to chat with friends and communicate with loved ones back home via Skype. I noticed that many were taking great pleasure in sharing plastic tubs of food. This makes sense, as they tend to eat whatever food they prepare for their employers for six days of the week, but on Sundays they get to indulge in food from their homeland.

Recently, many domestic helpers have used Sundays to protest the conditions that they are often subjected to. There have been harrowing accounts of physical and mental abuse, as well as the lack of workers' rights. It certainly made me grateful of my life in England. I look forward to a couple of days off each weekend when I can go to the theatre or a nice restaurant. These workers were simply happy to temporarily escape their employers' home, even if this meant sitting on cardboard in the street.

The Peak Tram offers the most direct route to Victoria Peak, which at over 550 metres above sea level is the highest point on Hong Kong Island. It also provides passengers with splendid views over the harbour and the city. This historic funicular railway is a legacy of British colonial rule, with the service having been open to the public since 1888. Its original purpose was to provide transportation for the residents of Victoria Peak, who tended to be wealthy British families desperate to escape the chaos of the city.

The construction of the funicular railway is considered to have been a revolutionary feat of engineering that was unlike anything previously built in Asia. Alexander Findlay Smith had travelled around Europe and North America whilst learning about various aspects of mountain railway projects that could be incorporated into his design. There were many doubters, but the distinctive red trams have successfully transported people up and down Victoria Peak, initially powered by steam before the switch to electric motors, for over 130 years.

Upon arrival at the station, it was apparent that we would have to wait a considerable amount of time before we became the latest people to ascend The Peak via this form of transportation. Perhaps a visit to one of Hong Kong's most popular tourist attractions on a Sunday was not the best idea.

Mum and I were stood in the queue with the sun beating down on us for what felt like an eternity. We spent over two hours waiting; we could have had several rides on the world's longest outdoor covered escalator system during that time! What a waste!

It felt rather exciting when we finally got to board one of the iconic trams. The journey was as scenic as I had hoped it would be, with the occasional gap in our lush surroundings providing a glimpse of the city below. It was only when we were travelling on the tram that I realised how steep the incline was, further underlining how impressive it had been to have completed this project in the nineteenth century. The only disappointment was that the journey lasted less than ten minutes. We had spent over two hours queueing for an eight-minute journey!

We alighted at the upper terminus within the Peak Tower. The unusual shape of the building, which houses a shopping centre, a viewing platform and a Madame Tussauds, became apparent once we stepped outside. The top section looked like a boat that was resting upon the central tower, but it is apparently supposed to resemble a wok.

There was a replica funicular tram in the public space near the tower but given that we had just experienced the real thing, we had no desire to inspect it at close quarters. Instead, we decided to check out the Peak Circle Walk, which is a 3.5-kilometre hiking trail that loops around the hill. As we made our way along the route, there were several approaches to large houses that caught our attention.

"Rich British people used to live up here during the colonial era. They would be situated above us Chinese, but now there are lots of wealthy locals who reside in these properties," Mum proudly stated.

The walk was pleasant and not too taxing. It took around an hour to complete the trail, but we could have done it quicker if I had not stopped to take so many photographs. It was a shame that it was so misty that the city was barely visible. This was not unexpected, given the level of air-pollution that exists in this part of the world.

We returned to the Peak Tower, where we briefly browsed the shops. A travel book caught my eye; actually, it was *The Travel Book*. No, I am not talking about *The Adventures of an Introvert* by David R.Y.W. Chapman; this was Lonely Planet's latest offering that covered every country on Earth. I resisted the urge to purchase a copy, mainly because I would have to carry this huge book around with me for the rest of the day.

After a week of Chinese cuisine, I fancied some junk food. McDonald's was the obvious place for this, so we headed straight for the golden arches. There was no sign of any McRefugees, but I guess that homeless people are less likely to be taking up temporary residence upon a hill that is hundreds of metres above sea level, where the houses are ludicrously expensive and hidden away from the public. I noticed some interesting items on the menu, including rice and noodles, but I stuck to the standard fare of a Big Mac and fries. I did spice things up with some wasabi salt though. It is always strangely satisfying to see the different options available in McDonald's restaurants around the world. In case you were wondering, the wasabi salt was delicious.

After dinner, we made our way to the top of the tower where Sky Terrace 428 is located. It is the tallest viewing platform on Hong Kong Island; unsurprisingly, it is 428 metres above sea level. Darkness had not yet descended, so I was able to take some photographs of the city in natural light, and then a short while later, whilst the cityscape was being lit up by electricity.

We were in the most photographed spot in Hong Kong, and I seemed to be taking the most photographs of any person in Hong Kong. The terrace was heaving with fellow tourists, all vying for the best position for taking pictures. The view was beautiful, but it was difficult to capture a high-quality image due to the lack of natural light. Although there was a professional photographer on hand, I was too much of a cheapskate to pay for his services.

"It is just a tourist trap," I declared.

I would regret that decision, as I would have to wait until my next visit to Hong Kong before I was able to acquire a perfect photograph of the two of us stood in front of one of the most impressive views in Asia. Thankfully, we did not have to wait another two hours for the tram journey back down from The Peak. It had been a wonderful day, even if we had spent a considerable amount of time standing on elevators and in queues.

*   *   *

Fiona had used most of the week to catch up with old friends in Hong Kong, but my cousin spent the following day with me. She decided that there were a couple of places that she would like to visit in the Nathan Road area. Despite her being a few years my junior, she was more streetwise, more familiar with Hong Kong and had a better grasp of the Cantonese language. Basically, she was an adult, whereas I had the social skills of a teenager.

As we travelled through the city, I contemplated how Hong Kong is a place of contrasting fortunes. There are lavish skyscrapers surrounded by rundown residential buildings. The streets are often dirty, but tourist hotspots are usually kept in pristine condition. I had already discovered how the housing market affects those on either side of the financial spectrum.

The first place which Fiona wanted to visit offered a glimpse of life for those who I had not previously paid much consideration. Many people emigrate to the financial powerhouse of Hong Kong in order to make money. For Europeans and Americans, this usually means a well-paid job within banking or the international business sector. For those who have travelled here from poorer nations in Africa and South Asia, however, the reality is completely different.

Chungking Mansions was completed in 1961, with the subsequent decades seeing the building complex develop into a hub for ethnic minorities. The black and gold sign above the main entrance resembled that of a casino, which led me to the conclusion that the place was going to be more presentable than Fiona had previously indicated. She saw that I was still a little apprehensive, so she attempted to reassure me: "It will be really interesting to see this unique place. It is supposed to be relatively safe…I think."

Passing on second-hand knowledge that is was "relatively safe," and showing little conviction in her assertion, did little to ease my anxiety. Still, I put my trust in her as we entered the building. It immediately felt like we had been transported to a market in Africa. There were stalls in every direction as far as I could see, with the goods on offer varying from clothing, food, jewellery, and an assortment of traditional African and South Asian products. One of the most striking aspects was the contrast between the ethnic background of people here compared to the rest of Hong Kong, where just under ninety-five per cent of people identify as being ethnic Chinese. In Chungking Mansions, however, the situation is reversed, with the vast majority of people being immigrants of some description. It is often said that this place is like a separate city within Hong Kong.

Many of the vendors approached us and presented their sales pitch, which often included items such as a 'copy watch.' This was perhaps not the best place to be window shopping.

"So, is this place a market?" I asked Fiona.

"This section is, but thousands of people live in the floors above. There are some backpackers, but most are immigrants, both legal and illegal. It has also become synonymous with crime, mostly drug dealing I think."

It appeared that Fiona had completely abandoned any attempts to reassure me of our safety. She was correct though; there are numerous guesthouses that offer an affordable place to stay in a region where property prices and traditional hotel fares are out of reach for many. Crammed together within this crowded complex, the residents experience unsanitary conditions and live with the knowledge that the place is a firetrap. The authorities reviewed public safety regulations following a fire in 1988 that resulted in the death of a Danish tourist, but it had still seemed extremely hazardous during our brief visit.

It is estimated that around 10,000 people pass through the building each day, with many of them purchasing goods or food from the stalls that Fiona and I were browsing. With an influx of immigrants travelling from all over the world to make a living there, Chunking Mansions has been described as an example of 'low-end globalisation.'

Many of the vendors are working illegally due to their immigration status and the nature of the goods that they sell, which helps to keep the prices lower than one would find outside of the complex. Whilst most people here are just trying to make enough money to support their family, there are some who take advantage of this chaotic place to sell drugs in the hidden corners of the building. Part me of was fascinated by this melting pot of different cultures; however, the sheer number of people gathered in an unfamiliar and somewhat unsafe setting was enough to make me feel uncomfortable.

Fiona agreed: "I am not sure that I want to explore any further. We will leave now. There are some old trees nearby."

I ignored the fact that the prospect of visiting some "old trees" hardly filled me with excitement, as I was just relieved to be leaving this chaotic place. Fiona had been referring to the Banyan Trees that line a section of Nathan Road near Kowloon Mosque and the Former Kowloon British School. These large trees offer shade from the intense afternoon sun, as well as the opportunity to admire their beauty. I found the above-ground roots of the trees to be fascinating, as they seemed to have spread and twisted across anything that was close by. There were concrete platforms and brick walls that were covered by the sprawling roots of the Banyan Trees.

We visited Times Square later that evening. In case you are wondering, I am not capable of teleportation and I have not forgotten which city I am writing about. Sharing a name with the famous square in New York, this is in fact a luxury shopping centre and office tower complex in Causeway Bay. The location was once considered undesirable, but the redeveloped area is now coveted.

As Mum and I exited the MTR station, it was immediately noticeable how this shopping centre differed from the typical model found in Western countries. Like most places in Hong Kong, space is hard to come by and land prices are high; therefore, the decision to configure the retail space over nine storeys makes perfect sense. Tower One, the tallest of the two, consists of forty-six floors, with most of the space used for offices.

The area may not be as eye-catching as Times Square in New York, but the artificial lighting under the darkness of night and the steady flow of distinctive red and white Hong Kong taxis presented some decent photographic opportunities. I found the interior of the shopping centre to be lacking in character. It had a modern and clinical look that matched up with its high-end target audience, but it felt like we could have been anywhere in the world. The endless series of escalators and sheer number of visitors was also unappealing to me.

Night markets are a prominent feature of Hong Kong culture, with many people gathering in these bustling open-air spaces to shop, eat, sing and partake in a wide range of activities such as fortune-telling. The markets now attract plenty of tourists who are keen to sample this vibrant atmosphere. Mum and I visited Ladies' Market in Mong Kok, which is one of the most famous marketplaces in Hong Kong.

Mong Kok, which loosely translates as 'crowded corner,' has an extremely high population density and it is the busiest district in the world according to *Guinness World Records*. A heaving market within the busiest district in the world is hardly my idea of heaven, but I was nevertheless interested in experiencing this iconic bazaar. The stalls have traditionally sold ladies' clothing and accessories; hence, the name.

One can now also find menswear, jewellery, electronics, food, toys and souvenirs. We noticed that there was a fair amount of counterfeit goods on offer too. I had no intention of buying anything, which was probably for the best since I have a deep-rooted fear of bartering. I would most likely have paid whatever extortionate price was first quoted, which would even have shocked the vendors.

As I was preparing to leave the market, Mum spotted something of interest: one stall was selling traditional Chinese male clothing. After a brief discussion with the vendor, Mum purchased a 'changshan' for me and another for my brother. Traditionally, these jackets are made from silk, but I am not sure what fabric was used for our cheap garments. My jacket was reversible, with one side black and the other gold. I still have mine, although I have only worn it once for a fancy-dress party.

We heard some people singing, which prompted Mum to ask: "Would you like to go to Temple Street Market? It is not far from here. It is famous for people singing Cantonese opera."

"OK, that sounds interesting," I replied.

My willingness to visit another market shows how my mindset switches to tourist-mode whenever I am abroad. I would never have agreed to this back in Manchester! This was a smaller market, but we were only here for the singing. I began to worry that I would be expected to join in. Thankfully, this was not the case.

Instead, we joined our fellow tourists by filming those who were singing their hearts out. The skill level at the markets varies from individuals just wanting to enjoy themselves to aspiring amateur artists who are honing their talent. Apparently, some professional opera singers performed here before their careers had taken off. I did not have a clue as to what they were singing about, but I enjoyed the spectacle, nevertheless. It was a pleasant way to end our final day in Hong Kong before the next leg of our Asian adventure. The Land of the Rising Sun awaited us in the morning.

CHAPTER 12: A HI-TECH TOILET AND A CHAOTIC CROSSING
TOKYO, JAPAN
NOVEMBER 2012

Given the fascinating history and culture of the country, I had wanted to visit Japan for a long time. It had been isolated from the rest of the world for most of its existence, retaining a strong sense of tradition that is unique to this nation. We have all seen countless films depicting samurai, ninjas, shoguns and geishas. The distinctive attire and customs had been ingrained in my mind for many years prior to our trip to Japan's capital city; I just hoped that we would be able to see a glimpse of this in the modern metropolis of Tokyo.

Japan's engagement with the wider world increased in the twentieth century, with the Imperial regime setting its sights on replicating Western powers by invading other countries. This dark period of the country's history, which of course culminated in the Second World War, was followed by sustained growth, peace and prosperity. I had an image of Japan as a place where cutting-edge technology was developed, which added a futuristic element to a country that retained so much of its history and culture.

The flight from Hong Kong to Tokyo took around four hours. I had become accustomed to being told by security staff at various airports around the world that family members could approach the passport control desk as one group; therefore, I displayed a rare moment of confidence by walking up to a border patrol booth alongside Mum in Narita International Airport. I was immediately reprimanded for doing this, with a stern looking Japanese officer pointing towards the sign that read: 'Approach the desk one at a time.' This reinforced my belief that I should avoid showing any hint of assertiveness and that I should continue my introverted ways.

We took the train to Shinjuku, where our hotel was located. Unfortunately, this was not one of Japan's famous bullet trains, so our journey took around an hour. Upon alighting, it was clear that we had arrived at a huge and chaotic station. Just as you would expect in a transport hub that has been recognised as the world's busiest by *Guinness World Records*, people were scurrying about in all directions. In what was to be a recurring theme of our stay in Tokyo, finding the required route out of the station proved to be a laborious task. There are over two hundred exits in total! After multiple failed attempts, we decided to leave the station through the next opening, regardless of whether it was the one we needed, then try to find our way from there.

Walking at a steady pace, it took less than ten minutes to reach the Keio Plaza Hotel. Although they were not joining us on the trip, Uncle Sydney and Rosalie had arranged our flights and accommodation. Having stayed in a nice hotel that they had selected for us in Macao, we had a good idea that it was going to be of high quality.

Our room, which was about thirty floors up, was undoubtedly better than what we would have ended up with if I had been tasked with organising our trip. It was not the pleasant décor, the plasma television or the comfortable beds that grabbed my attention. It was the toilet. This was not because I was suffering from food poisoning and in dire need of using the facilities; rather, it was because this appeared to be a toilet that had been sent back in time from some point in the distant future.

"Mum, the toilet has a remote controller!" I shouted with far too much enthusiasm.

"The Japanese are renowned for their ingenuity. You seem to be impressed!"

"I have never seen a toilet like this! This button warms the seat, this one sprays water like a bidet..."

As I was waxing lyrical, the toilet lid lifted when I stepped closer to it. The magnitude of what had just occurred caused me to halt my description of this futuristic bathroom appliance.

"The toilet has motion sensors! John would love this!" I declared. I was referring to my brother, which was quite fitting given his name.

I took a series of photographs and videos that I knew John would appreciate. The ancient shrines and modern skyscrapers of Tokyo would have to wait; my focus was locked in on a toilet. I can only imagine what anyone would have thought if they had gained possession of my phone and browsed through my photos and videos.

After seeing all of the available functions, there was no way that I was going to pass urine in the traditional masculine way. Instead, I put the lid back down, retreated and then stepped forward so that it automatically lifted. I sat down, pressed the seat-warming button and wondered how I had previously coped without this. After flushing the toilet using the remote controller, I marvelled at the possibility of going to the toilet without having to touch anything with one's hands, other than the controller. Mind you, who knows how many germs were living on that. I never thought that I would be giving a play-by-play account of using a toilet in a book that is available for the whole world to read! Although the pessimist in me doubts that much of the world's population will be reading this anyway.

We noticed that the Tokyo Metropolitan Government Building was directly opposite the hotel. I had read that there was an observation deck that tourists could visit without charge. The building, which has two towers that give it the shape of a typical Gothic cathedral, was the tallest in Tokyo until 2007.

"Do you fancy going there after dinner tonight?" I asked.

"Yes, that would be nice. I will leave the itinerary up to you."

Looking out of a hotel room window high above the city made me think of the film *Lost in Translation*. I could see on our map that the Park Hyatt hotel and the New York Bar, which were places that the lead characters played by Bill Murray and Scarlett Johansson visited, were within walking distance. I pondered whether to add these swanky locations to our itinerary, but ultimately decided against it. Instead, I consoled myself with the knowledge that most of what we said to locals during our stay here would indeed be lost in translation.

Mum and I headed out into this heaving metropolis in search of dinner whilst using the excursion to gain our bearings of the surrounding area. A truck pulled up by the side of the road. It was either owned by One Direction's biggest fan or it was being used to advertise the teen pop group. As the vehicle was adorned with a huge poster advertising tour dates and it had music blasting out at a dangerously high volume, I decided it was the latter. I must have been out of touch with modern pop culture, as I remember feeling surprised to learn that some kids who were on a British reality show were now global superstars. Back then, I would have scoffed at the notion of a reality television star becoming President of the United States of America. Now I just cry.

Continuing the theme of globalisation and the prevalence of Western culture in this Asian city, I noticed that we had already walked past a couple of 7-Eleven stores. We had also seen plenty of them in Hong Kong. Despite its American origin, the chain of convenience stores was bought by a Japanese company in 2005. This explained why there were so many of their stores in this part of the world. Indeed, there are more 7-Eleven's in Japan than in any other country.

Having spent our first evening obsessing over a toilet, One Direction and 7-Eleven, I was determined to find a restaurant that at least resembled some aspect of Japanese culture. Thankfully, there were lots of sushi bars to choose from. We entered a reasonable-looking establishment that had caught my eye due to its clever use of limited space. Just as I had seen on television, diners were sat around the bar whilst a chef prepared their food in front of them. I noticed that many of the patrons were dining alone, which for some reason added to the charm. The idea of individuals popping in for some sushi on the way home from work was strangely endearing. Perhaps I am just odd.

We sat on a couple of stools by the bar and performed the standard greeting of a gentle nod of the head. The chef guided his hand along the counter display of various sushi, indicating to us that there was a wide range of tasty treats on offer. I was just pleased that we had gotten this far without having to verbally communicate with anyone. We pointed at a few items and asked for tea whilst performing hand gestures that were supposed to represent drinking from a cup. He seemed to understand our request and started preparing this for us. By this point, it must have been clear to him that we were of Chinese origin rather than Japanese. Either that or he thought that we were not of sound mind.

Sushi, which translates as 'sour-tasting,' has become popular around the world in recent decades. We enjoyed our rolls of seafood, rice and seaweed, but I was not so keen on the sashimi that Mum ordered. My palate had developed considerably during my travels, but it was not sophisticated enough to appreciate these thinly sliced cuts of raw fish. I resorted to the childish tactic of smothering the undesirable food item with a condiment. In this case, it was wasabi, which resulted in an intense burning sensation in my nose. It was like consuming a spoonful of English mustard!

The conclusion of our dining experience involved asking for the bill by making the universal hand gesture of signing a cheque. I always feel like an ignorant buffoon whenever I do this, but it does seem to be the quickest way of cutting through any communication issues. Otherwise, we could have ended up with another pot of tea.

The ten-minute stroll to the Tokyo Metropolitan Government Building allowed us to walk off our dinner before visiting one of the observation decks. There is one in each tower, but I am unable to recall which of them we ascended. In any case, we were treated to a spectacular view of the bright lights of the city under the darkness of night. Most importantly, it was free.

"We will be exploring this metropolis over the next few days," I stated.

"You are responsible for navigating our way around the city. I trust you."

Mum seemed to have more faith in my abilities than was warranted. I had become comfortable during our time in Asia, as I had let her, or our relatives and friends, plan the itinerary. Now it was my turn. As usual, I felt excited but also nervous. I was determined to see as much of Tokyo as possible during our brief stay, and I was aware that it was up to me to ensure that this occurred.

As we passed some payphones in the hotel lobby on our way back to our room, one of the multilingual signs caught my eye. It referred to business hours of, if my memory is correct, six o'clock in the morning until ten o'clock at night.

"Do Japanese people work such long hours?!" I asked Mum.

"I don't think so, but they do a lot of overtime."

She was right. Most employees generally work the standard nine to five shift pattern that we are used to in Western society, but there is a much greater expectation that they undertake a large amount of overtime. According to a 2016 government survey, nearly a quarter of Japanese companies required employees to work more than eighty additional hours per month, often unpaid.

It is not just a case of employers cracking the whip; employees have been conditioned to take on a personal responsibility for their work. Another study found that many Japanese workers do not use all of their annual leave, and often feel guilty when they take holidays. There is even a Japanese word called 'karoshi,' which translates as 'death by overwork.' This is a recognised legal term that can be attributed to a cause of death. Whilst this word generally refers to sudden deaths such as heart attacks and strokes, the mental toll of this lifestyle has been equally devastating.

This is just one of many reasons why Japan has one of the highest suicide rates of any developed country. In addition to the issues of overworking and isolation, other contributary factors appear to include the traditional belief that there is often honour in taking one's own life rather than burdening others, and the fact that complaining is not regarded as being part of Japanese culture. For context, the suicide rate is around three times higher than the comparative figure for the United Kingdom.

A famous example of a work-related suicide occurred in 2015 when an employee of a major advertising firm took her own life. She had allegedly been forced to work one hundred hours of overtime per month, which contributed to her depression. Such tragic events have led to a recognition that this culture of overworking needs to change. This has been reflected by the introduction of extra public holidays, and regulation requiring employees to take a certain number of holidays and time off between shifts.

We watched some television upon returning to our room. The news reports covered various world events such as the fallout from Barack

Obama's re-election and an escalation of the violence in Syria. I will spare you from another play-by-play account of my toilet-related activities.

* * *

Mum and I returned to Shinjuku Station the following morning with the intention of travelling to the Shibuya area. We faced the problem of trying to figure out which train we required whilst overcoming the language barrier. There are fifty-three platforms that cater to the various transport networks that operate out of the station, so finding the correct one was not going to be straightforward. I tried my best to avoid any human interaction, but I was unable to conclusively work out which train we required. Unfortunately, this meant that we had to ask a member of staff.

"Will you ask?" I suggested to Mum.

I am unsure if this request was due to my usual shyness, or whether I inexplicably expected Mum to be able to communicate in Japanese better than I could merely because she was fluent in Cantonese and Mandarin.

"I think you should ask. It will be good for your character," Mum replied.

Great. She had chosen this moment to give me a nudge into behaving like an adult. I gingerly approached one of the booths within the ticket office and tried to summon the courage to complete this impossible assignment.

"We are planning on travelling to Shibuya, then travel to Harajuku and some other areas later. I am unsure which train to get. Please can you advise?"

The elderly gentleman behind the Perspex screen stared at me without displaying a hint of emotion. It was clear that he did not have a clue what I was saying. This was always a likely scenario given that less than thirty per cent of Japanese people are able to communicate in English. I had travelled extensively across the world, but the one time that I was being forced to verbally communicate with someone was in a country where few people spoke my language. My ignorance and laziness had led me to rely on enough people speaking English wherever I travelled to, but it was coming back to haunt me now.

"You are being too detailed. I spent several years working as an interpreter, so I am used to communicating with people who only have a basic grasp of a language. It is best to just say the essential words and be direct," Mum advised.

She could see my distress, so she jumped in to save her beloved son.

"Shibuya. Two tickets," Mum said to the ticket office employee.

After being handed our tickets in exchange for a few hundred Japanese Yen, Mum asked one more question.

"Where?"

The man pointed in the general direction of the JR Yamanote line. Thankfully, this is a circuit that runs both clockwise and anticlockwise. We were down to two out of fifty-three possibilities.

Mum and I followed the signage until we reached the platforms that served the JR Yamanote line. We decided to board the train that had just arrived, knowing that we had a fifty-fifty chance of having to go the long way round the circuit. Fortunately, it was soon clear that we only had to travel the shorter distance, which would take around ten minutes.

I was also pleased that although the service was busy, it was nowhere near as crowded as it can get. Prior to our trip, I had seen videos of the employees who are tasked with pushing people onto overcrowded trains. If you are attempting to board a service that is already running far beyond its capacity, an individual wearing white gloves may well push you onto the train. This has become less prevalent during the last couple of decades, with the expanded transport networks helping to ease congestion. There is no need to be alarmed if someone pushes you whilst you are on a train platform in Japan, but it would be more worrying if this happened in England! It would most likely be a football hooligan trying to cause harm to a rival club's supporter!

We alighted at Shibuya Station, which has a couple of attractions that have been immortalised in popular culture. We were soon stood by one of them. Along with a crowd of fellow tourists, we were admiring the Hachikō statue. This beloved landmark depicts the Akita dog that has become part of Japanese folklore. Hachikō is said to have been adopted by Professor Eizaburo Ueno in the early 1920s.

The professor would be accompanied by his loyal companion as he made his way to Shibuya Station each morning before he undertook his daily commute to Tokyo Imperial University. Hachikō would then be waiting for his master when he arrived back at the station. After Ueno suffered a fatal cerebral haemorrhage whilst at work in 1925, his loyal dog still turned up at the station every day to greet him. Undeterred by this daily disappointment, Hachikō is said to have continued to do this until his own death in 1935.

The story of this faithful dog is often used as an example of loyalty that is held in high regard in Japanese culture. There have been numerous films made about this tragic yet heartwarming turn of events. The legend spread globally, eventually resulting in a Hollywood remake featuring Richard Gere. My wife cried her eyes out upon watching *Hachi: A Dog's Tale*. Although I did not shed any tears, I was a gibbering wreck inside.

I patiently waited for my turn to pose alongside Hachikō whilst Mum took my photograph. The irony is that I would not have gone near him in real life, as I am allergic to dog and cat hair. At least if the dog were real, my allergies would have served as a good excuse if I finally succumbed to emotion and tears began streaming from my eyes.

A couple of hundred metres away from the statue, the most famous spectacle in Shibuya, and one of the most well-known in Japan, was unfolding in front of our eyes. Huge waves of human beings were moving in all directions in what was one of the most chaotic scenes that I had ever witnessed. Shibuya Crossing is the world's most recognisable scramble crossing.

In addition to the standard four pedestrian crossings that form a square, there is a diagonal crossing. Like any other scramble crossing, the traffic lights are coordinated so that all vehicles passing through the area come to a halt at the same time, allowing pedestrians to cross in all directions. This was just on a ridiculous scale. It has been reported that up to 2,500 people cross every few minutes when the ten lanes of traffic are waiting behind red signals. The daily average for people using the crossing is over two million!

Scramble crossings are not as common as they once were, with many people feeling that they lead to traffic congestion due to the long delays whilst all vehicles are stationary. Supporters of this type of crossing cite the increased safety that they bring due to the simple system of only pedestrians or vehicles being permitted to cross the intersection at any given time. One thing that must be considered when deciding whether to introduce such a system is that there needs to be enough space on the pavement for the build-up of pedestrians every few minutes. People are also required to strictly follow the rules for it to remain safe.

From what I saw, this was not an issue at Shibuya Crossing, as waiting for your turn to cross appeared to be part of this novel experience. My excitement levels increased as each second went by, knowing that it would soon be time to cross this wonderful junction. The huge electronic advertising screens above street level reminded me of Times Square in New York and Piccadilly Circus in London. The flow of vehicles ceased, then it was time to go! Of course, we had chosen the most glamorous option of using the diagonal crossing. Even though we were walking, it felt like we were being swept along by a stream of people.

I had planned on taking some photographs of us crossing, but there was little chance of that. Instead, I lifted my camera above my head and took as many photos as possible, hoping that some would turn out well. I inspected the images, but whilst some were of an acceptable standard, none of them truly captured the chaos that had unfolded around us.

Fortunately, I had read that the best view of Shibuya Crossing can be found within the huge Starbucks that is situated next to the scramble. We ordered a couple of cappuccinos and headed upstairs. I was surprised and delighted to see that a couple were just leaving their window seats as we entered. We had caught a lucky break, as I had read that it can be difficult to grab the seats that directly overlook Shibuya Crossing. It is well-known that people come here for the view; the coffee is just a bonus. Starbucks will not care, as they are guaranteed a constant flow of customers. We took up our coveted position facing the window, whilst feeling the glare of those not fortunate enough to have walked straight into this opportunity.

"The view is as good as I had hoped it would be," I commented.

"Yes, you can see it all unfolding from here. We were amongst the chaos just a few minutes ago, and now we can watch it from our comfortable position."

I became conscious of voicing our pleasure too loudly. Instead, I got my camera out and waited for the madness to resume. I felt the excitement building up, even though we were merely spectators this time. The flow of vehicles came to a halt, and after a brief pause, the mass of pedestrians hurtled across the intersection in all directions. Perhaps citizens of Tokyo were not such big fans of One Direction after all! It felt like I was watching a time-lapse sequence, but this was happening in real-time, right before our eyes.

I took as many photographs and videos as I could before the traffic lights brought an end to this temporary human mass migration. A woman took up the next available window seat, which happened to be beside us. She noticed the camera in my hand and the look of enthrallment that was written all over my face.

"Every time that I arrive in Tokyo, I start by coming here and taking in this view. It is nice to have a coffee and witness this crazy scene," She informed us.

"It is a strange but wonderful thing to watch," Mum replied.

"I am from the Netherlands. How about you?"

"England," I replied. I think that short response fulfilled my minimum obligation to engage in conversation.

"People come from all over the world to sit in a Starbucks!" the woman said with a chuckle.

We laughed then prepared for the next wave of pedestrians. I am unsure of how many times I repeated the cycle of taking photographs and videos every few minutes, but I know that I sipped my coffee so slowly that it was cold by the end of our stay. Our seats were snapped up within seconds of us making our move towards the exit.

The Harajuku district was only a ten-minute walk from Shibuya Crossing. This part of the city is regarded as being a representation of Japanese youth culture, with fashionable and quirky boutiques nestled between high-end retail outlets. I had my doubts as to whether I would fit in with this trendy scene, especially whilst I was being accompanied by my mother. It was a scenario that was rather reminiscent of my teenage years!

Takeshita Street may sound like an ominous name for English-speaking visitors, but it is one of the most fashionable streets in the Japanese capital. Upon arrival, it was clear that it was far too popular for my liking. Although the street was only a few hundred metres long, it was jam-packed with colourful stalls, cafes and clothing shops.

Apparently, this is one of the key locations of Kawaii. This refers to a culture of cuteness that can be applied to people and material goods. Whilst teenagers in Western society often aim to appear 'grown up,' a large proportion of the youth of Japan have a long history of adopting the image associated with a child. Teenagers and young adults in England generally hate being told that they are cute, but this is taken as a compliment in Japan. Even pop stars appreciate being given this label. Cuddly toys, Hello Kitty merchandise and the prevalence of pink items of clothing are aspects of the Kawaii culture, which has outgrown Japan's borders to become a global subculture.

The way that teenagers, and even adults, dress can be striking. The image of Japanese women wearing schoolgirl attire is well-known throughout the world, although there are many other styles that are part of this culture. Lolita fashion, which is inspired by the Victorian period, sees women attempt to achieve the porcelain doll look. It is also common for men to adopt Kawaii culture by wearing makeup and false eyelashes, and by shaving their legs. It was safe to say that Mum and I were not here for a makeover!

If we had been looking to dive right into Kawaii culture, we could have made our way over to Kiddy Land. This multi-storey building in Harajuku has been supplying the people of Tokyo with character goods since the 1950s. I guess that the world needed more cuteness after the horrors that it had just endured. This iconic store sells a plethora of items that depict characters featured in Pokémon, Manga, Hello Kitty and just about any animated range you can think of.

We could also have gone to Cat Street, which has a quieter, chicer vibe than Takeshita. It has nothing to do with anything feline, but given that I am allergic to cats, the name alone was enough to put me off visiting. It was probably for the best, as there was nothing chic about my style back then. Or now.

We visited the nearby Meiji Shrine, which is, unsurprisingly, a shrine to Emperor Meiji and Empress Shōken. It was completed and dedicated to their deified spirits in 1920, eight years after Meiji's passing. The country was modernised under his rule, increasing its engagement with the wider world and becoming a global power in the process.

We were not visiting the original shrine, as this was destroyed during the air raids on Tokyo during the Second World War. Due to some of the horrific actions of the Japanese Imperial regime, people often ignore the fact that its capital city suffered extensive damage during the war. Operation Meetinghouse is the single most destructive bombing raid in human history. Sixteen square miles of central Tokyo were destroyed during one night in March 1945. Around 100,000 people were killed, many of whom were civilians, with a further one million made homeless.

The devastation caused by events such as Operation Meetinghouse, and the atomic bombing of Hiroshima and Nagasaki that killed up to 250,000 people and left many suffering from the effects of the radiation, is often ignored by those outside of Japan. There is almost a feeling that people are not allowed to mourn the casualties in the same manner that other nations grieve the loss of their loved ones during the war. Another reason why talking about such tragic events is often avoided can be explained by the traditional Japanese belief that it is important not to burden your loved ones. For this reason, many people choose to 'swallow their grief' rather than to talk to their family about their suffering.

The subject of the bombing of Japan is rather delicate, with many people in Asia, and the world in general, feeling a certain level of resentment towards the Japanese Imperial regime that leads them to the conclusion that such events were justified. Regardless of the sins committed by those who were in power within Japan, one must feel an incredible sadness for the suffering caused by these devastating events. The fact that their deaths are treated differently because of this makes it even more tragic.

We entered through a Torii, which is a traditional gate that is often found at the entrance, and within the grounds, of a Shinto shrine. This wooden Torii has one of the standard shapes consisting of two tall pillars, a horizontal crossbar, and another bar that dips in the centre. Forgive my rather clumsy description, for I am not a Torii expert. Anyway, they are regarded as the gateways to the home of the gods.

We were surrounded by trees, which made it hard to believe that we were in one of the busiest cities in the world. The shrine, which is adjacent to Yoyogi Park, is within a forested area that covers seventy hectares. It is thought that around 100,000 trees were planted during the construction of the complex. Perhaps the world needs to build a few more shrines of this nature in order to tackle climate change! Mum and I casually strolled through the grounds until we encountered a large stash of alcohol. We had not discovered the most unlikely location for a Bargain Booze store; rather, we were stood in front of row upon row of beautifully decorated barrels of sake.

This rice wine is not only the national beverage of Japan, but it is seen as connecting its people with their gods. Decorative barrels, such as the ones at Meiji Shrine, are intended to honour the gods and have become a symbol for happiness and prosperity. We noticed a large collection of barrels of Burgundy wine that had been donated from France. I am not sure why they had been given, but a recovering alcoholic may be wise to avoid visiting the shrine!

We passed through numerous other Torii as we made our way towards the centre of the complex. Apparently, the level of holiness of the gates increases as one gets closer to the inner sanctuary of the shrine. We eventually stumbled upon a square that had a tree in its centre. There were hundreds of wooden plaques attached to a stand that enclosed all sides of the tree. On closer inspection, it became apparent that people had written their wishes and prayers on these plaques. Most seemed to be written in Japanese, but there were enough adorned with other languages to indicate that tourists from all over the world had become aware of this tradition.

Apparently, these plaques are known as 'ema,' and are based on the traditional Shinto belief that horses could carry messages to the gods. Ema, which roughly translates as 'picture-horse,' were eventually adopted for practical reasons. This was probably for the best, as the prospect of over 125 million people using horses to carry messages would be rather chaotic! Regardless of my lack of knowledge of this tradition, these beautifully decorated plaques were a charming sight, especially as it was clear that this represented an outpouring of positivity and love from around the world.

Without any warning, a group of children dressed in kimonos and other traditional attire walked past us. I did not know it at the time, but this must have been connected to Shichi-Go-San, which celebrates the traditional rite of passage held in mid-November. This practice, which often involves visiting a shrine for the first time, eventually became to be seen as a way of driving out evil spirits and ensuring a long, healthy life.

No matter how adorable the children looked in their colourful clothing, I could not bring myself to take any photographs of them. The parents were happy for strangers to take pictures of their offspring, as this is often regarded as part of the ritual, but I still felt uncomfortable with the prospect of taking photographs of children.

"You were cuter than them when you were that age," Mum commented, proving that mothers are undoubtedly biased towards their own brood.

The main buildings in the centre of the shrine complex were much quieter and more peaceful than the temples that I had seen in Hong Kong. For this reason, my memory of the shrine is less vivid than of the aforementioned temples, which had been a hive of activity filled with incense and colourful lanterns.

Upon exiting the complex, we took a train to the Chiyoda ward. This is where the grounds of the Imperial Palace, which occupies 1.15 square kilometres of land, can be found. Sadly, the public transport network in Chiyoda was targeted by terrorists in 1995. The Japanese doomsday cult Aum Shinnrikyo carried out a series of coordinated attacks, which involved releasing sarin on three lines of the Tokyo subway during rush hour. Twelve people were killed, with a further fifty severely injured. Nearly a thousand others suffered a temporary problem with their vision after coming into contact with the nerve agent.

Chiyoda is also notable for being the site of several political assassinations and attempted coups, which is not too surprising given that the Imperial Palace occupies most of the ward. I put such deadly events to the back of my mind and led us into the vast palace grounds. I felt that it resembled a city park more than the home of the Emperor. Perhaps that was because the section that we were in was separated from the palace by a moat.

I took some photographs of the visible sections of the palace, which did not look as extravagant as the equivalent buildings that one may encounter in various countries around the world. Its main body has a clean-cut European style whilst some of its elements incorporate traditional Japanese architecture, with its shape resembling a pagoda. Despite its somewhat understated appearance, the palace grounds were once attributed with a higher value than all of the real estate in California put together. This was during the peak of the 1980s Japanese property bubble that saw greatly inflated prices. The bubble eventually burst in the early 1990s, leading to economic stagnation.

Established at the site of the old Edo Castle in 1868, the palace has undergone many changes and suffered extensive damage during its long history, including having a barrage of American bombs dropped on it during the Second World War. The part of the grounds that we were in, the East Gardens, were open to the public. I had been pleasantly surprised that we had already visited two large areas within this hectic metropolis where it was possible to escape the fast pace of city life.

The National Diet of Japan was next on our agenda. I am not referring to a sushi warehouse or a super-charged Slimming World group; this is the main legislature of Japan. The National Diet Building, located just south of the palace grounds, is where the House of Representatives and the House of

Councillors meet. The gates leading to the building were closed, which meant that we had to take photographs through the bars. It may not have made a difference if they were open in any case, considering that the central entrance to the building has such restricted access that it is known as 'the door that never opens.' Perhaps it really was a secretive Slimming World group! Either way, it was yet another diet with an unattainable goal.

It has a similar look to American government buildings, with concrete and granite used during the construction, which was completed in 1936. The most interesting aspect of its external appearance is the pyramid-shaped roof. This was likely influenced by the popularity of European-East Asian hybrid designs at the time.

"Why is it called the National Diet Building?" Mum asked.

This was the opportunity to unleash a joke about dieting in Japan that I had been waiting for.

"It looks like a government building. I bet that is what it is," Mum added; thus, once again scuppering my plans to say something funny.

"Yes, I first encountered this term in Berlin. Diet is taken from Latin and it was once commonly used to describe an assembly. I thought that it was odd when I first heard the word used in this context," I explained.

Like many others, I had not realised that another shrine was close by. Hie Shrine is only a short distance from the National Diet Building, but it is almost hidden in plain sight. The main Torii is located amongst trees that are nestled between the glass-laden city buildings. I was not disappointed about missing out on visiting the shrine itself, as this is a small and modest structure. Apparently, the most delightful aspect of making a trip to the shrine is when one ascends the stairway. This is framed by a series of ninety red Torri that provide visitors with beautiful photographic opportunities. They look nice on Instagram anyway.

After a busy day of sightseeing, we took the train back to our hotel. Over the course of the day, it had become clear that the public transport system of Tokyo was extremely impressive and efficient. Trains always seemed to arrive at the scheduled time, and everything appeared to run smoothly. In order to give an idea of how punctual the trains are in Japan, there have been several apologies made in recent years due to services departing around twenty seconds early. As someone who relies on the rail networks of Britain, this seems incomprehensible. British trains are so unreliable that one can, in what is surely a complete contradiction to the word, come to rely on a service arriving at least five minutes after the scheduled departure time. Therefore, there is no need to panic if you arrive a few minutes late.

Upon our return to Shinjuku Station, however, we were faced with the familiar problem of locating our required exit.

"Logic dictates that it must be somewhere in this general direction. I am confident that we will be in more or less the right place if we use this exit," I proclaimed.

Upon leaving the station, of course, we did not recognise where we were.

"I do not understand how we have ended up here. We may as well just choose any random exit next time. We will have a one-in-two-hundred chance of ending up where we need to be, which doesn't seem any worse than how things have panned out so far!"

"It is very confusing," Mum agreed.

"The station is either some sort of maze or its exits have teleportation devices that transport you to a randomly selected location within Tokyo! In any case, the security guards must be entertained by the regular sight of clueless tourists trying in vain to find their desired exit!"

"Maybe we will get the hang of it by the end of our trip," Mum suggested. I did not share her optimism.

After a delicious meal consisting of yakisoba, which is a fried noodle dish, and some yakitori, which are chicken and vegetable skewers, we headed to Kabukichō. This is Tokyo's most notorious red-light district, which had once garnered the dubious recognition of being Asia's largest adult entertainment district. At the turn of the century, many of the establishments were under Yakuza control. There have been efforts to clean up the area and drive out organised crime during the past couple of decades, with a focus on attracting tourists like us. To what degree this has been achieved is debateable.

The more pressing question that is probably on everyone's mind is: 'Why on earth did you take your Mum to a red-light district that has historical links to the Yakuza?!'

The answer is simple: I saw an impressive picture of the Kabukichō Ichiban-gai gate in my guidebook. I was prepared to deal with any organised crime groups that got in the way of my attempt to recreate the photograph. Well, I was willing to let my Mum give them a telling off! God help them if they dropped any litter on the floor whilst she was around!

A fifteen-minute walk allowed us to burn some of the calories that we had consumed during dinner, as well as giving me the time to contemplate the unlikely possibility that we would encounter a scene that belonged in a grisly crime thriller. In reality, the area looked fairly similar to what we had seen during the last couple of weeks in the Far East. Busy streets and neon lights had become the norm; this was just an enhanced version. More importantly, we were, as far as I could tell, surrounded by tourists rather than violent criminals. At least none that were easily identifiable.

I took the photograph of the famous red gate before we began walking through this vibrant district. Neon lights and video screens were all around us, mostly advertising consumer goods and food. The further we walked, the more I noticed the odd seedy sign. There were some that said things along the lines of 'XXX Girls' and showed pictures of a group of women dressed as schoolgirls. It was hardly Bangla Street in Phuket or De Wallen in Amsterdam, but there were enough reminders that we were in an historically seedy area.

There were people trying to entice passers-by into their establishment with the promise of cheap drinks; however, there was no sign of any prostitutes. That was probably for the best, as I may have died with embarrassment if Mum and I had been approached by a sex worker.

We enjoyed walking through the entertainment district, even if we did not really do anything of note. We did not even visit Omoide Yokocho. This is a narrow street lined with lots of small restaurants and bars that is affectionately known as 'Piss Alley.' Unsurprisingly, this is because one is likely to encounter people passing urine in the street due to the lack of public toilets. With the hi-tech toilets that exist in Japan, why would anyone resort to relieving themselves in the street? I once again seemed to have steered my narrative towards toilet-related activity in Tokyo. I can assure you that there are plenty of other things to do in Japan's capital city!

*   *   *

I had read that it was better to visit the observation deck of Mori Tower rather than ascend the iconic Tokyo Tower. This provided you with the opportunity to take in a view of the city skyline that included the latter. What I had not considered was the geographical position of Mori Tower. It is only a couple of kilometres away from Chiyoda, so we could have included this as part of the previous day's itinerary if I had planned it better. I guess that it can be difficult to plan your activities in an unfamiliar city.

After once again conquering the public transport system and the language barrier, we arrived at Roppongi Hills. This huge complex of offices, restaurants, shops and apartments was developed by building tycoon Minoru Mori; therefore, it is unsurprising that the fifty-four-storey tower that is its centrepiece bears his name.

What was unexpected, and a little unnerving, was the sight of a huge spider at the base of the tower. Thankfully, this thirty-feet-high arachnid was not alive; hence, there was no chance of it wreaking havoc in the city or scaling the tower in a scene reminiscent of one of the numerous *Godzilla* movies. Instead, we were looking at one of Louise Bourgeois' *Maman* sculptures. Other incarnations can be found in London, Bilbao, Doha and various other cities across the world.

I summoned the courage to overcome my arachnophobia by walking between its long legs and gazing up at its abdomen, which had a sac containing over thirty marble eggs. The artist has described how she has used spiders as an ode to her late mother. The strength, skill and cleverness of the spider, combined with its nurturing and protective instincts, are characteristics that she recognised in her mother.

The tower, which is the sixth tallest building in Tokyo, seemed to have been constructed using a lot of steel and glass. To my mind, it did not appear to have many distinguishing features. It contains office space, retail units and restaurants. The highest floors are occupied by the Mori Arts Centre and Art Museum, as well as the Tokyo City View observation deck. We took the elevator up to the latter, where we were immediately presented with a panoramic view of the capital city.

Whilst it had been pleasant to take in a night-time view of Tokyo during our first evening, it was far more interesting to be able to look over the city in daylight. The large windows that encircle it ensure a bright and open feel to the observation deck. With the help of the information boards, we could pick out certain landmarks and gain a better understanding of the layout of the city. The Tokyo Skytree had been completed earlier in the year, replacing Tokyo Tower as the tallest artificial structure in the city. It was situated further afield, but I was more interested in the older model anyway.

Completed in 1958, Tokyo Tower stood out from its surroundings, not only due to its height, but because of its colour. It looked like a version of the Eiffel Tower that had been painted red and white. The official colour is 'international orange,' which is used in the aerospace industry to make objects more visible from their surroundings. The Golden Gate Bridge in San Francisco is another famous example of a structure adorned with this colour. The tower may have been painted this way due to air safety reasons rather than anything more poignant or symbolic, but it made it stand out in a similar way to the little girl's coat in *Schindler's List*.

After walking around the observation deck and enjoying the view from every available window, we decided to have our picture taken. The professional photographer captured our image, which would be made available to purchase from the shop. He made a rookie mistake though: in a most surprising turn of events, he offered to take another photograph with my camera. It saved us a couple of thousand Yen, and probably led to a stern word in his ear from his superiors.

There is also an open-air observation deck on the rooftop, but we declined the opportunity to visit. Instead, we took the train to Asakusa. We had travelled here to visit Sensō-ji, which is Tokyo's oldest temple. Legend states that two brothers retrieved a statue of bodhisattva Kannon, who is associated with compassion and mercy, out of the Sumida River. Each time that they put it back in the water, it returned to them. The chief of the village then transformed his house into a small temple for the locals to worship Kannon.

The first incarnation of Sensō-ji was erected in 645 AD. It suffered damage during various fires throughout the years, and survived the Great Kanto Earthquake in 1923, before it was completely destroyed by the U.S. firebombing raids that were part of Operation Meetinghouse. The reconstruction of the temple was regarded as symbolic of Japan's post-war rebirth and the establishment of peace.

I was impressed by the outer entrance gate, known as Kaminarimon, or 'Thunder Gate.' Standing at over eleven metres tall, this imposing red structure has some interesting elements. Statues depicting the Shinto gods of wind and thunder are situated in the alcoves either side of the entranceway. The most striking feature is the humongous red lantern that hangs under the centre of the gate. It is just under four metres tall and just over three metres wide. Slightly bigger than the lantern I hang up at home for Chinese New Year!

I was slightly concerned that the lantern, which weighs approximately 700 kilograms, would somehow become detached from its fixing and crush us to death. Mercifully, we managed to walk through the gate without the gods of wind and thunder deciding to bring a premature end to our lives.

Beyond the gate, there was a busy street lined with stalls. Nakamise-dori, or 'Inside Street,' is approximately 250 metres long, and it is thought to have existed since the early eighteenth century. I guess that the high volume of footfall provided a good business opportunity for many local people. The stalls were selling a variety of snacks and the usual souvenirs that were available throughout Japan. I ended up buying a little Geisha doll for Carol. I must have chosen well, as she has held on to it for all these years. And she has not discarded me either!

The second gate, the Hōzōmon, can be found at the end of Nakamise-dori. It has two storeys, with the upper level containing the temple's treasures. This makes sense, given that its name roughly translates as 'Treasure-House Gate.' There are statues on either side of the gate depicting the guardians of the Buddha. This gate has three lanterns, but they are slightly smaller than the one that we had walked under a few minutes beforehand.

Aside from this spectacular gate, perhaps the most eye-catching part of the temple complex was the five-storey pagoda to our left. Standing at over fifty-three metres tall and with a history dating back to the tenth century, it is one of the most famous pagodas in Japan. It houses memorial tablets of thousands of families and individuals, but as it was closed to the general public, we were unable to see for ourselves. I made do with a photograph outside of this wonderful red pagoda. Maybe I will be memorialised inside once my time on Earth has come to an end. Perhaps not.

I did not think that the main hall was as visually impressive as the other structures within the complex, as the tall sloping roof seemed to cover most of the building. The incense burner in front of the hall was more interesting. A crowd had gathered around it and people appeared to be trying to cover themselves with the smoke that was billowing out of it. Many people believe that this has healing powers. It just made me cough and my eyes itch!

The wooden décor and calligraphy inside of the main hall reminded me of an upmarket Chinese restaurant in Manchester, which I am sure was not the intended design. There were small groups gathered with their hands clasped in front of various locations within the grounds. I believe that they were not only paying homage to Kannon, but also the two fishermen and the village elder who created the original temple.

Leaving the shrines and incense behind, Mum and I moved on to the Edo-Tokyo Museum. We decided to stretch our legs by undertaking the two-kilometre walk to the Ryōgoku district rather than using the busy public transport system again. Our route took us over, and then along, the Sumida River. And past numerous 7-Eleven stores.

The museum is housed in an unusual building that reminded me of a character from the *Transformers* film series. Apparently, it is supposed to resemble a traditional rice storehouse and it is the same height as Edo Castle. I prefer my comparison.

The museum provides an insight into life in this region, ranging from when it was known as Edo prior to the late 1860s to its modern existence. Like the Hong Kong Museum of History, it contains interactive displays and recreations of famous buildings that represent Japanese history.

It was strange to see a full-scale replica of the Hōzōmon gate that we had just visited at Senso-Ji. Even this copy version looked impressive. We enjoyed walking over the museum's recreation of the original seventeenth-century Nihonbashi Bridge whilst looking down over some of the replica buildings. The wooden bridge, which was replaced by a twin-arch stone version in the early twentieth century, has long been regarded as a crucial point along the route in and out of the city.

The miniature replica scenes, including tiny figurines depicting people going about daily life in historical periods, were interesting and charming in equal measure. We spent an hour or two walking around the multiple floors of the museum, enriching our knowledge of Japanese history in the process.

We decided to spend the evening on the artificial island of Obaida. When I say that we decided, what I really mean is that I dragged my poor mother on an unnecessary mission to locate a miniature statue far away from our hotel. I had seen a photograph of a replica of the Statue of Liberty in front of a suspension bridge in my guidebook, which prompted me to take the decision to track it down and recreate the image.

Obaida was originally a group of small islands that served a defensive purpose before being transformed into a tourist and leisure zone following various landfill projects. It initially proved unpopular for businesses due to the relative difficulty in reaching the area from the city centre. We found this out to some degree, as we had to switch to the Yurikamome line, which required the purchase of separate tickets. With an elevated rail line and no driver on board, it is Tokyo's first fully automated transit system.

We exited the station that I hoped was closest to the statue, but there was no sign of it nearby. In fact, I could not see anything of interest. Mum and I began travelling in what we hoped was the correct direction, eventually feeling relieved when we reached the waterfront. We followed the walkway until we came across the statue, which at forty feet tall, is smaller than I had anticipated. The angle from which the photograph in my guidebook had been taken made it look much bigger than it was, but it was still satisfying to take in this view of the replica Statue of Liberty in front of the Rainbow Bridge, which was being lit up against the backdrop of the night sky.

I took my own photographs, which proved useful during a quiz that I organised at work a few years after our trip. I took great pleasure in seeing people fall into my trap by confidently answering 'New York' during the 'name the location of the photograph' round. Yes, I am that sad.

With our mission complete, it was time to find somewhere to eat. We enjoyed some tasty ramen, which is a Japanese noodle soup, before ambling through one of the small shopping centres. There was an arcade that, partly due to its location by the waterfront, brought back childhood memories of trying to win cuddly toys by conquering impossible challenges and begging my parents for more tokens to use on video games. As there was not much of interest to us, we headed back to our hotel. Considering that we had an early start the following morning, this was probably for the best.

*   *   *

It was five o'clock in the morning when my alarm went off. I immediately questioned my sanity. Why had I been so determined to wake up this early in order to visit a fish market? I would never dream of doing anything like this in England. But when I visit other countries, I am desperate to see every possible tourist attraction or notable landmark. Even a fish market.

Until most of the market relocated to Toyosu in 2018, Tsukiji Fish Market was the world's largest and busiest seafood market. The biggest attraction for many lies in the form of the live tuna auctions, but visitors are required to arrive at an ungodly hour to receive one of the 120 coveted slots. People turn up as early as two o'clock in the morning, with the first auction not commencing for another three hours. I was not tempted to follow suit; after all, there are some limits to my tourist-related obsessions!

Seafood enthusiasts and businesspeople are allowed to inspect the size and quality of the fish prior to the auction. To illustrate how big the tuna can be, and how much they are valued in Japan, one man paid 333.6 million Yen for a 278-kilogram bluefin at the new market in 2019. That is the equivalent of just under £2.5 million!

Business had started to wind down by the time that we arrived, which I think was around nine o'clock, but there were still enough fish and it was busy enough for us to get a taste of the market. Well, not in the literal sense. Walking into the cavernous building, bleary-eyed, it felt like we were clocking in at the start of a shift working in a warehouse rather than a tourist attraction. After all, this was primarily a place where people shop for seafood rather than pose for photographs. It was interesting to see this thriving trade in action, and it gave us an insight into the scale of the market. I took as many photographs as I could whilst trying to avoid any of the workers noticing. They must be used to it, but it felt odd to be taking pictures of people selling fish!

We had some brunch in a nearby sushi restaurant. Given the proximity, it would be nice to think that they got their produce from the market.

"The food in Japan has been really good," I commented.

"Yes, Japanese food is delicious. I was unsure of whether you would like it though."

"A few years ago, I would not even have tried the food. Back then, I just liked burgers and chips!"

"Travelling has broadened your palate. I am pleased to see you trying different food now."

"Have you enjoyed our trip?" I asked.

"Yes, it has been great. So interesting. How about you?"

"The past couple of weeks have been wonderful. Macao, Hong Kong and Tokyo are all fascinating places. I would have liked to have seen Mount Fuji, but it was just too far away to squeeze into our short stay. I would also have liked to have attended a Sumo event, but I could not force my mum to stare at a bunch of fat men in nappies all night!"

We had to overcome the challenge of exiting Shinjuku Station one more time before heading to the airport for our return flight to Hong Kong. Mum had previously stated her belief that we would get to grips with the layout of the station and find the exit closest to our hotel by the end of the trip. Needless to say, this was not the case. If we had persevered in trying to find the correct exit, we probably would have missed our flight; therefore, we resorted to our tried and trusted method of leaving the station wherever we could then gaining our bearings from there. If I spent a year living in Tokyo, I doubt that I would be able to find the correct exit!

* * *

Following our trip to Tokyo, I flew back to Manchester from Hong Kong a couple of weeks before Mum made her return. I spent most of the twelve-hour journey worrying about the dried seafood that Mum had asked me to smuggle back into the country. By the time that the plane had landed at Manchester Airport, my imagination had run wild, leading me to believe that I would be apprehended by border control and thrown into prison indefinitely.

In reality, the worst that could have happened was that the goods would be seized and maybe I would be given a small fine. However, my anxiety had caused me to become a quivering wreck by the time that I had collected my suitcase. I walked through customs, undoubtedly looking guilty as sin. If any officials had been nearby, I would have confessed without prompting and begged for forgiveness. I had seen enough episodes of *Border Force* to know that nervous behaviour in the baggage reclaim area is often enough to provoke a search of a passenger's luggage, and possibly an interrogation. Fortunately, the area seemed to be unattended and I walked straight through. This experience was enough to remove any doubt from my mind that I would make the world's worst drugs mule.

CHAPTER 13: THANK YOU
CLOSING WORDS FROM THE UNITED KINGDOM
OCTOBER 2020

"Hi," I mumbled to a passer-by. I was met with silence and a blank expression. Following my return from Asia, I had been forcing myself to engage with the fellow residents of Manchester, with mixed results. Perhaps I would have been wiser to have attempted this exercise in Wigan.

"Hello," I murmured to the next person that I encountered.

This time, my greeting was returned. Success! I was still very much an introvert, but at least I was making an effort to speak to people. I felt that I needed to do this; after all, how could I explore the planet without interacting with its inhabitants?

This was merely a tiny step on my personal journey, just as the trips featured in this book form only a small part of my global adventures. There was much more of the world to see, and there was a considerable amount of personal development required to make the most of such opportunities. I have been fortunate enough to visit many wonderful places across the planet during the eight years since my trip to Tokyo; I like to think that the journeys featured in this book have helped to draw me out of my shell to some degree. I still generally avoid small talk though!

Four months after the trip to Hong Kong, Macao and Tokyo, I would be embarking on a grand adventure: a seven-day trek along the Great Wall of China. Not only was this going to be my most spectacular journey to date, I was undertaking this task with over forty strangers! This would have been unthinkable a few years beforehand, but I had well and truly caught the travel bug. This will make you do things that you had never thought possible, such as occasionally exchanging conversation with strangers!

*   *   *

The world has changed considerably since I went on the trips featured in this book. Like everyone else, I am currently being encouraged to follow social distancing guidelines, whereas before it was merely the product of my shyness and anxiety. I have already gone almost a full calendar year without venturing overseas. Whilst I have missed walking along tropical beaches and admiring historic cities across the world, one must at least attempt to take the positives from this situation. I have seized the opportunity to explore the country that I live in whilst the planet, and the people within it, have taken some much-needed time to heal.

When things return to normal, perhaps I will be even more grateful for the opportunity to explore our beautiful planet and the people who call it home. Although I doubt that I will become an extrovert, I look forward to making the most of my time on Earth. Just do not ask me to give any public speeches!

*   *   *

I must once again thank the people closest to me who have demonstrated admirable patience and understanding whilst I have spent hour upon hour sat in front of my laptop trying to delve deep into my memory banks to write about events that happened such a long time ago. My wife, Carol, deserves praise for putting up with me even when she knew that my mind was preoccupied with the book. The love she consistently shows me inspires me to become a better person, and to complete any project that I undertake.

Mum and Dad have continued to offer words of encouragement and support during the moments when I have questioned whether people will appreciate my writing. They have also tried their best to answer any questions regarding missing details of the trips that we enjoyed many years ago.

My friends and family have provided much-appreciated support since I announced that I was going to release my first book last year. It was heartwarming to see people respond so positively. I also feel compelled to thank anyone who has purchased either of my books up until this point. It was a leap into the unknown, but the fact that the first one has been well received has given me the impetus to carry on writing. The kind words from people who have read it have meant a lot to me. Hopefully, you have enjoyed this book too.

*   *   *

The most effective way that you can show your appreciation is by leaving a review on Amazon. This is extremely helpful for an independent author like me.

If you have enjoyed this book you may want to check out my debut offering:

The Adventures of an Introvert: Ten Countries, Four Continents; Minimal Eye Contact

You can keep up to date with the latest news regarding upcoming projects, read my regular blog posts and find links to my social media accounts (where I frequently post photographs from my trips) via my website:

https://theadventuresofanintrovert.com

Printed in Great Britain
by Amazon

23071744R00121